D1214409

BROKE AND THE SHANNON

An account of the eight years during which
Captain Philip Bowes Vere Broke
commanded His Britannic Majesty's frigate *Shannon*,
of how the man made the ship
and the ship the man.
Also of Captain James Lawrence
and the United States' frigate *Chesapeake*
who met them in chivalrous combat off Boston
and made history.

Broke
and the Shannon

PETER PADFIELD

HODDER AND STOUGHTON

SBN 340 02511 5

Printed in Great Britain for Hodder and Stoughton Limited,
St. Paul's House, Warwick Lane, London, E.C.4
by Richard Clay (The Chaucer Press) Ltd, Bungay, Suffolk.

FOR BUN

NOTE

ALL the conversation attributed to Broke in these pages is, with unimportant exceptions, taken either from his letters to various people or from accounts by witnesses to the action. Where the conversation is from his letters no attempt has been made to keep to the *date* of the letters; they may have been written years after or years before the cruise of the *Shannon*. They are nevertheless representative of Broke's views on the subject under discussion. The seeker after their *chronological* truth is provided with detailed notes in a Chronological Index at the back, showing where each quotation comes from and when.

ACKNOWLEDGEMENTS

I HAVE had a great deal of help from many people, but if one has to be singled out first I should like to thank Mr. Graham Hunt, who has made a study of Broke and of the *Chesapeake* action over a number of years, and who very generously made his hard-earned knowledge available to me when I began work on the book, afterwards criticising the draft in minute detail, making many valuable corrections and suggestions, and also lending me some rare books and pamphlets from his collection, and various ship plans. I also received a lot of incidental background knowledge of the period from my talks with him.

The Hon. Mrs. Llewellen Palmer, a direct descendant of Broke through his fifth son, Charles Acton Broke (born 30th June 1818), who spent her early years at Broke Hall, gave me a great deal of help and encouragement and loaned or made available books from her famous ancestor's personal collection. She also read and criticised the first draft of my book and made many helpful suggestions. I am grateful too for permission to reproduce pictures and documents from her home.

Mrs. Palmer's brother, the Hon. J. V. B. Saumarez of Shrubland Park (Louisa Broke's birthplace), allowed me to reproduce several pictures, including the set of superb watercolours of the *Chesapeake* action – which unfortunately lose through printing in black and white. I am also grateful to Mr. Saumarez for permission to quote freely from the Saumarez papers (which include all Philip Broke's papers) on loan to the East Suffolk County Archives.

The County Archivist, Mr. D. Charman, and all his assistants at the County Record Office were most helpful at all stages and made great efforts to catalogue the papers in time for me to start work, for which I am most grateful. It is unfortunate that another possibly very useful source of material, the Hyde Parker papers, could not be similarly hurried forward. It was not possible to see these papers as pressure of archivists' work precluded their being sorted and catalogued for some time, but I feel that as Captain Hyde Parker of the *Tenedos* frigate was Broke's 'constant companion' throughout the long blockade leading up to the *Chesapeake* action, they might well reveal some more intimate details of the period. I recommend them to the next author or historian who may tackle the American War or

Philip Broke; for my part, as an imperfect perfectionist, I am disappointed.

From the United States of America, I should first like to thank Rear-Admiral E. M. Eller, Director of Naval History, Washington, for making available microfilm of the *Chesapeake* Courts Martial, and the muster and payrolls of the *Chesapeake* and *Constitution*, and for his valuable help throughout my research. I should also like to thank the New York Historical Society for the microfilm of Admiral R. H. King's diary, in their possession, and Mr. John D. Cushing of the Massachusetts Historical Society, and Mr. P. C. Foster Smith of the Peabody Museum, Salem, for their help on historical and geographical details.

From Canada, my grateful thanks to Admiral Hugh Pullen, who was working simultaneously on a book about the *Chesapeake* action, but who generously criticised my draft chapters concerned with the action, made many helpful suggestions and sent photocopies of documents. I should also like to thank Dr. Bruce Fergusson, Archivist, Public Archives of Nova Scotia.

From the gunnery angle, which was the original motivation for this book, I should once again like to thank the Captain and officers of H.M.S. *Excellent* for very generously allowing me to take away valuable old gunnery manuals and students' notebooks from their library and study them at home, and also for help over various details (as unlikely as the actual colour of gun smoke in 1813!). I should also like to thank Mr. A. W. H. Pearsall of the National Maritime Museum, Greenwich, who has made a study of gunnery, and who read the chapters concerned with Broke's practice of the art, and clarified some doubtful points. Also Mr. Dudley Pope for help with gunnery references, and also for writing his excellent *Guns*.

Dr. John Stevens of Aldeburgh did some valuable eye- and camera-research on the spot around the coastline from Boston to Cape Ann, and lent me some helpful books about the seamanship of the period and the American sailing Navy, for which I am most grateful.

I should also like to thank the librarians of the Admiralty Library, the very helpful staff of the National Maritime Museum, the West Suffolk Education Committee and the East Suffolk Education Committee, and of course the truly splendid Interlending Service which enabled me to study at least one book which is not available in this country.

If there is anyone I have forgotten, I apologise for the oversight.

ILLUSTRATIONS

[1] Hon. Mrs. Llewellen Palmer
[2] Hon. J.U.B. Saumarez
[3] Saumarez Papers

Here's a health, brave Broke to you, to your officers and crew
Who aboard the *Shannon* fri – gate fought so han – dy O!
And may it always prove, that in fighting and in love,
The British tar for ever is the dan – dy O!

Last verse of the sea shanty, *Shannon and
Chesapeake*, still popular at the turn of the
century.

PROLOGUE

BROKE HALL stands four square and battlemented close by the river Orwell below the little village of Nacton in Suffolk. It is an unpretending house. The main gates are plain. The drive leads straight, shadowed and scented by limes either side, a long way before the plain oak front door. To the right the sun flashes off broad reaches of the river; ahead the ground rises and folds around the square house, the old flagstones and the lawns. Oak trees and evergreens complete its shelter from sea winds. Birds sing among them.

From the gentle high ground beneath these trees the view of the river and the far banks breathes England; there is nothing harsh, nothing swift, no feverish rapids, no sparkling pools, only the broad, easy stream leading in lazy curves to the sea. The far bank about a mile away rises alternately wooded and swelling with green and rich brown fields, pointed up with white houses, more trees, village churches, nothing to jar nature.

The only strange notes in all this peace are provided by the gulls; they pipe as shrilly and excitedly as ever a swarm of Boatswain's Mates, mingling their sea noises with the land birds. For this is a meeting-place – rural Suffolk with maritime England. A hundred sail and more have been anchored between those green banks within cannon shot of the house – Britannia's shield, their canvas-clouded masts have thrilled generations of slow farmers and labourers and villagers of Nacton, and their great guns in salute have startled the gentlemen's deer in those fields – once parks – and caused pheasants to rise and drum away like Frenchmen.

Leading from Broke Hall down to the river there is an avenue of lime trees. It ends at a sand beach scattered with shingle which runs along the shore, narrowly dividing the grass banks and knotted roots of Suffolk from the mud flats at low water. Sea wrack in the mazy indentations. Salt smell of estuaries. Here is a silence and peace that is not of the twentieth century.

Here we can drift back through the years without intrusion, through generations of Brokes, through this century and the last until we come upon a boy wandering this same sand, his eyes filled with this expanse of water, his mind with great thoughts of the ships that pass upon it. He is dreaming of the day he can get to sea himself – of the high, giddy adventure and romance of life under those raking

I

spars, the far ports, the Indies, the skirmishes with Monsieur Crapaud, the brave epaulettes of an officer of the King, those *tall* ships! It is not unusual for East Coast boys to be seized in this way.

This boy is Philip Bowes Vere Broke, elder son of Philip Bowes Broke, Esquire, a solid, landed gentleman with literary tastes – not wealthy but able to maintain his seat and his station comfortably from the few farms in Essex and Suffolk which go with the Broke estate. He has ambitions for a liberal education for his sons, Winchester, his old school perhaps, or Eton. But Philip is under the spell of the ships.

Young Philip has red hair from his mother, who is a parson's daughter, and from her also a firm religious grounding which admits of no uncertainties – he is representative, perhaps, of the last generation of educated Englishmen who can go through life without doubt. From his mother and father and the extensive library at Broke Hall he has a taste for books and the Latin poets in their own tongue. He will carry with him through life as surely as his red hair this taste for literature, these classical ideas, this absolute faith in one God all mixed in with the quiet and beauty of Suffolk, the wild flowers along the edges of the fields and narrow, windy, tree-hung lanes, the slow herds – the sea wind, keen from across the Orwell. He will also carry the stability and sense of station of a Broke descended from countless landed Brokes tracing back to Saxon times, from William de Doyto del Brooke, son of Adam, Lord of Leighton in Cheshire, through the Chief Baron of the Exchequer, Sir Richard Broke, builder of Broke Hall in 1526, and Captain Packington Broke, slain while in command of the frigate *Fforesight* at the battle of Solebay in 1665. Young Philip will feel the privilege of his position and the responsibilities that this privilege carries, one of which is to set an example in defence of his country – even with his life.

We have moved on from the boy on the sand. He does not comprehend all this yet, and is only concerned with persuading his father that there is really only one career for him, His Majesty's Navy. His father, disappointed, makes a compromise: young Philip may attend the Naval Academy at Portsmouth; this, although a most unfashionable way of entering the sea service and frowned upon by stalwarts of the old school as 'a sink of vice and abomination', is probably a kinder introduction for a lad than the fearful squalor of the gunroom in a man-of-war – certainly more likely to encourage study.

So from the age of twelve until he is fifteen Philip studies the theory and high art of seamanship under canvas and obtains some glimpses into the New Principles of Gunnery, which have been propounded recently by an Englishman named Benjamin Robins, and which bring the light of science to this hitherto mysterious practice: the flight of a ball does *not* conform to a parabola in flight, but is continuously retarded by the air it pushes, and most surprising, the spin imparted to a ball by contact with one or other side of the bore as it leaves the muzzle will cause it to curve towards that side during its flight.

The Naval College instructors are not convinced of the practicality of this science, knowing well that the art of *Naval* gunnery consists in laying the ship so close to the enemy that the shot cannot miss however it leaves the barrel and whatever it does thereafter. More important is the composition of the powder and its preservation in the damp magazines below the waterline.

"Your attention, gentlemen! We take saltpetre, sulphur, well-fired charcoal that has been burned in a cylinder, not a pit, and we break them into fine powders, thus – we mix in the proportions seventy-five, ten, fifteen – or seventy-five, nine and a half, fifteen and a half if you follow Monsieur Crapaud! Now, moisten the composition with water or vinegar – or for the real potency urine from a wine-bibbing priest – and beat it into a fine, grey paste. Afterwards, gentlemen, we reduce the grains by passing through a sieve of copper wires. This is gunpowder!"

Young Philip learns that the explosive force of the mixture derives from its endeavours to expand when transformed into a gaseous substance by the application of a lighted match – or the very latest innovation in the Naval Service, a spark struck from a flint-lock. The expansion takes place with equal force in every direction; thus while the ball is impelled out of the mouth of the cannon, the cannon itself is driven in the reverse direction, their separate velocities being inversely proportional to their respective weights.

"The best guns for our ships, gentlemen, will therefore be fixed by the working space available on our deck. In the great ships of the line which have considerable beam will be found the long two- and thirty-pounders. Our frigates, being less beamy – and less able to carry such weights – do mount twelve- or eighteen-pounders upon the gun deck."

Philip's mind is fired by the details of his future profession. The ships he sees riding the Orwell, formerly just brave symbols of grace and adventure over wider horizons than the Broke estate, take on added interest now that he can see the bones and vital organs beneath their fair curve and canvas. His is an essentially practical mind; his lessons in the craft of seamanship and gunnery have given it something to bite on, and now we can see him down by the river's edge fitting out a fleet of wooden model ships and staging a general action, experimenting with gunpowder to fire their small cannon, on one occasion constructing a raft and setting out upon the tide to visit a ship at anchor. This fascination with the mechanics of seamanship and gunnery, this bent for experiment awakened at the Naval College will also last him throughout his life.

The years pass quickly while he is learning until in 1792, at the age of fifteen, he is appointed Midshipman in the *Bulldog* sloop-of-war, and we can see nothing of him at the Hall. Only his letters arrive frequently. They are long with descriptions of the strange, brutal, yet intensely stimulating new life he has been plunged into. Reading between the lines he is a little lonely when he finds the time, for there are not too many lads of similar interests and education in His Majesty's ships. But his eagerness to acquire knowledge and master every smallest detail of the profession soon makes him a favourite, and his Captain, George Hope, later a good friend at the Admiralty, takes him under his wing; when Hope is appointed to another vessel, he will take young Philip with him.

But before that – war. The French have beheaded their King, and a number of good Naval officers beside, and are attempting to spread their hateful revolutionary doctrine through Europe and the world. Young Philip is not only a seaman now but a crusader, convinced with all the fervour of a romantic youth – and heir to landed estate – that the war with France is a 'sacred cause'. At the same time his letters home come alive with more tales of adventure than he ever dreamed of by the quiet Orwell, stories of the chase, and cutting-out parties in small boats, of boarding merchantmen and being placed in command of prizes, of hunting down sharp privateers, or sailing in close to the enemy's batteries as the eyes of the fleet. As a fighting sailor he is fortunate; he is breathing in almost with his first draughts of deep sea air the trade of war, which no peace-time exercises can simulate. He is learning naturally and barely consciously the disciplines and aggressive attitudes that go to make the British the most formidable sea-fighters in all Europe.

After three years of small-ship time as a Midshipman, Philip Broke receives a commission as Third Lieutenant to the *Southampton* frigate; still we miss him at the Hall except in letters. He is cruising in the Mediterranean with Nelson's squadron. At the battle off Cape St. Vincent his frigate is employed towing the Spaniards off when they can stand the pounding no longer. But the French have not yet been driven into their harbours and there is excitement aplenty in which the frigates take a more active part almost every week.

At last, after more than five years' continuous absence, Philip

4

returns to Nacton for his twenty-first birthday, received to a hero's welcome – and rightly so for he is now a seasoned fighting officer. The great portraits in the Hall look down on him with approval – and some expectation perhaps. Another fighting Broke to restore the family estates to their former eminence? Philip gazes up at the moustachioed Captain Packington Broke and feels he knows him better now; so little have the arts of seamanship and gunnery changed that they could exchange a yarn or two and never notice the passage of the centuries.

After some months breathing the quiet of Suffolk and feeling his pulses slowing to the old, familiar beat of the country, Philip – always a small-ship man and proud of it – is appointed to the *Amelia* frigate, Captain the Hon. C. Herbert. Herbert is a man of some literary taste and talent, and Philip finds the atmosphere congenial. He serves two years here, experiencing another general fleet engagement and many other excitements before obtaining his promotion to Commander.

Now, while his father, who is a staunch Tory party worker, schemes with his political friends to ensure his son's promotion to Post rank, young Broke experiences his first independent commands, some inconsequential fire brigs and convoy sloops, before his father's 'interest' gains him the coveted step to Post Captain in February 1801. Now his career is assured; at twenty-four years old he has his foot unshakeably on the promotion ladder and can look forward, with or without ships to command, to a steady ascent by seniority up the Captain's list and stage by stage through the Rear-Admirals and the Vice-Admirals to the very top of his profession – if he can survive that long.

He returns to Broke Hall on half-pay, a well-built young man over six feet tall. His weathered face wears a pleasant expression; his speech is assured, and he carries himself with a confidence born of ten years of very active service and the knowledge of his own capabilities this has brought. There is no vanity though. The anecdotes of the chase and capture, of storms and foreign ports with which he entertains his avid family are modestly understated. His red hair hangs naturally and shows no powder; his dress is unassuming. In company he goes out of his way to be pleasant and cheerful.

And now he is often down by the river with his young friend, Sarah Louisa, second daughter of Sir William Middleton, Baronet, of Shrubland Park, not far from Ipswich; she is a fair-haired girl with a sheltered complexion and very blue eyes – a shy creature in company, but it is obvious that she is very much in love with the Naval hero, and he with her. They marry in November 1802.

They are ideally happy together, but as the months on half-pay lengthen into years, Philip becomes increasingly nostalgic about those fine, free days at sea, and increasingly impatient of idleness. He writes to Lord Melville at the Admiralty, reminding him of his presence and his eagerness to take advantage of any Post command that might fall vacant, and in the meantime he satisfies his restless mind by forming and training a body of local peasantry to arms against the day when old 'Boney' might attempt an invasion of the last free country in Europe.

At last, in the spring of 1805, after he has been four years on half-pay, Lord Melville finds him a frigate, not a new or imposing one to be sure, and grossly undermanned like so many of His Majesty's ships in these hard times. It is certain also that no volunteers will come flying to join at the sound of her new Captain's name as they would for Lord Cochrane or one of your other glamorous frigate commanders.

Broke, sir? Who is he?

But for Philip she is a ship beyond all ships – his first Post command. He is nearly twenty-nine years old, in the prime of manhood, and his brilliant prospects are all before him. Elated by the thought, but suddenly very sad at having to leave his delightful Looloo and the two children she has borne him, Philip enters the coach for London, his cases packed with a new Captain's uniform, table service and various flints and locks and sights for great guns with which he has been experimenting at home.

And again, for an even longer period, we see almost nothing of him by the Orwell – only Louisa coming down to the beach with their children in the summer to read his letters, and wondering, as the years pass, when she will be granted another such long honeymoon to enjoy her husband before they are both old and the children grown up and gone. Philip wonders too. In quiet intervals in the loneliness of command he suffers painful visions of his youth with his family fading into one continuous cruise – years which could never be recaptured.

"My dear, beloved Looloo . . . My Sunday devotions bear me home to my Loo: I wish I could pray by her side. Alas! I shall see *no primroses* this May to remind me of my gentle Loo. When shall I sit and read to her again in the shade whilst she ties up the violets? Poor Nacton. 'Tis far away; I must not think of it till I am on my return.

"But I must close up this and attend to my wooden mistress.

6

She is a *great tyrant*! Give my love to the dear little cherubs around you and Heaven protect you all!"

.   .   .

There is a church at Nacton with a plain, square steeple dwarfed by high pines and firs which stand outside its ground. Opening into the south side of this church is the Broke Chapel, and beneath lie all that remains of Philip Bowes Vere Broke and his wife, Louisa. In the skull of the man, by the left temple, there is a sabre gash four inches long, parting the bone down to the brain cavity. And on the memorial tablet in the Chapel above, the Lords of the Admiralty – who are not given to overstatement – mark in him a "professional skill and gallantry which has seldom been equalled and certainly never surpassed".

CHAPTER ONE

NELSON was dead, but the elements he had defied so long neither knew nor cared. 1806 blew in as bitterly as ever. The northern seas were tumbled, spun with foam, bleak, inhospitable, constantly amove, constantly impersonal. And in them and part of them, moving, tossing, jerking, the rheumy old wooden ships of England kept watch in the Channel and around the ports of France, wallowing and scudding under bare poles or a rag of an old storm trysail, hung and crusted with salt, little lonely islands of hard life in all this blown water.

One of these was *Druid*, a worn sieve of a frigate rated 32 guns, with a second sheathing of fir to keep some of the water out. Aft in her meandering cabin Captain Philip Bowes Vere Broke tried to catch up with his Journal:

"The cruize we made after leaving the convoy in the Downs was one constant series of bad weather; we were generally driving about in strong gales between Cape Clear and 48° North and in 10° or 11° West. Afterwards in between Scilly and the Irish Channel till we were obliged to bear up round Land's End. As mentioned in the Log, I never witnessed heavier gales or more violent storms than we weathered during this period. The most material disadvantage we suffered was our being totally prevented from exercising our young crew either in handling their arms or their sails . . ."

1806 was a sad year for England. On 9th January a silence as profound as many had ever heard fell on the streets of London as Nelson's body was borne to St. Paul's to the slow beat of the Dead March. Behind the funeral car tramped the crew of the *Victory* and the sight of them drew tears of emotion from the crowds. They were not yet aware of the full and decisive consequences of Trafalgar, but they instinctively knew the value of this man they had lost.

On 23rd January Pitt died. As Nelson had been the embodiment of Britain's Naval defiance, so Pitt was identified with the country's political will to stand – and if need be, stand alone – against the tyranny across the Channel. Fox took over the government. He was a man of peace, and he started discussions with Napoleon, but soon found that words had no more meaning than air with the Corsican upstart, while treaties and agreements were simply weapons to further what could not be gained by war. It became apparent that there could be no end to the fighting until either Napoleon or Great Britain was overthrown.

In September Fox died, the last of the 'Giant Race', and any faint, lingering hope of peace died with him. It seemed to many people then that war was the natural state of the world, and peace, if it ever came, would simply be a brief and charming interlude, a transient pause for breath and time to gather strength for the next great effort. For this was the ultimate in the stalemate years. Napoleon's armies were as apparently invincible on land as Nelson's band of brothers at sea. The elephant versus the whale. Where was the decision to come? Arthur Wellesley, later Duke of Wellington, was no more than a sepoy general, and Portugal, although a problem, was scarcely a threat to Napoleon.

The only threat he recognised was the Royal Navy – the ships of the Royal Navy hanging like so many sea urchins around his continental fortress, each one kept in station by morale and seamanship and leadership of a high order – each one so cumbersome and vulnerable by itself, but in total, *such a force*!

The Royal Navy was at the very pinnacle of its achievement. For centuries the English had claimed sovereignty over the waters of the world; for decades – and perhaps because of this conceit! – they had achieved it. And now that they had achieved it they accepted it as 'from the laws of God and of Nature'. William Mountaine, prefacing his *Seaman's Vade Mecum* thirty years back had stated it: "That the Monarchs of Great Britain have a peculiar and sovereign authority upon the Ocean is a right so ancient and undeniable that it never was publickly disputed . . ." In some of the most decisive fleet actions in history the Royal Navy had knocked out the Dutch, the Danes, the Spanish and the French, while in single-ship encounters it had become very exceptional for a British man-of-war to be taken unless fought to a standstill by overwhelming force. Professor Lewis has calculated the line where overwhelming force began as something like five to three against in weight of broadside, size and complement; British method and morale could overcome any less *matériel* superiority. British defeats on equal terms since the revolution could be counted on the fingers. As a result organised French shipping had now been swept from the seas, and only sneaky privateers and frigates ventured out when the wind blew their jailors momentarily away.

This had led the French into a vicious spiral of defeat; the more they were kept in their harbours, the less they could practise their ships and crews; the less they could practise, the worse they became.

They were half-beaten at the mere sight of a British Naval ensign. And Royal Naval officers stood jauntily, white-breached on their quarterdecks and bore their ships in chase like huntsmen, disdaining manoeuvre, pointing their bows straight on interception courses and never doubting the outcome if they could only reach within pistol shot.

Captain Broke was lecturing his First Lieutenant on this peculiarity of the times as the onset of milder weather in the spring of the year left his mind freer, and elevated his spirits. They paced the weather side of the quarterdeck in the first fresh rays of the early morning sun, the Lieutenant, unused to this familiarity on duty, matched his stride to Broke's eager pace.

"But all scientific manoeuvre has become apparently superfluous," Broke was saying. "This was not always so. It is evident in the pages of our Naval history that this thorough disregard of all caution in the approach to action is only a character of the present days. The old officers who commanded our ships before the Glorious First of June not only displayed much more caution in the preparation of their ships for action, but they talked *with respect* of the art of manoeuvring for position. I remember Sir William Fairfax mentioning once that on his succeeding the celebrated Lockhart Ross in the *Tartar* and being reminded – I think by Lord Rodney – of the high character that ship had to maintain, he applied himself most jealously to the practice of all the warlike exercises – but particularly to manoeuvring for position. He used to hoist his barge out at sea and work *round her* as if she was an enemy's ship, or back and fill to know his own ship's exact ability in thus gaining advantage for *raking* or for superior *bearing of guns*."

The Lieutenant broke in as he paused. "Of course if the enemy is only bent on flight, sir—"

"Exactly! That is exactly the position we have reached. Sure as we are that having only the superiority in sailing we are certain of bringing the enemy to close action – when British seamanship and courage will rapidly triumph – what need of manoeuvre! Under such circumstances, for a British Captain to attempt manoeuvring for position, even in the most approved and *scientific* way, would be at great risk to his character."

"The enemy might escape."

"He might escape, and the British commander would be severely censured – justly so – for losing by his *theories* a victory which the ability of his officers and seamen would have almost assured had they only been boldly led up to an abrupt, impetuous attack."

Broke sighed, half-regretful of those former days when an action might have been decided as much by thought and planning beforehand as by the steady courage of the British sailor. It was almost too easy these days – provided, of course, that one could *catch* the enemy. Their frigates were certainly better built and faster, and it was rare enough to see one now that the British superiority was so marked. Still – his day must come —

His thoughts were interrupted by a stirring cry from the fore royal yard, "Sail ho!"

Journal, "May 1st: At 8 a.m. chased a brig to leeward. Wind SSW. She bore up and made sail . . . we made all sail, it blew fresh and we followed her at the rate of 12 and 13 knots coming up fast. It was thick weather with rainy squalls in the evening; at 10 we fired a 6 pdr. at her, being within 1½ miles distance. Whilst preparing to shorten sail and run alongside her we suddenly found ourselves in the midst of Admiral Stirling's fleet, who was cruizing. We were at 11 within musket shot of the chace and had barely time to discover that the strange ships around us were men-of-war when the Admiral fired a shot across us and one at the chace . . ."

The *Druid* fortunately missed the flagship as she stormed past almost under the great quarter galleries, and was hailed to heave to or she would be sunk. All sail was lowered in confusion and the wheel hastily put down. The frigate rounded to, driving her lee gunwale under so that the main and lower decks were flooded and several guns broke loose from their tackles and were only prevented from hurtling across the ship by their breeching ropes. Fortunately the chase was also surprised into giving herself up, and when the situation was resolved Broke found that he had a fine 18-gun privateer, *La Pandora*, as a prize.

The following day, having taken leave of the Admiral with his prize in company, a large sail was reported to leeward and he was off again on the breeze with his studding sails set like wings; alas, this one lost him in the Passage du Raz. He found afterwards that she had been *La Topaze*. Perhaps it was as well he never caught her.

Midshipman King recollected:

"The *Topaze* of at least 1100 tons against our 700, of 340 men at least against about 180, say 60 of whom were Greenwich College men – of 50 guns against our 38 – of 44 pdr. carronades against our 12 pdr. long guns, and so forth . . . could a 12 pdr. shot have seriously injured such a ship as the *Topaze*?"

Broke was wont to call the *Druid* a 'point of honour' ship – too small to fight and too large to run away. But he made it a point to safeguard his honour by thorough, repeated, exhaustive training both with small arms and with the great guns. They may have chased like sportsmen, these British Captains, thirsting for glory or prize money or both, but they were not amateurs.

All the same there were hints of complacency beginning to show among some of them, and hints of that imbalance between their attitudes towards seamanship and gunnery which became so exaggerated in favour of seamanship in the later years of the century. This was especially marked among some of the younger officers who had never known a time when a Frenchman would seriously dispute command of the sea with an Englishman, and had come to regard their superiority, like William Mountaine, as given by God rather than the great cannon. As the French nearly always ran at the sight of English ships of force, more attention began to be paid to training the men at the sails than at the guns.

Broke never permitted this attitude to develop in his ships. From the first beat to quarters he drummed it into his Lieutenants that officers who were satisfied with the general state of gunnery in British ships would never improve either themselves or the men under them. And they must not assume that the Royal Navy had achieved its superiority over other Marine Forces by improved practice. Quite the reverse.

"It appears to me most evident that our success is entirely owing to the deprivation of our enemy's crews in all professional skill. Our seamen fight bravely as they have always done, but looking back to the practice of Hood's and Rodney's fleets, to the service effected by our fire in the actions of those days, and to what *our ships then suffered* in combat with *even enemies* there appears ample proof that the other modern European Navies have much deteriorated. Why, after an action of one of our largest frigates with a French ship of the same force it was ascertained that all the mischief suffered in killed and wounded by the British was effected by two rounds from a quarterdeck 9 pdr. – laid by a French artillery officer on board? Such is our enemy's state!"

Instead of allowing this lamentable showing by the opposition to breed satisfaction, Broke seemed to regard it as a spur to show what *could* be done with scientific gunnery. He was an enthusiast. "The essential point I look for," he told his officers, "is zeal in the cause of great gunnery, and *conviction of its importance*." There was never any doubt about his own conviction. He had the same thrill from seeing

13

one of the beef casks which were thrown overboard for target practice disintegrating under cannon fire as he had from bringing down a woodcock with a sporting gun. He was constantly employed with his carpenters and armourers making improvements to the great-gun sights, which were provided at his own expense, making adjustments to the gun carriages to permit wider arcs of training, greater angles of elevation or depression, faster service; his notebooks and the backs of old letters or scrap paper on his writing table were covered with sketches of different ideas he had for his guns. His lectures to his Midshipmen, whose education he regarded as one of his first duties, were studded with the theory and practice of gunnery as he had found it through his service.

"It is certainly advisable – particularly with an enemy who is likely to try to escape or manoeuvre for position to always have some guns appropriated for dismantling service. I remember this system was acted upon in the *Southampton* frigate under Captain Shield. As you have observed, I always adopt it in my plan of exercise. To some guns best situated for the purpose, and which have ample room for training clear of chainplates and other encumbrances, are allotted all the double-bar shot and an additional supply of grape and case to each so that they are always ready to turn their fire upon yards, masts or rigging with the ammunition which is most efficient for that service."

Broke was one of a small band of officers who recognised that improvements in the manufacture and equipment of the great guns which had come about during the previous century had made *accurate* fire a possibility, at least for close action. The most important changes came from the increased accuracy of the bore of the cannon caused by drilling out *after* casting – rather than the earlier method of casting the metal around a core of timber, which was liable to get out of parallel – and the adoption of the flint-lock. Before the lock had been introduced, guns had been fired by putting a slow match to a trail of bruised powder which spluttered along to the vent and thence down to the cartridge; this meant an appreciable time lag between the action of firing and the discharge of the piece, time during which the roll of the ship would probably throw the elevation out several degrees. With the much quicker discharge from the lock's spark, the possibility of realistic aiming became greater.

The tools were there, and Broke's first action on taking command was always to fit his guns with sights, then to set about training his officers, and through them the men, in their use. This was a somewhat unusual practice; most commanders, brought up on the inaccuracy of Naval fire, considered that the only cure was to lay themselves so close alongside the enemy that missing was impossible. In these circumstances sights were not only unnecessary but a distinct nuisance; they were liable to get knocked off as the guns went crashing in and out through the ports; they tended to divert the attention of gun captains from rapid fire, which ought to be their primary object – and in any case they would be quite forgotten in the maddening excitement of action.

The last objection scarcely applied to Broke's men. They were exercised at gun drill every day at sea except Saturday and Sunday, and the use of the sights became as much a habit as any other part of the loading and firing procedure, and was unlikely to fail in the test of action. As for the other objections, Broke never disagreed with the principle of close action. It was always his teaching, and he for ever stressed that the King's enemies "have not the same composed courage under close fire . . . as our impetuous seamen". His purpose in sighting his guns was simply to make close action even *more* fearsome and destructive to the enemy. All his sights and exercises were only designed to ensure that whatever the roll or list on the ship, each gun would be aimed so precisely horizontal that its ball would skim flat above the surface into the corresponding gun deck of the enemy.

"It is of course in action between single-decked ships that precision in this practice is most indispensable. A bad gunner firing at a 74 has two to one in his favour against the gunner firing at a frigate. It is in actions between the smaller classes where faults in gunnery are most fatal."

He considered as a 'fault' in gunnery any shot that went above or below the men on the enemy's gun decks. Dismasting or unrigging practice he regarded with contempt unless effected by the special dismantling service guns which he ordered on the enemy's wheel or yards. Each shot, each charge of grape or canister from his main batteries he considered as wasted unless coolly aimed to kill men – not to sink or disable ships; all his efforts were therefore directed towards securing 'the greatest power of horizontal fire in all situations'.

There was nothing unusual in these aims – they were entirely in accord with British doctrine handed down from one generation of fighting sailors to the next – it was only in method that he went far beyond contemporary practice.

Broke was a sociable man; his diary in port was always filled with dinner engagements – he was modest, unpretending, almost invariably good-humoured – and yet there is a suspicion that with gunnery he had more than a share of that splendid discontent which characterised his famous successor in ordnance reform, Percy Scott. Not that he would have been so ill-mannered as to mention his ideas un-solicited to any of his brother Captains; he was not an evangelist in the wide sense – sufficient for him to spread the good word among his own officers and the Midshipmen, his 'sea children'.

Some Captains came away from a tour of his gun deck convinced that he was a faddist, others went and copied his methods in their own ships; it mattered little to Broke. Whatever their reaction, he seldom doubted that their zeal for the service equalled his own, and that was all that really mattered. And although he was a highly cultivated man, and one of the comparatively small but growing band of officers who carried an extensive library to sea with him and read Latin with facility, he never despised or underrated the 'tarpaulins' who had come up through the hawes-hole and from the merchant service.

"You say some of your messmates are *mere seamen*," he remarked to one of his 'sea children' from a gentle background who complained one day of the quality of manners and conversation in the gunroom. "But I assure you such comrades if well dispositioned are very valu-able *aids* to any young officer commencing his career." He motioned the lad to one of the heavy and austere dining chairs by the lashed 12-pounder against the side.

"My first gunroom mess was just the same. I should have liked some more generally informed friends – but in the acquirement of professional knowledge I found their value. You see, it is impossible in our line for *any man* of *any age* to become so perfect a seaman that he may not – to the last hours of his life – have a chance of gleaning some very useful knowledge from other seamen who have sailed in other *climates* and other *circumstances*. And very useful, I observed, was the *graft in* of the old merchant seaman *master* who used to fill that office – if sober! He generally had long experience and practice of difficulties which rarely do, but always may, happen to a man-of-war. From the scanty supply of stores or of men in merchant ships, he had often been obliged to exert his utmost energies and his invention in extricating himself from dangers and difficulties."

He looked keenly at the lad and saw that his words had stirred some new animation and interest in his eyes. He rose, and stepping the few paces to him, clapped a hand on his shoulder as he shot upright from his seat in response. "You will have plenty of time to smooth and polish when by and by you are a half-pay Captain. Now you are in the service of *Nelson*!"

As the boy left he said kindly, " 'Tis difficulties that make good men!"

One of Broke's own chief difficulties in the *Druid* was the manning problem. It was the same with all His Majesty's increasing great fleet of ships in this fourteenth year of war, but that made it no easier to bear. As the summer set in he was despatched on another tour of impressment.

Journal. "July 25th: AM light breeze & cloudy at daylight. Saw a sail on the ld. beam at 3.20. Tacked in chase at 9 to the West. At noon fresh breezes and cloudy, chase ESE 8 or 9 miles. PM at 6.30 fired a shot at the chace; at 8 tacked; soon after chace bore up and stood towards us, hove too, boarded her, found her to be the *Barry* of Grimsby. Impressed 9 men from her ...

"Monday, Aug. 4th: At 5.30 boarded a Greenland ship. Impressed 9 men from her ...

"Tuesday, Aug. 5th: At 7 boarded an English brig from Picto to Hull. Impressed 2 men from her and sent 2 men in lieu ... at 2.50 saw 2 sail in the SSW. At 5.40 hove too two Greenland ships. Impressed 2 men."

It was about this time that a new surgeon, Dr. A. C. Hutchison, arrived to take up duties in the *Druid*. He had not been aboard long before he came to suspect that the Cook's mate, who had been on light duties for some months on account of an apparently locked elbow joint, was an imposter. He reported this conviction to Broke.

"But notwithstanding that I continued so to report him for upwards of two months, that worthy man – for in whatever ship Broke sailed, he was the father of his people – would not follow my advice and make an example of him, allegeing that I might be mistaken, and that he should never forgive himself if he were to punish a man who might afterwards be found to be innocent."

However, Hutchison eventually managed to persuade Broke to trick the man into revealing himself; after mustering all hands on deck, the Cook's mate was called out in front of them and questioned seriously by Broke on various subjects designed to take his mind off his bent and useless arm. Hutchison hovered near by, and when he saw that the Captain's questions had succeeded in diverting the man's attention, he suddenly seized the arm and straightened it with ease. The man was so surprised that he involuntarily raised the afflicted arm to his forehead, entreating forgiveness. He was lashed to the gratings and flogged.

One day during the *Druid*'s human fishing cruise she overhauled a Guernsey privateer cutter of 18 guns called the *Providence*. As they closed it became apparent that the vessel's masts were cut about, her sails riddled with holes from grape and canister shot, and when boarded her Captain explained that this was the result of an action two weeks back near Bilbao in which he had beaten off a French 18-gun brig. Hearing this Broke refused to take any men from her.

"A gallant fellow! Let him go, sir, and no doubt he may serve Monsieur Crapaud as well again!"

"Wednesday, Aug. 6th: Exercised great guns . . . exercised small arms . . .

"Thursday, Aug. 7th: Exercised the great guns . . ."

.   .   .

On 29th August the *Druid* was lying in Cork Harbour and Broke learned that he was appointed to the *Shannon* frigate now fitting out after building at Chatham. This was undoubtedly a step up; she was one of a new class of 18-pounder frigates being built to the draught of the *Leda*, whose lines had been taken from a captured French frigate called the *Hebe*. It was well known that the French built better, faster ships, and undoubtedly the *Shannon* would be a fit reward for his arduous two years' service and the pains of rheumatism he had suffered in *Druid* – not that he lacked affection for the cranky old lady. How could he ever forget the eager hopes of his first Post command! But now, with a *modern* ship . . .

He spent the next day packing and wrote a hurried letter to Louisa to tell her the good news and – even better so far as she was concerned – that he would have a short break with her in Suffolk between commands. On 1st September he noted in his pocket diary "W 2 L^d G^r sailed in *Savage*".

These terse entries which he made in the minute leaves of his diaries every day of his life were in a simple code; thus 'W' meant 'wrote to', 'R', 'received from'; 'L' was for Louisa, his beloved Looloo, and the L^d G^r just noted referred to his Commander-in-Chief, Admiral Lord Gambier. There is an entry a few days later on 15th September which fits no known code; it may perhaps be left to the imagination. His Majesty's Navy was a cruel master, especially for a young married man who was so ideally happy with his wife and family, and so ambitious that he could never consider refusing a command lest he might be put on half-pay for the rest of his time.

"Sept 7 Off Start . . . anchored at Spithead
       PM came ashore
     8 Came to Cobham
     9 Came to London   W Horton   took up comm^n
       Came to Ipswich."

A bare four days with his wife and little Philip, beginning to be a great amusement at two and a half, and Loolins aged eighteen months, taking staggering steps towards her strange big daddy, were all he was allowed before the demands of his new mistress, *Shannon*, called him away.

> "14 Came to London
> "15 Came to Sheerness   W L   rainy
>   broke down   W L
> "16 took comm^d of *Shannon* . . ."

The oarsmen lent their backs into the stroke. The slim white barge fairly quivered through the tide off the Nore, but because of the rate of it made disappointing progress. Broke sat in the sternsheets, his body moving easily like a horseman with each pull of the sweeps. He had shipped his quarterdeck face again for the first time since leaving the old *Druid* but there was anticipation written large upon it, and he could barely restrain the upward tilt of his lips as he gazed over the bow at his new command.

Shannon! How prettily she sat the tide! Those wide yards, far overreaching her beam; he imagined them clothed in chase. Her sides with the line of closed gunports, swelled out to the river, and he saw the new copper glinting above the rip of the water. She was light. Few stores in her yet; she had only recently left the fitting-out hulk. Her paintwork shone in the autumn sun. Quite new! And all his own! What a run she had; how the tide must be bubbling about her apple-cheeked bows. She had fine, fast lines beneath though – built for speed.

The rain of yesterday was swept clean from the sky. His fortune was in the making; this was a ship to be proud of. He could mould her from the beginning – set her up as taut as a swifter so that when the time came her batteries of 18-pounder long guns and 32-pounder carronades would concentrate on one point like a burning-glass; he had new ideas to try out and schemes of practice amended from the *Druid*.

He shivered momentarily. He would need more men than he ever had in *Druid* to do this new plaything justice – yet the real sailors were spread so thinly now. With so many ships in commission to lock Bonaparte up, with the wastage from disease, desertion and fighting consequent upon this interminable war, and with the Americans taking so many prime men into their own marine, a Captain had to be thankful enough for whatever he could sweep off the streets into his berth deck – vagrants, jail sweepings, quota men, young boys, whatever. It was an anxious time for England that she had to rely on such wretches.

The sea air soon toughened them though, the regular meals, hard and spare as they were, soon put brawn on, the discipline shook them down – and when it came to a pounding they had that steady courage which is a characteristic of their race. They could be moulded. Just so long as there was a hard core of sailors and topmen to start with.

He glanced at a copy of Lord Keith's standing orders which he had received.

"Princess of Orange

"As some homeward bound East and West India ships and Southsea men may be hourly expected in the Downs, every exertion is to be made by the officers commanding H.M. ships and vessels at this anchorage to impress men from them, care being taken that none be impressed who are protected by Act of Parliament and that a sufficient number of men-of-war's men are left on board the several vessels for the purpose of taking care of them until they can be relieved by the Ticket men who are to assist in navigating them to the river . . ."

So many sailors on the very point of seeing their homes and families after a long foreign voyage, so summarily seized and put under the iron discipline of a man-of-war, without any shore leave, with the only prospects before them blockade or a foreign station, or under the terrible misfortune of a bad Captain the prospect of a living hell afloat from which only death or desertion could ever release them. And if they were caught after deserting, it was a noose from the yardarm . . .

It was not surprising that many sailors mutilated their own persons or tried to feign serious disease as the only means of escape.

Dr. Hutchison: "I beg to state that two men were brought to the Hospital from ships of war in the Downs – the one having cut off half his foot with an axe, and the other his four fingers close to his hand merely for the purpose of obtaining their discharge, in which object however they failed, it having been deemed highly advisable to check such wicked practices in the Fleet."

Powdered alum, lime and tobacco juice were some of the dreadful irritants which men introduced into their own eyes, often blinding themselves in order to obtain a discharge with pension for loss of an eye. Paralysis and epilepsy were common hoaxes, continuous vomiting produced by drugs, or coughing up blood purchased for the purpose at butchers' shops, usually by the womenfolk, were less drastic devices.

A staggering paradox that England, the lonely stronghold of freedom and individual liberty on the edge of Napoleon's Europe, could only preserve her ideals at the cost of the inhuman bondage that drove men to these lengths. Fox's last effort and success before his death had been devoted to pushing through both Houses of Parliament a resolution to end the human commerce in Negroes; yet the policemen – the men-of-wars' men – to carry this ideal into practice enjoyed less freedom than any slave on a West Indian plantation and worked often harder, certainly more perilous hours for their hard, salt tack, their ration of the 'cat'.

The paradoxes we may note were scarcely apparent to Broke. He was an intelligent man and a thoughtful man, but his reflections never extended to questioning fundamental truths. The laws of God and of Nature ordained that the King ruled the country by right, that the nobility and the common people each served in the separate, immutable stations to which it had pleased God to call them and Britannia ruled the wide oceans by the same token. To do so she found it necessary to impress some poor wretches who had little enough to look for in this life in any event. Bonaparte conscripted men for the *Grande Armée* – where was the difference? The pressed men should be proud to serve in the 'sacred cause'. They would be, too, after some months under his command.

Of greater practical import was the unfortunate effect the British claim to the right of impressment had on American opinion. For America, as the chief neutral seafaring nation, and a country whose nationals were scarcely, if at all, distinguishable from Britishers, suffered most severely from the arrogant demands of the Royal Navy, mistress of the seas – and so conscious of it. If an American seaman had lost his papers or was otherwise suspect of British nationality a Royal Naval boarding officer under instructions to secure a certain number of prime seamen would always give *himself* the benefit of any doubt, and take the man. American feelings were constantly outraged. And there were few such enlightened British Admirals as Collingwood, who would place themselves in imagination in the American position and ask themselves: "What should we say if the Russians were to man themselves out of English ships?" Collingwood considered the affair with America "extremely improvident and unfortunate as in the issue it may involve us in a contest which it would be wisdom to avoid . . ."

"Toss oars!"

The stem of the barge nosed past the entry steps leading up the tumble home of the *Shannon*'s side. Broke stood and grasped the baize-covered side ropes which had been run down for his arrival, stepped out on to the lowest rung and mounted quickly, hauling up hand over hand. He was an athletic man, at thirty in the prime of life. The Boatswain's pipe shrilled and quavered above; the guard of Marines with scarlet tunics, white pipe-clayed cross-belts, brass fittings a-glimmer, white breeches, stood to attention with fixed bayonets, toeing a seam of the quarterdeck; the hands who had been employed about the deck stood away forward; Lieutenant James Bray, in temporary command, stood, together with Midshipmen and the Lieutenants of Marines, near the entrance port.

As Broke's foot touched the deck, the officers' heads were uncovered, the guard snapped to the present and the uniformed side boys stood rigidly. He turned and raised his hat briefly to the ensign flapping hugely from the stern. A Captain in His Britannic Majesty's Navy – a man of the highest importance – a minor god, clothed in dignity and awe.

His gaze swept back across the ship – the statuesque quarterdeck party eyeing him with interest, the great bitts opposite with each rope from above belayed on its pin and coiled neatly, the dull ochre mainmast rising solidly from the deck, ringed with black mast hoops, black blocks shining amidst the rigging; forward a disarray of spars fresh from the pickle vats, coils of rope, a jumble of opened casks, a launch in the act of hoisting, canvas spread over the parallel black seams of caulking to prevent paint discolouring the deck, bulwarks partly obscured by the glistening carronades lashed alongside them to be out of the way.

He stepped aft. There was a fresh smell about her compounded of turpentine and varnish, hemp, paint, sawn timber, tar, and that indefinable shipyard and river smell that took him straight back to his boyhood and the quays at Ipswich.

Nacton. He wished Louisa could see him now. How she hated him leaving her – yet if she could just smell this shapely new frigate of his and know what it meant – of course she did know. But it didn't make it any easier.

He beckoned to the First Lieutenant. "Have the hands mustered, Mr. Bray, if you please!"

Capitaine Jurien de la Gravière: "It is impossible to avoid seeing in the capture of the *Chesapeake* a new proof of the enormous power of good organisation, when it has received the consecration

22

of a few years actual service at sea . . . on the 16th September, 1806, the day when he took command of his frigate, Captain Broke had begun to prepare the glorious termination to this bloody affair. The Americans were wrong to accuse fortune . . ."

CHAPTER TWO

BROKE stayed aboard at night for the first time on 22nd September. The frigate was all ready for sea. The larboard bower anchor was hove short, the pilot was lying in the cot which had been rigged for him, the decks were quiet and quite dark. The only gentle sounds which entered Broke's sleeping-cabin were from the Thames gurgling past the side below and fussing around the rudder, imparting fractional movement to the timbers – independent life to this new ribbed and planked sea creature of his. On the deck above a Marine sentinel was keeping himself awake with a steady pacing – eleven steps up – pause – eleven steps back . . .

Broke was thankful to be sailing. The half-and-half affair of lodgings and inns ashore was not to his liking. It offered neither the comforts and delights of home and Looloo and the children nor the stirring prospect of action. And he disliked the atmosphere of a ship in port, which so lacked the crisp orderliness and routine of the life at sea: instead there were dockyard officials and scoundrelly victualling officers with their gear and stores about the decks and a laxness among the hands due to their generally debauched condition as they made up for months of deprivation at sea in a few short days. Not that he begrudged them their licentious sport with women and drink on the berth deck. The poor devils had little enough else to enjoy in this life.

He was lucky to have so many at this stage. In addition to the Marines and the few hands he was allowed from his previous command, mostly Petty officers and Midshipmen, he had a draft from the *Zealand*, guardship at the Nore, whither many of the London-pressed men were taken and incarcerated until one of His Majesty's vessels required them. They were a mixed crowd with few prime seamen among them. But which Captain had enough seamen in these times?

In fact there were barely seventy who had been trained to the sea; of the rest there were 2 shipwrights, 2 sawyers, 5 carpenters, 1 cabinet maker, 1 wheelwright, 4 coopers, 1 lathmaker, 4 ropemakers,

C

8 watermen, 2 sailmakers, 2 blacksmiths, 1 whitesmith, 1 nailer, 1 tinman, 1 brickmaker, 1 miner, 2 tanners, 5 husbandmen, 49 labourers, 1 stationer, 1 pen cutter, 1 printer's pattern maker, 1 jeweller, 1 steward, 32 servants – including boys – 1 butcher, 1 cook, 1 miller, 3 bakers, 1 brewer, 3 fishermen, 4 gardeners, 1 cotton-spinner, 7 weavers, 1 fustian cutter, 2 wool-combers, 1 framework-maker, 2 framework-knitters, 1 cloth-dresser, 7 tailors, 11 shoemakers, 1 hatter, 1 barber, 1 whipmaker, 2 horse lackies, 1 ostler and 1 chimney sweep. These landsmen were mostly English with a good sprinkling of Scots and Irish, and just four Welsh, but the sailors comprised many nationalities, among them Portuguese, Italians, Hamburgers, West Indians, as many as eleven North Americans and even strangely a Frenchman. The sea was an international profession.

The average height of the crew thus formed was a mere 5 feet 6½ inches and of the total of two hundred and fifty-odd, only forty-two topped 5 feet 8 inches, and of these only seven were over 5 feet 10 inches. These figures were by no means extraordinary; the pitiful diet of the poor of the country had so stunted their growth that by comparison with the established middle and upper classes many were poor physical specimens. They would soon grow hard and muscular at sea, though, or go under in a sewn hammock with round-shot at their feet.

The main thing was that they were hands to be moulded, and sufficient of them. Broke drifted off to sleep with an untroubled mind, lulled by the familiar music of the tide.

The frigate woke to life early the following morning. The Boatswain's Mates and Midshipmen cursed and chivvied and 'started' the sluggards out of their close hammocks with short ropes' ends. The landsmen would learn soon enough. Directly after the frantic rush to the upper deck to stow their hammocks in the nettings lining either side at the waist, and above the fo'c'sle and quarterdeck bulwarks, the pipes were shrilling again for unmooring stations. The carpenters shipped the capstan bars; the fifer took up his position close by, the messenger rope was turned around the drum of the capstan, taken right forward around a roller and led back astern to its own eye and lashed to form a continuous bight; meantime the men with the rope nippers lashed its forward part to the anchor cable where it came in through the round, heavily timbered bow – and the tramping began.

"Merrily now, my lads! Walk away with her!"

Round and round the capstan in time to the tune, feet stamping the deck, and a cheer from the seasoned hands each time the nippers were unlashed and replaced farther forward on the dripping cable. As the strain came on each section the muddy Thames water oozed out of the strands and made rivulets along the deck. The rope quivered aft without a pause. Down in the close, hemp and adzed oak atmosphere of the cable hold the tierers sweated the slack of it round in great wet coils while the *Shannon* crept slowly forward over the tide.

Broke stood in uniform and cocked hat on the quarterdeck listening to the sounds of departure coming up through the hatchway from the maindeck. There was more noise than he liked to hear, and he guessed that the Boatswain's Mates were using their 'starters' over-zealously. But it was necessary to break these new hands in quickly – time enough to relax the bullying when they thoroughly knew what they were about.

He started walking along the gangway towards the fo'c'sle where the pilot was standing on a carronade, watching the cable creak in through the hawse-hole. The morning air was fresh, tinged with river smells. He felt keenly alive. Now that the break had been made he only wished to be away, to wash the shore and all its associations from the decks with salt water. And the sooner he was away, the sooner he might return – if it pleased God, return with some distinction.

He saw the pilot straighten and jump down from the gun. The anchor must be aweigh. A cry of "Up and down!" confirmed it, and the next moment the First Lieutenant on the quarterdeck was shouting orders through his speaking trumpet to make sail. In an instant there was a rattling and thudding of feet over the ladders and decks from below and the shrouds were swarming with men grasping the lower ratlines – awaiting the next word. More men formed themselves up by the fore- and mainmasts, some casting off ropes from the pins, others who had little idea of their positions were harried like sheep by the Boatswain's Mates. He shuddered at the disorderly riot of movement and shouting. One poor wretch stumbled in the confusion and was savagely beaten over the shoulders by a petty officer, which only made his confusion worse. Broke made a note to reprimand the petty officer. There would be no unnecessary violence in his ship.

The First Lieutenant called "Away Aloft!" and the men in the shrouds started up like acrobats, shaking the rigging in their haste, racing to be first over the tops – these were the sailors. A pause during which the stragglers caught up, then "Trice up and lay out!" and the reaching yards were alive with figures creeping out along the foot-ropes – one man from the foretop was running out along the yard itself. As they reached their positions they untied and cast off the gaskets, and took the weight of the sails thus released in their arms.

"Let fall! Sheet home! Hoist Away!"

"This is one of the spectacles that charm the trade of war . . . the instant flashing effect is magical and magnificant; the minute-ago-naked masts, beams and yards, the whole of the uptowering scaffolding and beautiful skeleton is clothed in fifteen thousand feet of graceful drapery, so perfectly fitted and so admirably put on. Then out it swells and curves in the wind; it is beauty itself."

The Marines of the starboard watch were running aft with the topsail halyards – the blocks rattled and the sheaves spun as the yards stretched their canvas aloft.

"Belay!"

Quiet again, as the *Shannon* leant over to the breeze and started paying off across the tide. The First Lieutenant ripped out more orders to man the braces as she came round, and the Quartermaster at the wheel moved the spokes to test if the rudder was biting yet. Broke leaned over the side and watched the dark water sliding past, gathering speed – she had a fine, long run. The rigging snapped taut as she heeled over fractionally more to a gust, and the yards creaked and grunted into position, the wheel ropes squeaked through their blocks below – then she was round and away, headed for the Queen's Channel and the open estuary, picking up her skirts and walking out over the chop on the water.

The wind freshened all the time as she ran out over the Kentish Flats. Clouds formed together in the sky. The low shoreline of Essex was lost to sight, Thanet lay to starboard, the ruined towers of Reculver standing up boldly as they had for centuries to guide mariners inside the sands. Ships and small craft, the trade of the world – and mostly in British and American bottoms – beat up past them towards London, lowering their topsails briefly in salute. *Shannon* was feeling the open sea now, rising to it and dipping gracefully, and the buxom white figurehead took her first splashes of deep salt water.

Broke was well pleased with his ship. He paced the weather side of the quarterdeck feeling the need to talk to someone about her – how easily she skipped along on her new copper. Perhaps he would invite the First Lieutenant to dine. But out here on deck protocol must be maintained, and a few brief phrases to which James Bray would reply respectfully, non-committally, would have to serve as conversation.

A Captain kept aloof from his officers. It was decreed by tradition and necessity; too close a familiarity in the confined spaces of a man-of-war and he would soon become drawn into the strands of their lives and lose that god-like detachment and jealously guarded superiority upon which he might have to rely in moments of crisis, disaffection and boredom. He was accorded the status and privileges of a monarch; it was necessary to observe the constraints.

. . .

"Sept 23 Came to Downs R L saw
Admls Holl^{y} Whin^{ts} here
"24 Ashore PM Gale
"25 R Orders . . ."

The following day, the weather being fine again with light westerly breezes, the topmasts and yards which had been struck for the gale were sent aloft and the *Shannon* proceeded to Dungeness Bay to take on water, fresh beef and other victuals. She stayed here for some weeks, and Broke took the opportunity personally to supervise the laying and sighting of his great guns.

The first task was to measure the 'dispart' of each one of the 28 long 18-pounder cannon which formed the maindeck battery, 14 each side. Cannon were cast in such a way that the outside diameter at the breech was greater than at the muzzle ring, and thus any aim taken along 'the line of metal' inevitably angled the bore of the gun some degrees above the direct line to the object aimed at – this was one of the reasons why the masts and rigging of engaged vessels often suffered more than their hulls. To counteract this natural angle of elevation, or dispart, many officers fitted a short metal upright, in effect a foresight, somewhere along the barrel – perhaps the most common place was upon the muzzle ring itself. Broke had his armourer fit the sight halfway along the gun atop the trunnion ring so that it would be less liable to accidental damage when the gun was run out or in through the port.

Having disparted the pieces, the next step was to ensure a simple and effective method of having the guns laid horizontally under all conditions of visibility, both for point-blank firing if the ship happened to be upright, and to act as a 'zero' mark when it was required to elevate or depress the guns according to the heel under canvas, or the range of the target. The first step here was to get the ship upright as observed on a plum-line hung from aloft down the main hatchway – easily done on a calm day by moving weights across the deck. Then a timber in the shape of a large 'T' square, the 'T' being set exactly at right angles to the main length and having a small plumb-line hanging down it, was thrust into the bore of each piece in turn, and the gun elevated or depressed by moving the wedge-shaped quoin under its breech out or in until the plumb showed the bore to be horizontal. At this point scores were cut into the quoin and its bed which were sufficiently deep for each gun captain to lay his piece for horizontal fire by night or in the smoke simply by touch. Two more deep scores, either side of this 'horizontal' mark, were added after some months at sea. One of these was for:

"That level on which the gun would be point blank for the horizon when it was on the lee side and the ship under the heaviest press of sail on a wind under which it was probable she would engage in a chase or running fight; this would be an elevation of from 6 to 9 degrees according to the stiffness of the ship."

The other score was for similar conditions when the gun was on the windward side of the ship. But that is going ahead. Having all his main battery lined horizontally in Dungeness Bay, Broke began fitting tangent scales to them. These scales, of which there are several differing sketches in his notebooks, were probably simply upright pieces of wood fixed at the breech of each gun, and having horizontal scores cut across them for different degrees of elevation. Instead of lining up the breech ring top with the forward dispart sight, the captain of the gun would line up whichever score corresponded to the ordered elevation. Other sketches show more complicated structures, which are in effect 'V' backsights moving up or down between uprights marked for the different elevations.

These sighting arrangements underwent constant modification later as Broke watched and analysed their success at target practice, and before the end of the cruise the tangent scales were replaced or made secondary to wooden quadrants marked with the degrees of elevation, fixed on the side of each breech, each having a plumb-bob to give the vertical line.

All these modifications were carried out on the main battery of long 18-pounders on the gun deck. Above them, on the quarterdeck and fo'c'sle, were the carronades, stumpy, wide-bored pieces for short-range work. These fired a 32-pounder ball – as large as the shot from the main batteries of line-of-battle ships – but being very short in the barrel they did not carry very far. They were often considered to be inaccurate, but as their bores were drilled to allow less space around the shot – technically, less 'windage' on the ball – than the long guns, they were often far more accurate for close-range work with solid shot than the long guns. Their real advantages, however, were extreme lightness, and ease of operation by a smaller crew than was required for one of the long-carriage guns. Because of their short barrels they could also be loaded in faster time than a long gun – and when within range they became fearful weapons, spewing enormous quantities of grape or canister from their wide mouths.

Their elevation was altered by a screw instead of a timber quoin, and instead of being mounted on conventional carriages their trunnions were held on a baulk of timber which moved along another length of timber called the slide. This slide was pivoted at the outboard end so that the gun could be trained.

For these pieces Broke had the 'horizontal' mark and the degrees of elevation and depression painted around the screw thread. But as supplied by the Ordnance Department the carronades could not be depressed more than about five degrees – entirely insufficient for firing horizontally to windward under canvas in anything like a fresh breeze – and so he had his carpenters make special chocks to fit snugly under the inboard ends of the slides to raise them when firing to windward and allow a depression below the 'zero' mark of some 10° or 11°. These chocks could be fixed in an instant by only two men, one holding the slide up, the other placing the chock beneath.

Now, having achieved his uniform scales to ensure that each gun would be precisely aligned to the number of degrees ordered, Broke set about his master scheme, probably the first example of what came to be known later as 'director firing'. This was a system to allow the guns to be concentrated on any given spot within their arc of fire by night or in thick smoke, when the individual gun captains could not see the target. Opposite each of the maindeck gunports inboard of the gun carriages, lines of bearing were cut into the deck planking, the centre line aimed at a point directly abeam at point-blank range – thus at the forward ports this line would be pointing slightly aft, and at the after ports slightly forward to concentrate the fire. The scores were filled with white putty and marked in degrees. Amidships on the upper deck just before the mainmast a large compass was inscribed in lead with marks of bearing corresponding to those at the gunports.

"To suppose a case: you are coming up with your enemy on a dark night; the Captain judges what her distance *will be* and how many degrees of the wooden quadrant (tangent scale) will give that distance. Then he orders the guns to be so elevated and trained to so many points before the beam. All being ready the Captain watches the bearing of the enemy by the compass on the tank (before the mainmast) and when that bearing corresponds with the point to which the guns are trained, he gives the order to fire."

This was a system of incredible refinement for the day and with the equipment available. To appreciate the advance it marked it is necessary to realise that at this time the Admiralty was still rejecting applications for gun sights on the ground that "such novelties" were "not according to the regulation of the service".

Broke even went to the length of having his carpenters compensate for the sheer of his gun deck – that is the slope towards the waist from the bow and stern – by cutting down the high side of each carriage until the bed was horizontal as observed on a spirit level. No detail was too small to be overlooked.

.   .   .

There was a brief interlude for action in October when the *Shannon* was ordered to join a squadron attacking Boulogne with Mr. Congreve's rockets, long, iron-encased projectiles capable of such destruction that the *Naval Chronicle* found it "scarcely possible to describe the effect they produce on the mind".

Broke noted in his pocket diary:

> "Oct 6 received fireworks
> "   8 Went to Boulogne with squadron – attacked with rockets – burnt a house
> "   9 W L."

They returned to Dungeness and continued provisioning and preparing the ship for a cruise. In November came a consignment of stores for the Boatswain: brooms 36; brushes, tar, 10; hides in the hair in lieu of junk for mats on the yards, foot of sails and rigging, 10; junk to complete points, gaskets, rope bands, nippers, plats, mats on the gunwales; leather buckets 25; rope or twice-laid stuff, hammocks and old rags for service, spunyarn 6 cwt. . . .

Shannon sailed soon after and spent the rest of the winter in routine blockade duties in the Channel, seldom seeing an enemy's ship unless at anchor in her own harbour, but working the raw hands up to a pitch of excellence with the guns and sights and small arms – drilling for the day when their chance would come.

In the early spring Broke received orders for Greenland with the object of protecting the British whaling fleet which had suffered from the depredations of a French squadron the previous year. The *Meleager* frigate, Captain Broughton, was placed under his command.

He sailed up to Yarmouth to complete for the voyage at the beginning of April, and on Sunday 26th, the *Meleager* having joined, the two vessels weighed and set course northwards in light winds and clear weather. Broke had aboard, in addition to full holds of casked, salted foodstuffs, six live bullocks "and a sufficiency of vegetables to serve the crew about three weeks, besides the officers' private stock of sheep".

He went with an eager mind. It promised to be an interesting cruise in a region he had never seen during all his time at sea, and there were prospects of chase and action if the French decided to repeat their efforts of last year; above all, he was for the first time in his career under no superior orders. *Shannon* and *Meleager* were his to do with as he saw fit, far from any control by the Admiralty or local Commanders-in-Chief. And after the brief dissipations of the shore, he returned with fresh heart to making his people as expert at all the warlike drills as patience and thought could ensure. In the lengthening evenings he sought to relieve the ache at leaving his delightful family once again by retiring into his books, or the education of his 'sea children'. He liked to stimulate their young minds to the enjoyment of authors and poets who gave him pleasure.

"I am glad you delight in Horace," he remarked to one of his more cultivated lads, who came to borrow from his library one day, "there is no work to which one can recur for a vacant quarter of an hour – or even for a few minutes – with so much pleasure. Such imagination! Such colouring and such elegance of expression! Every brief ode is a *beautiful gem*, flashing a sudden, pleasing light and glow over the mind instantaneously and leaving it in a sort of happy harmony. What a beautiful resource for a man in active life, who can now and then only snatch a moment to listen to the *magic of poesy!*"

He wondered if he had relaxed his stern façade too much. "That is," he added, "his enchanting odes, and his pleasing, social and elegant letters. But excellent as his satires are, I could wish he had never written them. All satirists at times get so *sour* that one *cannot love them.*"

. . .

The two frigates strode northwards over a calm and misty North Sea. There were no excitements to break the unremitting routine except for those provided by the ships' companies themselves.

On 28th April a man named William Franklin was caught stealing from a messmate and sentenced to the 'cat', the thirteenth man to be so punished since Broke had taken command six months earlier, not a record of extraordinary leniency, but certainly not tyranny or sadism as practised by a number of His Majesty's commanders in the sacred name of discipline.

The pipes shrilled and the Boatswain's hoarse voice carried over the ship, up the masts, down the ladders, through the berth deck and the mazy, heavy-timbered dark alleyways and storerooms below, "All hands ahoy to witness punishment!"

The Marines, shining with polish, formed up under their sergeant, and fixed bayonets to a snap of brief, almost musical orders, while the crew shuffled or were harried by the Boatswain's Mates into groups forward of them either side of the main deck. Broke and his officers in full uniform with side arms stood splendidly on the quarterdeck as the wretched Franklin, dressed in his best jacket and trousers in the faint hope that it might help him with his plea, was led forward to make a defence. Broke listened with a stony face. The officers were silent. The Master at Arms led the man back to the grating which had been prepared in a vertical position against the gangway and helped him to remove his jacket and shirt. Two Quartermasters sprang to his wrists and seized them to the grating above his head with lengths of spunyarn, then bent and lashed his ankles.

Broke watched the scene without expression as he had watched so many hundreds of similar, often far worse degradations throughout his career. It was the part of his duty he relished least, but it was a very essential part if the mixed collection of sailors, vagrants, jail sweepings, dissatisfied tradesmen and scoundrels aboard were to be ordered into a harmonious and respectful crew. For certain offences the men expected it – not as some Captains laid it on for any minor deviation, but as a stern reminder that the code did not countenance mutinous talk, insolence, insubordination, theft, excessive drunkenness or 'filthiness'. In the cooped-up rough and tumble of a frigate's sweating berth deck it was necessary to have occasional demonstrations of this frightful severity of the law.

Franklin's back was very white against the teak grating. The Boatswain's mate, whose turn it was to administer punishment, had removed his own coat and rolled his shirt-sleeves to the elbow. He extracted the 'thieves' cat' from its baize bag and ran his fingers through the nine tails, combing them out by habit although there was no blood yet to clot them. The knots down each strand were larger and harder than those on the normal 'cat'. Theft, although a commonplace below decks, could not be tolerated when caught.

". . . any man who would whip his horse with this instrument of torture would commit an outrage which the moral feelings of any community would not tolerate . . ."

The Boatswain's Mate positioned himself carefully a few feet from the grating, legs flexed slightly apart, and glanced briefly at his white target, which was motionless except for the nervous rise and fall of the lungs. Suddenly he swept the 'cat' back behind his neck and in the next instant lunged forward with his whole weight behind his arm as he brought it down. The ropes and knots hissed briefly and landed with a cutting sound about Franklin's ribs; his breath left his body in a shocked, involuntary gasp.

The Boatswain's Mate regained his balance and lunged again. The white flesh blushed in streaks, patches of blood broke through where the knots had struck. Franklin writhed from his wrists. The ropes landed again, and this time the deck was spotted with red, and more red on the Boatswain's mate's fingers as he drew the strands out, then tossed them behind his back. They hissed again – cut! Franklin leaped in his confinement and oathed to keep himself from screaming. The first blushes on his back were swelling into angry purple weals as the 'cat' fell again – and again – and again . . .

". . . the lacerated back looks inhuman; it resembles roasted meat burnt nearly black before a scalding fire; yet still the lashes fall; the Captain continues merciless . . ."

Twenty-four full-weight, athletic lashes, two hundred and sixteen closely spaced weals, three times that number of places where the knots had bitten in – a raw battleground of furrows overlaid and sticky with gore. Franklin would carry the marks of it for life. He was cut down from the grating and led away to the sick bay, staining his path with drops of blood, while the rest of the hands departed silently to the pipe down.

On the following day the scene was re-enacted with a man named Woodward in Franklin's place at the grating – again for theft – again twenty-four lashes.

.   .   .

By 7th May the two frigates had reached a latitude of 70° N and fallen in with the first drifts of loose ice. The thermometer, which had been falling steadily, now sank and remained below zero even at noon, and the poultry started dying of cold; those fowls that survived, they killed and hung in a boat towed astern, hoping that the snow might preserve them. Snow and sleet showers became frequent. The sea rose in squalls and froze in beads and daggers of ice along the lower rigging, chains and head nettings. And when the hands attempted to wash decks in the early morning the water iced up and had to be removed with shovels. Whales rose and blew around them.

"On the 15th May, being standing to the Northward in lat 73° 15′ N and long 12° 50′ E, we met with a heavy body of ice, stretching from the NW to SE as far as we could see from the mastheads, and apparently of great breadth as we could see no horizon beyond it; the background of this drift was broken into high hummocks, the most distant of which appeared like land; much loose ice was connected with this bank and streamed away to the SW. We sailed along the skirts of it for two days and then stood away to get further off as foul weather came on . . .

"21st . . . the groups became closer as we advanced – the masses were frequently of the length of the ship and as high out of the water as our maindeck guns, or about ten or twelve feet . . . the smaller pieces were much lower; they were all covered alike with frozen snow – we saw seals basking upon many of them. Their groups were often so closely crowded that we could not steer the ship between them without her striking, which she several times did with considerable violence, though we kept steering under easy sail, and picking our way with great caution . . . Having myself seen so much ice in the Eastward I was now convinced that we could not get up to the fishery off Spitzbergen without forcing our way through it, which our pilots thought would be a dangerous attempt for the frigates as they were not prepared for this kind of navigation by sheathing and filling as the whalers' ships are, or furnished with ice hooks etc for securing them to the ice in case of necessity. We had already experienced some smart shocks from the larger pieces and thought it advisable under these circumstances to extricate ourselves and recover the open sea before any foul weather should come on . . ."

Broke decided to tack his ships and sail westward for Jan Mayen's Island in the hope of intercepting any enemy's vessels which might choose that route to the fisheries off Spitzbergen. But again he found himself blocked by ice.

During all this period of tacking and filling in arctic conditions with the haze off the ice never far distant he took pains to keep his people dry, warm and fit so far as he was able. Whenever rain or squalls threatened, he shortened to easy sail in order that they would not need to go aloft in dangerous conditions; whenever the sun shone he exercised them on deck at warlike practices with the great guns and small arms at a target, cutlass drill, singlestick. As a result of his care, the sick list was confined to four men, all suffering from accidental hurts; as a result of his meticulous attention to every detail of drill with the great guns the *Shannon* was fast becoming a formidably destructive opponent.

"June 1st   PM   Exercised the Great Guns . . ."

The drum rolled to quarters. Immediately the hands were doubling to their well-rehearsed stations. Shortly afterwards silence again – broken only by the waves hissing and swirling past the side, the creak of a yard, the strain of a tiller rope over its lignum-vitae roller. All down the clear, curving length of the maindeck the guns' crews of the larboard battery were ranged quietly by their pieces; four men each side of each barrel, facing their opposite numbers over the metal. And staring down the lines from each breech, the captains of the guns awaited the first order. Beside them were the powder boys, so many of them looking too young and too slight to be companions to these monstrous cylinders of black iron – the barrels were safely trussed up now by their necks above the closed ports, but once loose and given a taste of powder they would take on an independent leaping life of their own . . .

The men stood easily to attention, legs braced against the easy list and roll; in contrast to the waxwork stiff lines of Marines on the gangways above them they were flexible and relaxed – but alert. Nearest the ship's side in each crew the loader faced the loader's mate – there were no numbers in Broke's plan of quarters, only names associated with duties. Next to these two came the small-arms man opposite the fireman, who was also a sail trimmer when the occasion demanded; third in the lines the second loader, who was also a sail trimmer and boarder, stood opposite to the second captain of the gun, who was also a boarder, and nearest to the breech of each piece, the tackle man faced the lanthorn man.

The Second Lieutenant, officer of the forward maindeck quarters, stood with his Midshipman aides watching over the guns numbered 1 to 7; the Third Lieutenant, officer of the after quarters, guns from 8 to 14, waited under the skylight from the quarterdeck for the next command.

"Clear for action!"

The stillness had been unnatural. Now it broke into a riot of movement – no voices, but hurrying feet, blocks dropping on deck, the chink of hooks and bolts going home, reaching hands unhitching the sponges, worms and rammers from the beams just above head height and laying them on deck in parallel, flexible rope handles towards the ship's side, others placing the metal-ended handspikes and crows each side of their carriage; second captains lighting their long rope slow matches and placing the glowing ends securely in the notches cut into the rims of their match tubs; loaders and loaders' mates casting off the muzzle ring lashings, the hands on the tackles choking any movement of the great pieces with quick turns around the cleats; gun captains removing their vent covers, placing the flint-locks, adjusting the flints, collecting their first tin tubes of priming powder and a pouch of spare flints from the shot lockers; small arms men collecting cutlasses for the boarders, handed up to them from chests below, placing them abreast of each gun well clear of its jumping space; lanthorn men collecting nettings of wads, powder boys scurrying from the magazine scuttle with their salt boxes each containing one flannel cartridge, cloth jackets spread over the boxes to prevent sparks entering – no detail was too small even for practice. Drill and drill and drill would stand the fearful test of action where thinking would fail.

Now the upper halves of the gunport lids had been unshipped and sunlight was striking in diagonals across the roll and casting the unlit, dull-stone painted timbers of the ship's side into gloom by comparison. The arctic breeze swept in. The dogs were knocked off the lower halves of the port lids and they were unshipped and placed inboard out of the way.

The movement began to dissolve again and the men, warm from their activity, waited silently in position. They would be warmer soon despite the chill wind, and exhausted by the immense efforts required of them. The 18-pdrs., nine feet long, weighed more than two tons apiece, and the friction in the tackle blocks and axletrees increased this – they had to be drawn smartly too . . .

"Cast loose the guns!"

Commotion once more. The lashings were freed, tompions unplugged, and while the cannon were held in position by the side tackles opposing the train tackles from the backs of the carriages to eyebolts inboard, the second captains and second loaders lifted the breeches, using their handspikes as levers over the stepped timbers of the carriage; the gun captains inserted their quoin beneath, pushing it home to the third deep score – horizontal firing to windward.

"Run out the guns!"

Each gun captain, a foot placed on the back of his carriage, seized its breeching rope and pulled it up clear as the crews lent their weight to the tackles and the trucks went rumbling outboard, carrying the muzzles through the ports. The carriages thumped up against the lower port sills. The captains laid the slack of their breeching rope in bights either side of the piece so that there would be no fouling when the guns leaped in recoil. After that the priming wires – thin metal spikes – were poked down the vents to prick the cartridge inside the breech and expose the powder. The cannon were always kept loaded at sea. A priming tube filled with good-quality dry powder was thrust into each vent after the priming wire had been withdrawn and inspected for traces of cartridge – then more powder sprinkled from the horn into the pan of the flint-lock which would fire it. Bruise the powder with the end of the horn – hang the horn from a beam.

The gun captains, taking their firing lanyards in hand, stepped back to the full extent of the line, some six feet safe from the breech.

"Point!"

They bent their right knees to lower their eyes to the level of the breech ring, keeping their left feet extended to the side, well clear of the probable line of recoil, and shouted terse instructions to the second captains and second loaders, who levered the carriages bodily and clumsily over the deck with handspikes to train them. The other hands kept a strain on the side tackles.

"Fire!"

A pause as the ship yawed off course and the dispart sights swung ahead of the small, rising and dipping barrel target. The second captains crouched by their pieces prepared to leap clear as the gun fired, but held their slow matches ready to plunge them on to the priming powder if the lock should fail – they blew on the ends to keep the glow fierce. The men on the side tackles prepared to let go everything.

The frigate came back slowly and as the sights veered towards the target again the firing lanyards tightened in anticipation – then jerked taut. Sparks from the lock's snap – a series of deafening crashes – vents spitting flame – jumping black metal – side-tackle ropes racing round their sheaves, train-tackle men hauling in on the slack until the flying guns were held up on their breeching ropes – the carriages slapped and cracked back to the deck at all angles. Haul taut the side tackles! Hold her now – steady – steady again!

The loaders were thrusting their sponge handles out through the grey-white smoke clouding in at the ports and then ramming the sponge down the muzzle in one motion – three quick turns all the same way, and withdrawing it – the new cartridge had been handed by the second loader – thrust in, seam downwards, tied-up end outwards – rammer handle out through the port and in again over the cartridge, pushing it home – well home – an extra shove – then the cannon ball itself sent rolling down after the cartridge as the ship heeled – a wad of rope yarn after it to hold it in position and then the rammer again – push it home – three smart taps to make sure . . .

The loading numbers were sweating now.

Broke paced the weather side of the quarterdeck above, past the carronade crews who had not yet fired, and gazed good-humouredly at the target barrel still floating unscathed forward of the beam as the *Shannon* reached slowly through the water. The shooting had been good, but it would have taken an exceptional or an exceptionally lucky shot to have hit so small an object at more than a cable's length in these conditions. They were closer now. Perhaps the next broadside . . .

He was delighted with the progress his people were making. They were responding to good treatment as all Britons would, and there was a bite and invigoration about this ungenial climate that seemed to put an edge to their keenness.

The First Lieutenant was looking at him, waiting to know if he should give the order to fire again. Broke nodded, and stopped his pacing to face the target.

The first gun from somewhere way forward crashed out shortly afterwards and the others followed closely in a jagged din of explosions which shook the deck. Flame tinged the smoke as it blew back over the gangways and fo'c'sle, and he saw the balls from the ports below the quarterdeck flying outwards, dark specks over the waves. A forest of waterspouts stood up, mostly beyond the target – and then quite suddenly one ball hit. The barrel leaped clear of the surface like a porpoise, disintegrating into its component staves, and bringing a spontaneous cheer from the carronade men, shortly echoed from below as the gun captains realised that the sea was empty again.

The First Lieutenant bawled down the skylight for an end to the noise. Broke insisted on absolute silence during every evolution, for if everyone was cheering and giving instructions the proper orders from the officers might not get through.

When the Lieutenant had lowered his speaking trumpet Broke called out, "The enemy is falling foul of our larboard bow, Mr. Bray. Prepare to repel boarders!"

Bray turned to instruct one of his midshipman aides before raising his trumpet again. When he had called the boarders away Broke told him to have another barrel target put over to give the carronade men their sport. And if they could not hit it – his own fingers were itching to pull a lock lanyard.

So it went week by week. Succeeding barrels tossed in storms of waterspouts until they were finally torn apart, sometimes by Broke himself at his quarterdeck aiming carronade. During aiming practice every man hitting the target was rewarded with half a pound of tobacco – at Broke's expense – and those men promoted to captain of a gun were given the status of Petty Officers and similar rights to shares of prize money. Broke's aim was to give each one confidence in his own single power of destruction if he would only aim and fire as coolly in battle as he did at practice. And to give the old hands confidence in his scheme for 'blindfold', or director, firing, he arranged occasional demonstrations without a target – ordering a set elevation and angle of bearing, and giving the order to fire as the side rolled up. The men soon got used to seeing the balls ploughing into the water almost as closely bunched as at target practice with a barrel.

When the hands were employed about the ship on necessary maintenance duties Broke often had his Lieutenants and Midshipmen themselves at one of the cannon or quarterdeck carronades, and encouraged a free discussion afterwards so that "some *advance* was generally making towards perfect service orders".

He never allowed these drills to deteriorate into formalism. Unexpected hypothetical situations were constantly thrust on his officers in the middle of the general practices, and they were expected to react on their own initiative.

"Nobody can tell how an action will be fought. Our honour is never safe unless we are ready for any turn that the enemy's desperation or *'fortune de guerre'* may give to the contest. We must always be ready to meet a fellow in any way he may fancy to try us."

"June 8th, 11 pm saw a bark and a brig – whalers. They bore off and ran, but showed British colours. We did not chase them, not wishing to drive them into the ice. At midnight it blew a hard gale with a huge, rolling sea. The sun was as brilliant as it ever is in England at noon, and the sky a pure, cloudless azure.

"9th 10 pm fine, but the sun had not power enough to melt the icy gems which cased our rigging in many places like a beautiful spar.

10th A fine, bright summer's noon at midnight. The sun gave a perceptable warmth through glass though the air was keenly frosty. The water was smooth, and the blue verge of it finely contrasted with the bright effulgence rising from the distant ice, and gradually blending with the pure, clear sky . . ."

Broke found the conditions of this cruise both novel and exciting. He recorded in his Journal, besides day-to-day occurrences, descriptions of the ice fields and their extent, the prevailing currents and winds, the methods of cautious navigation he was learning from his pilots and from experience, the antics of his compasses, which gave such wildly different variations from those recorded on his charts, and

D

details of any matters which he thought might prove useful to any successors or to the Lords of the Admiralty in London.

"The blink or brightness of the sky over the ice will often show its position long before the ice itself can be seen from the mastheads. It is well to take advantage of fine weather to ascertain the position of the ice in general that in thick or blowing weather a ship may know how far she can proceed with safety; and when cruising close on the skirts of the ice, or amongst drifts which lie apart from each other, it is proper to note down by heaving or a rough chart, the situation of the particular points and bays which the ice forms around you so that upon the sudden arrival of fogs or thick weather you may know which is the most likely way of extricating yourself. The ice will certainly not be quite stationary, but the separate larger drifts will nearly preserve their relative form and bearing for several days, unless they are directed in their driving by firm ice or the land to leeward, or scattered by long and obstinate gales . . . If caught with a fresh breeze between lee and weather drifts, or absolutely among heavy, driving masses of the ice, it is dangerous (in thick weather) to attempt to work or sail out again; the safest way is to lie and drive with the ice – backing and filling to avoid such pieces as you come near – in preference to wearing or bearing up to clear them, as the ship should never acquire headway enough to strike with violence. A man-of-war with her fore and main topsails aback will drive to leeward but a little faster than the heavier masses . . .

"If driving upon the shore it is certainly advisable to moor to a large mass of ice, as it will not only retard your drift, but probably take the ground in much deeper water than the ship will require to swim in; and if so will form her a smooth berth to ride in . . ."

By mid-June the *Shannon* and *Meleager* were still hovering off the ice pack, barred from northward progress, cruising among 'large, straggling islands of ice' and speaking several whaling vessels held up in the same way. The weather, which had been damp and foggy for much of the first part of the month, grew colder as the winds veered northerly. The fogs remained though; they hung about the vessels and froze where they settled, encasing every rope and yard in a sparkling sheath of ice. The sails stood out like glittering white boards, so stiff that when they were furled for the squalls which came frequently the canvas sometimes cracked across instead of bending. The men went warily along the footropes, and their hands became as tough and numb and cracked as the canvas itself.

In the third week of the month the fogs came down more densely still as the wind shifted into the south-east, freshening; the two frigates clawed their way off the floes, keeping company by firing a gun at intervals, but making little speed for fear of striking one of the huge bergs that would materialise suddenly out of the gloom – beautiful and sinister, seas washing and frothing white against the sides and driving spectacular caverns and grottoes through the solid walls, melting the ice into patterns of fantasy, coral branches and weird tree forms. Below the seething edge of the water great spurs stood outwards ready to impale any ship approaching too incautiously.

It was a relief when fine weather set in again, however briefly. And heading northwards once more they soon came upon geese and land birds whose calls and colours provided a welcome variation from the whales and herds of seals which had been their only companions among the wastes of mist and water they had passed through. The day after, 17th June, brought more of these shore visitors, and also the first glimpse of the land they came from, "a high, irregular chain of pyramidal mountains, their western ends glittering in the sun, probably clad in snow."

In blustery weather they cruised along the edge of the drift ice, which appeared to extend in solid formation between them and this high land, searching for a clear passage through, often becoming dangerously entangled as they probed up the shifting channels. White peaks reared on every hand, dazzling in the sun or hung with mist – jagged, grotesque shapes interspersed with channels and bays of deep water lifting with the swell – smoothed out under the lee of the ice, reflecting blue and stark white – constantly changing in pattern, narrowing, then widening unexpectedly, a maze of false trails to the north.

The bergs swung and drifted in the wind:

"... all lofty plains of ice covered with a smooth surface of snow, and filling up the gorges and vales between the mountains; they slope down to the seaside, and there terminate in abrupt precipices resembling cliffs of pure chalk, only more brilliant and partially tinged with the light blue colour of solid ice."

After another short spell of fogs Broke eventually found a way through the drifts on the 22nd June, and made such good progress along it – sailing through the night, which was as bright and clear as noon – that the two frigates were able to drop anchor in Magdalena Bay, Spitzbergen, on 23rd June.

Immediately they brought to, Broke had the launch hoisted from its stowage in the waist and lowered overside. He boarded it with his Master and several Midshipmen, and was pulled over to the *Meleager* to collect Captain Broughton, after which they spent laborious, chilling hours with the lead and line, sounding around the ships for uncharted rocks and shoals. Afterwards they went ashore to seek fresh water to replenish their own stale, casked supplies.

The next four days were similarly spent, sounding, exploring the land, surveying, until on the fifth day at anchor Broke was satisfied, and felt himself able to send his people ashore by watches to give them a break from routine.

They needed it. They landed from the boats and went mad. The air was keen and fresh, and with the sudden release from the harsh discipline aboard it acted on their spirits like alcohol. They gambolled and roared away up the snow-covered slopes, picking stones and chunks of ice and hurling them at the birds, which flapped up in swarms of alarm at this startling invasion of their territory. The men slipped and fell and shoved each other, small, hard, muscular, roughened and toughened men and youths, the stuff of the fiercest seafighters in Europe, swaggering game-cocks, many carrying indelible weals of the 'cat' across their ribs and shoulder-blades – now tumbling and shouting and laughing like boys released from school.

When the first, heady joys of freedom wore off, they became more cautious and took to stalking their game before hurling the rocks, or even catching the birds in their nests with bare hands. They returned to the ships in the evening in high humour with themselves, and over the following few days the monotonous, salt-hard meals took on fresh flavours.

Broke led parties of officers on to the islands after duck during the following days and they usually came back laden, Broke himself claiming fifty on one morning in early July. The boats' crews for their part knocked down several more with stones, and raided the nests for eggs – not such good sport as chasing the French, but a welcome diversion from cruising.

Broke spent a few more days surveying and gathering information from the whalers of all nationalities, Danes, Dutchmen, British, Hamburgers, that passed or sought shelter in the Bay, or anchored briefly to inter a man at Burial Ground Point, then, having heard no news of any enemy squadron and as the ice to the north was beginning to clear, he decided to push up for the Seven Isles, whither some of the more persevering whaling ships sometimes ventured; it was the direction in which Lord Mulgrave had recently been trapped while searching for a northern passage. Broke actually reached a latitude of

80° 5′ North before he was forced back around Amsterdam Island by the threat of being similarly blocked in by the shifting ice "without any certainty of being released again".

"July 12th – Began serving lemonade to our people, their vegetables having been some time exhausted. Each of them drank at the tub a large wineglassful *before* they took their afternoon grog. It was mixed with one sixth lime juice, the rest water, well sweetened with brown sugar. To be issued twice a week, which I now thought sufficient as we had no scorbutic symptoms among them."

Sailing back westerly towards Jan Mayen's Island, still without news of any enemy activity, they came again upon the area of wet, hazy weather and fogs which had plagued them on the way north. The fogs were so frequent now, and the winds so variable that Broke gave up his intention of reconnoitring the coast as he had at Spitzbergen, and hauled off eastwards instead. But they made little useful progress and on 2nd August, still surrounded by fogs and with both ships short of provisions, making it impossible for them to "risque the delay which might be occasioned by our getting entangled with the South East ice", Broke set course homewards.

"We continued beating to the southward without ever being clear of the fogs for above an hour at a time, till we got into 66° . . ."

Broke occupied himself recording summaries of what he had learned during the cruise with the precision and detail which invariably marked his despatches and reports. His notes were sent under various headings, 'Wooding and watering', 'Provisions', 'Navigation', 'The people', 'Fortifications', 'Inhabitants' . . .

". . . The Russians have resorted here for more than twenty years. They are hunters employed by the merchants at Archangel and come in small, lug-rigged vessels of about 70 or 80 tons burthen, of a clumsy construction . . . They bring their bread with them from Russia, and an ample supply of warm clothing, shoes and gloves, though they were mostly clad in their shirts, in deer skins rudely dressed, with the hair inwards. Besides bread, stockfish or salt fish was their chief food; their prejudices would not allow them to vary this diet by eating the bears or seahorses, or even the wildfowl, and they consequently lose some of their number every year by scurvy. They have never attempted to raise any vegetables, though it is probable that those of quick summer growth might be cultivated with success in the warmer spots . . .

"The profits of these annual hunting parties may possibly be an

43

object to the merchants of Archangel but they would hardly answer to Englishmen, as their equipment and expenses of wintering would be infinitely greater, and the returns by what I could collect were not of great value. The mass of their cargo is the oil which they procure from seals and seahorses, but one large whale would probably produce more than their annual shipload . . ."

On 15th August the mountains of Norway hove in sight from the mastheads of *Shannon* and *Meleager*, and the following day the *Shannon* spoke a little Hull brig bound for Archangel and heard of the recent peace signed between Napoleon and the Czar of Russia – it seemed as if all Europe would soon be ranged against Great Britain!

A week later the two frigates, their hulls bruised and scored from many collisions with the ice, and barely patched over with paint during the last stages of the voyage, made Kirkaldy Bay, Inch Keith. They anchored and made their numbers to the Admiral, and afterwards a boat came out to them with the latest news, including an account of a brief action fought in June off the eastern seaboard of the United States between His Majesty's ship *Leopard* and the United States frigate *Chesapeake*. It made little impression on Broke at the time and set against the larger news from Europe. Had he known, it was fraught with significance for him and the *Shannon*.

The *Chesapeake* affair did not immediately plunge America into war against Britain, nor was it the chief cause of the war which eventually came, but it was a slight and a humiliation which the Americans and particularly American Naval officers never forgot nor forgave; its psychological consequences were immense.

It was an entirely unexpected engagement, coming as it did between two ships of countries at peace with one another, and was perhaps just another symptom – more explosive than usual – of the arrogance which Britain's command of the sea had implanted in many of her Naval officers. It was also a symptom of the concern they felt over the numbers of prime seamen deserting their service for the U.S. flag. These seamen were lured by better pay and the allegedly better conditions in American ships, although this was in many cases a fallacy. However it was, they deserted. And the Royal Navy, which could not afford to lose any real sailors at such a stage of the death-grapple with France, insisted on the right to search for deserters aboard any vessels of whatever nationality on the high seas, and on the right to impress and punish with frightful severity any Britons so found. They enforced this right.

It was even the practice for a British squadron to blockade New

York itself and stop every vessel entering, British frigates running amok among the merchantmen and firing off warning guns indiscriminately in full sight of the inhabitants of the city. One such chance shot from H.M.S. *Leander* three years previously had struck an American vessel and killed the Mate, a man named John Pierce, whose mutilated body was afterwards raised on a platform by the New Yorkers and paraded around the city amidst a storm of indignation.

These instances of boarding and search were nearly all of merchantmen. When it came to stopping a ship of war . . .

The *Chesapeake* stood out to sea from Hampton Roads on a fine summer's morning without any thought of conflict. She sailed by the British squadron, which was blockading two Frenchmen inside, and noticed with scarcely more than passing interest that H.M.S. *Leopard* had been detached and appeared to be heading on a course to intercept her. Ten miles out the *Leopard* closed, and delivered a letter to Commodore Barron of the *Chesapeake* from the Admiral commanding the Halifax station, asking him to submit his men to inspection as it was believed that some were British deserters. Barron naturally refused.

Afterwards he 'observed some appearances of a hostile nature' from the *Leopard*, and sent his men to quarters – although he could scarcely believe that the British were serious in their intentions. He was soon undeceived. The *Leopard* fired a shot across his bows as he filled away, and followed it with a broadside or two – probably three – which killed or wounded 21 men, seriously wounded all the masts, shattered the fore- and mainsails and the lower shrouds and stays, planted 22 round shot in the hull and damaged 2 boats – a storm of fire from point-blank range.

The *Chesapeake* was caught entirely unprepared. There were no locks on her guns and her decks were still lumbered with coils of ropes and spars, while the passage to the magazine was obstructed with furniture and baggage belonging to passengers and bandsmen; she only managed to fire one gun in return, and this was set off by the heroic efforts of a Lieutenant carrying a burning coal in his hands from the galley. The *Leopard* ceased firing and waited a while, and Barron had no option but to submit. Four alleged deserters were removed, one of whom was hanged at the yardarm, and although the British Government later repudiated this intolerably high-handed action, the damage had been done. The *Chesapeake* returned to port in an agony of rage and shame.

The agony spread through the country, burning most fiercely in the few ships of the infant U.S. Navy.

Broke was a sensitive man, but the story awoke few pangs in him. After all, Britain's supremacy at sea was a fact of life, and if that supremacy was challenged even in such an insignificant way by their cousin Jonathan encouraging British sailors to desert, and then harbouring them . . . The *Chesapeake* no doubt deserved all she had got.

CHAPTER THREE

THE *Shannon* was despatched to winter in friendlier latitudes off Madeira. She went with a powerful squadron to take the island from the Portuguese garrison, and Broke was well pleased with the prospects of action and the chance of glory, however slight that might be for a frigate captain attached to such a force. In the event he saw neither. The Portuguese Governor, who had been wavering some time in the manner of his Government at home, eventually capitulated at the mere sight of the British sail running in to anchor off his walls on Christmas Eve. Major General Beresford landed four thousand troops unopposed. And two weeks later the *Shannon* was escorting the transports home again.

They arrived in Plymouth early in February. Broke learned that he would be attached to the Home Fleet under Lord Gambier, and took the opportunity to instal Louisa and the children in a house at Plymouth; they were his consolation and delight during the weary months that followed. Through dull cruises as convoy escort, on contraband duty or blockade work his thoughts constantly returned to them – and never more vividly than during the Sunday morning services he conducted. When the *Shannon* returned briefly to refit or take on provisions he never lost a moment to be with them.

Came the summer. July broiled and threatened to equal the heat of the previous year when the haymakers had been fainting in the fields; out in the Channel, where *Shannon* spent most of her time, seakeeping became less of a fight against the elements, and there was more time for experiment and drill – drill . . .

The masts circled lazily close off the French coast; aloft in the royal yards the lookouts searched the seaward horizon for glimpse of a sail. About the decks the hands were alert and unrecognisable from the sallow creatures, landsmen and white, emaciated jailbirds who had been drafted aboard two years earlier. Now their faces and arms were deep red from the wind and sun off the water, their hands like leather, their muscles great from heaving the cannon about; they walked with a wide gait and rolling motion to offset the heave of the decks, their flat varnished or straw hats were thrust back from their foreheads so that the rims would not interfere with sight aloft, and their clothes had that peculiar cut which immediately distinguished sailors – flowing dark neck scarves, checked or striped full shirts, blue trousers cut very tight around the hips, thence hanging long and loose to the ankles.

But the chief difference was inward; they were a team, a fighting team encouraged by humane treatment and meaningful competitions, and rehearsed for every eventuality that forethought could conceive from the hostile elements or the fortunes of war. They could fight their frigate one side or both sides together, lay for horizontal fire in heavy, rolling weather or flat calm, by day or at midnight; when they could see the target, when they could see nothing from the gun deck – if half the hands were dead or half the hands were boarding, when the gun captains were killed, when the flints in the locks broke, in a distant action or at pistol shot or lashed alongside, boarding or repelling boarders, covering the guns with pikes, charging with cutlasses, manoeuvring in action, manoeuvring for position, disabling the enemy's wheel and headyards, sweeping her decks with musquets and swivels from the gangways and tops – all had been practised over and over until they were second nature; the best marksmen had been identified and all hands had absolute confidence in their officers and in one another, the guns' crews had confidence in their own single powers of destruction.

The midshipmen and captains and second captains of guns were familiar through constant practice with all the business of setting their sights for the different elevations ordered or throwing in the quoins to the right depth quickly through a rolling motion; it was instilled in them all that they must never waste a shot. Better not to fire than throw the ball away.

"To fire on the weather or the lee roll is a most difficult question," Broke confided to his First Lieutenant after one exercise in particularly rough weather. "It would be well worth the expense to make some experiments on this question on one of our roadsteads where vessels frequently roll much with the swell opposed to the tide – an old wooden hulk might be used for a target."

After repeated experiments at sea without such a convenient hulk to fire at, Broke remained undecided. There were advantages to each roll, and while generally advising his *best* gun captains to fire to windward on the rise, taking the precaution of aiming at the lowest

47

extreme of the object aimed at, he was doubtful if this was effective except with highly trained men. Raw hands would send the shot winging way over the horizontal line. In general he gave his gunners leave to fire on whichever roll they pleased, providing that at the instant they pulled the lanyard they were just coming towards a perfect aim.

"I confess I quit this question of rolling fire with much doubt – but certainly our new young crews should fire on the roll *down* until they are cool, quick and expert enough to be trusted with their guns rising."

Alas, the opportunities to show their mettle in real action eluded the Shannons. To the southward great events were taking place: the Spaniards had risen to throw off the yoke of Napoleon, Sir Arthur Wellesley had been chosen to sieze the opportunity by landing and creating a diversion in Portugal, Lord Cochrane in the *Imperieuse* frigate had been despatched on a lone commission from the Mediterranean around the coasts of Spain, and was adding to his legend and his wealth in prize money – but for the Home Fleet and the Shannons it was blockade and convoy and more blockade with little relief. Few Frenchmen ventured out from the northern ports and when they did they were mostly small stuff, worth little in prize money and nothing in honour; glory was only to be obtained in equal or disadvantageous action – a French frigate, nothing less.

When the *Shannon* chased it was usually a brig or a schooner which hauled down its colours, and scarcely a shot needed. They were sent in to Broke's agent at Plymouth with a small prize crew, but raised little more money than he had already spent on his special sight and gun fittings, or paying for the weekly prizes of tobacco for his marksmen who hit the target. The lists of these were growing longer too.

So the summer wore uneventfully away. In the autumn Broke was sent as senior captain of a small force blockading two French frigates in the Loire, but it was a change of scene only – the Frenchmen seemed quite content with their berths and made no move to come out. As Lord Collingwood, farther south, observed, "It is lamentable to see what a desert the waters are become."

Broke, heartily sick of inaction, occupied himself and his boats' crews sounding and surveying the approaches to the French harbour! His was a practical and energetic mind – besides, idleness only encouraged frustrating thoughts of his wife and children, and to shut them out he kept himself continuously working, if not at the guns, then at navigation or some other practical professional subject. He worked out courses of interception for varying wind directions and relative speeds of chase and chaser – himself – and ruled up small cards to carry in his pocket to facilitate the rapid working out of sights after thick weather.

"This was often of high importance when our timekeepers were doubtful. The gale ceasing, it was our first duty to resume our blockade port, close to the enemy's harbour, *before daylight*; and nothing but a knowledge of our longitude could enable us to run in for the shore without great danger. A few sights *rapidly worked* and agreeing told us if we might trust our watches; but the point was to be settled quickly as tide and *darkness might urge*."

Broke's keen interest in navigation was no proof against the perils provided by friendly pilots on those occasions when the *Shannon* was relieved briefly to take on provisions at a home port. Broke was several times during his career put aground by these people, who were a notorious hazard around the coasts of the world; on one occasion in *Druid* the poor fellow taking her out of Cork Harbour had fallen to his knees on the quarterdeck and begged Broke to spare his life after the frigate, refusing to stay, had run gently ashore on a falling tide. Now, when the *Shannon* was relieved from her blockade duty in October, another pilot put her ashore in the Thames Estuary with far less excuse.

"*Shannon*
Downs, Oct 2nd 1808.

"The Elder Brethren and
"Master Wardens of the Trinity House Hall.
"Gentlemen, Francis Pierrepoint, a Branch pilot of your house, having run His Majesty's Ship *Shannon*, under my command upon the Onion shoal in open daylight with a free wind, and being convinced that he is extremely ignorant of his duty I had intended bringing him to Court Martial, but in consideration of his having a family dependent upon him I have allowed him to go on shore. I think it, however, my duty to state the circumstances to you that he may not be permitted to take charge of a ship again without being newly examined as to his qualifications. You will act accordingly, but I should by sorry that our indulgence to him should risque the lives or property of others.
"I am, gentlemen, yours etc etc P.B.V. Broke."

They kedged her off easily enough on the next tide, and Broke, after completing with fresh stores, was soon on station again. Early in

November he fell in at midnight with a British frigate Captain fortunate enough to have found and brought to action a French frigate of comparable force. The Britisher was the *Amethyst*, Captain Michael Seymour, and he had taken the *Thetis* after a bloody action ending a few minutes before the *Shannon* joined. Broke stayed with the two vessels during the night while the surgeons finished their dreadful work, and in the morning he helped to man the Frenchman with Shannons, afterwards taking her in tow as she was in too shattered a condition to sail. Before he went he talked at length with Captain Seymour, pressing him for details of the engagement. This conversation and the stories he heard from his officers on the voyage to Plymouth so impressed him with the gallantry displayed by the Amethysts that he decided to forfeit the share of prize money which would be due to him, and to press his people to do the same. His officers soon agreed when he told them of his decision, and the hands called to muster on deck were also persuaded.

After the briefest visit to his beloved Louisa and the children whom he missed so much and who changed between each homecoming, he sailed again for a new station off the Black Rocks at the entrance to the harbour of Brest. This time there were several French sail of the line besides frigates inside.

Midwinter – the Frenchmen remained snugly in their berths. Out in the roads the winds came screaming through the salted rigging of the British squadron, thudding against spars, driving spray aboard, setting everything in jangling motion against a constant caterwauling background of noise. When the weather abated in intervals the Captains and officers of the blockading ships dined each other aboard and vied with one another to produce the longest string of tenderly cooked dishes and the best bottles to wash them down. Broke, with his modest good humour, was always a favourite. The conditions were trying and monotonous and apt to lead to quarrels, especially among the many highly strung and individualistic captains the service produced, but Broke could be relied upon to do his utmost to avoid hot words himself, and to attempt to smooth them down in others. His red hair was no signal for temperament. And so far as senior officers were concerned, he had made it a rule throughout his service career never to quarrel with them, "and always to keep in the right, which always ended in our being friends, finding that we both had the same real interest in the Service".

The conditions for hospitality grew briefer as the winter gales set in. The swell came in serried mountain peaks from the Atlantic, tops flattened and creamed off in flying spindrift, lifting the creaky wooden ships and hurling them over in all directions; Broke's whole world for days together was a wet, grey-green vista of driven water and salt spray broken only by his wallowing consorts, weaving masts and bare yards in arcs against the low sky – and the bleak, washed Black Rocks and the shoreline of France hazed in squalls.

> "*Shannon*
> at sea Jan 2nd 1809
> "My dearest Loo, We have persevered in keeping the sea all these gales most obstinately and were today rewarded with a prize, a fine French cutter of fourteen guns and sixty men – *Le Poumereuil*. I have sent Mr. Davy home with her to Plymouth . . . and pray give Mr. Davy a good dinner if he stays . . ."

The *Shannon* was relieved shortly after this and returned to Plymouth herself to land prisoners. Broke had another flying visit to his family, before he was off again for the Black Rocks, which he had come to know almost as well as the Orwell below Broke Hall. He had no sooner made Ushant, however, than he was signalled that the French fleet had escaped, and after despatching two smaller vessels to convey the news to Plymouth and the Commander-in-Chief, Home Fleet, he sailed close in to Brest to see for himself. It was true; there was not a mast or spar of a warship to be seen.

Two days later the Home Fleet made Ushant and Lord Gambier detached eight sail of the line under Admiral Sir John Duckworth to hunt the Frenchmen down, detailing the *Shannon* and one other frigate as the eyes of the fleet. This was more promising work; the *Shannon* was sent far ahead on her own to reconnoitre. But it was not long before news came through that the French force had made for Rochefort and were under blockade again by a British squadron under Admiral Stopford. Disappointed, Duckworth and his squadron started homeward, but the *Shannon*, perhaps unused to sailing *with* the fleet after her flying duties ahead, collided with a 74 and had to put into Cadiz for repairs.

> "*Shannon*
> Cadiz March 15th 1809
> "My beloved Looloo . . . on the night of the 11th one of my watchmen ran us on board the *Elizabeth* – fortunately we did no harm to Queen Bess, but we carried away our own bowsprit and received some other trifling damage. *What a pity* it had not

happened near Plymouth, as you will say *now* it is so much good luck *thrown away* . . .

"I was at the Caraccas (the dockyard) yesterday and took a family dinner with General Mont Aragon, the Commissioner – he was extremely hospitable and polite and his Lady Donna Minuela is very pretty and lively, but unfortunately spoke nothing but Spanish – he talks good French – however she showed me her flower garden which was prettily filled and appeared to be her pride . . . I brought home a nosegay of geraniums and violets and mignonette . . . so much *real* politeness is not often met with here.

"As it is Lent we have no Opera at this time or any public amusements and as the Spaniards, though friendly in their way, do not mix with us we have little inducement to stay on shore – so all live aboard like good officers only landing in the morning to walk and hear the news."

His walking took him past the many paintings in the public buildings of the City, and years afterwards he could recall the delight the Murillos gave him.

From Cadiz the *Shannon* sailed for Madeira for orders, and thence home to Plymouth to anchor in the Sound on 2nd May. On the 13th she set sail again for her most protracted cruise to date, no less than thirty-three weeks hovering off Rochefort, Bourdeaux, Belleisle, with only the occasional chase or the arrival of the mail or dinner with another Captain to break the monotony. For Broke it was a severe test of the spirit. To be so near to England so constantly while yet another summer wore away, to imagine the roses in bloom around Broke Hall and Louisa and his children who had returned there playing on the lawns or down by the water's edge, and to visit them only in imagination. Another summer that could never be replaced. There were no flowers in the Channel; only the sun and wind striking off the green water.

> "*Shannon*
> Bourdeaux June 18th 1809
>
> "My beloved Loo . . . we have been 100 miles of Bx till today, but are now going in to make the land and see who is there and shall then resume our *solitude* again – to lie in wait for any sly things that may creep in from the East Indies or Guadaloupe, if that remains to them . . .
>
> "I got one volume of Haggitt's sermons amongst the books by *Seine* and am confirmed in the idea I had of these being the fittest discourses I know for a general congregation and particularly for

the middling and lower classes – I pray for my Loo and trust she is home, safe and well with the dear children . . . I hope you have found your park in order, that you may let the little ones loose to play in it – do not increase their *regular walking* again till they get *fat* – if they will creep about the grass, so much the better for them. I wish they had one of my little kids or a pet lamb to play with – if you can manage to, pray get them as much out in your phaeton as possible if your horse is steady . . .

"Please God that Boney may be beaten into a *peace*, we may manage otherwise and I come to see my *wife* instead of her coming to see me. God bless you and keep you in the meantime for your affect^te P. B. V. Broke."

He prayed most earnestly for his family – but perhaps scarcely less in his heart for a chance at a fat French frigate. One chance was enough. He knew his people would not let him down. They were as expert as he could make them and when it came to the point they would display all the fierce courage of their race; he knew that.

"Shannon
off Bourdx June 25th

"My beloved Looloo . . . we fished one night and meant to have another haul next day off Bordeaux, but spoke an American ship going to Boston with passengers who told us, I suspect, a *horrible lie* to get rid of us. I ought to have sent him to Plymouth to be examined, but hearing that he had sailed with two French corvettes and that they were very close to us in such a direction I left him and made haste to persue them. And after running three hundred miles saw *nothing* and think *cousin Jonathan* is a *knave* so we have ever since been beating back to recover our station . . .

"We have had beautiful weather this week and pleasant breezes – but we see *nobody*. I shall now range up to the land again and catch our men a dinner of Haikes and Soles and Skate – if we can get nothing better to amuse us and perhaps we may find a postman to carry our letters . . . if I meet another of these *lying Yankees* I will send him to England to punish him . . . God bless you all from your affect^te P. B. V. Broke."

Louisa was expecting her fifth child in August; Broke from his writing table in *Shannon* was full of advice.

". . . I have a strange, selfish wish that you should cultivate a sisterlike intimacy with Mary Coles as there is no she-thing I know

53

around you who can equal her in active kindness and friendly attentions, and my Loo will want such *friends at times* . . ."

He received the news of her safe delivery of a girl shortly afterwards, but the infant did not survive long.

The summer wore away, autumn winds set in again and still the *Shannon* hovered relentlessly off the French coast without a sight of England.

"My dearest Looloo . . . I am haunted by a soft, rosy-faced vision with a wreathe of May on its head, which makes me think of peace and retirement and all such simple fancies . . . We have passed the week in *solitude* . . . and sad, blustering weather to cheer our spirits – today wet and stormy – when it moderates I shall look for my Commodore to enquire if he has been in more sociable regions than ourselves . . . Evening and a heavy gale SW. Pleasant pastime! I hope my Loo got to Church today to pray for us all – I have been reading quietly at home . . . this week I have been tormented by the reflections and speculations of some abominable Scotch critics who are of opinion that we shall never have peace again – which idea does not suit my arrangements at all – though it may Bonaparte's . . . what a wicked world! Oh, amongst other books for your library I shall put Mr. Hugo's French Tales which you have not read yet, not that modern French can improve so elegant a Frenchwoman as *my Loo*."

"Sunday Nov 5th a *new month begun* & nothing *new* for us, not even a *prize* to celebrate gunpowder treason with, however we said our prayers quietly, the weather being still extremely fine. It blew strong gales two days but is now serene again, tho' so *chilling* cold that I fear our publick devotions will soon cease as I am only a *field preacher*. We have not seen anything this week *floating on the waters* but ourselves, which is very dismal and unsociable – but as the moon is now meagre and the nights are dark we hope every morning to see company, but our friends at Bourdeaux are rather shy . . . God bless you all wherever you are, love to all friends and kiss little dear ones for your affectionate fish   P. B. V. Broke (tell Philip tho' I have been 6 months in the sea I am not wet yet.)"

"Nov 26th off Bourdeaux
". . . it has been squally gales all today & quite *unSunday like* – but as it proceeds from NW we still hope it may waft us a *prize* – we must now *absolutely* take something before we return to Basque or we shall be *laughed at* . . ."

"My dearest beloved Looloo . . . the easterly winds have prevented us regaining our station and so we have spoken several vessels going to and fro – amongst others the *Indefatigable* and Captain Baker charitably gave us a little stock of poultry to save us from *immediate starvation* . . . I asked Captain Baker, who lately sailed, if he had heard of any such lady as Mrs. Broke at Plymouth, but he said no, so I fear Devonshire's not yet honoured with her presence, tho' I know the said lady does not make so much *noise* in the world, but she might be *very quietly* settled at Stonehouse without *all the frigates* in the Sound being acquainted with it . . .

"When other folks are murmering at their ill luck in taking no better prizes I *always* comfort myself with thinking what a dear, good, affectionate wife I have got to go home to and suppose it is all for our good – perhaps if I was to get *very rich* I should be ambitious of being a *political man* or some such *uncomfortable character* – but there is no danger of that at present . . . God bless and protect you all and the quartello. I'm pleasing myself with the hopes of finding them all quite riotous on my arrival . . . adieu, your affectionate sea thing   P. B. V. Broke."

At last on 30th December the *Shannon* put into Plymouth and anchored in the Sound. Broke was joyously reunited with his family for nearly two months while the major dilapidations of that interminable cruising were made good at the dockyard, and the damp holds, reeking of stale bilge water, were freshened and filled again with casks of salt meat, pease, biscuits, beer, rum, powder and all the bare necessities of the sailors' existence and the demands of their mistress *Shannon*. Then, on 20th February 1810, Broke was ordered out once more on blockade duty to his old station, the Black Rocks off Brest. Here there was even less activity than on the previous occasion.

". . . it certainly is not the *Shannon*'s turn yet but every dog has his day, so we live in hope."

All around the coasts of Napoleon's Continental fortress from the Baltic to the Mediterranean the tossing squadrons of the Royal Navy lived on hope fed by duty and a stubborn hatred of their adversary – 150 line-of-battle ships, 200 frigates and 500 smaller craft, 130,000 men in a living, floating, unbreakable chain. Above them all as a rock and inspiration was the towering figure of Vice-Admiral Collingwood, the Commander-in-Chief Mediterranean, wearing out his life in the *Victory*, dreaming, like Broke, of the wife and home he had not seen for seven years while setting an example of continuous service for his country which will stand for all time.

"Now that the French fleet is destroyed at Rochefort," he wrote to his wife, "they may surely select some officer to relieve me, for I am sadly worn. Tough as I have been I cannot last much longer. I have seen all the ships and men out two or three times . . . Many about me are yielding to the fatigue and confinement of a life which is not natural to man . . ."

Neither was it natural to the men's womenfolk left to while away the years at home. Perhaps because of this, perhaps for purely physical reasons, Louisa had begun to suffer from headaches which were to plague her for years. Occasionally she wrote to her husband about them, and Broke added this to his other worries and frustrations.

> "*Shannon* off Ushant June 20th
> ". . . but I always feel soothed in thinking of *your distresses* by the recollection of your mildness and resignation under them – all things have a bright side to contemplate as well as a dark one, & if they *will force themselves* on our consideration we must take the best view they will afford us – but I wish *the head* would please to be quiet and allow my Loo to feel cheerful & easy or that *little Emporer* would permit me to stay at home to amuse it."

At other times Broke was gently teasing to cheer her:

> "I don't know which most to admire – your devotion or your courage in going to Church on horseback! Particularly if it was a *real horse* that *moved its legs* . . .
> "I suppose your garden's only ornamental, I hope full of roses – I have two pretty ones in my cabin now – but they make me melancholy and I threaten to turn them out for making me waste so much time in idle regrets – I fear the poor things will get sick and die of the salt air before I have the courage to dismiss them – they are true Loo Indians and in full bloom now . . .

> "June 24th
> "No! these roses must not stay! they haunt my imagination with wifish ideas and won't leave me a moment for myself or King George. If it were even a picture I could shut it up, but these things *flaunt* their beauties in my face yet look so mild and innocent in their bloom that I can't help thinking of her. I certainly will

give them away to the first trustworthy body who will take care of them . . ."

He put the pen down and walked up his companionway to the quarterdeck. The officer of the watch, seeing him emerge, moved discreetly from the windward bulwarks to allow him to promenade alone. A perfect day. The wind was balmy and the sun striking off the wave tops. The decks were white from the holystone, the rigging taut and the sails swelling in beautiful curves from the yards. He never tired of the sight and the nostalgic thoughts dropped away from him as he paced past the lashed carronades and listened to the music of the water down the side below, feeling the life in his command through the soles of his feet. The past week of fine weather had brought a better humour to the ship and constant exercises at a mark with the aiming gun had toned his people up to new heights of enthusiasm at their own speed and accuracy. His blood quickened as he thought of what the *Shannon* could do if only she was granted the opportunity – if only . . .

He looked upwards as he reached the gangway.

"Masthead there!"

"Sir —"

"What do you see?"

A slight pause as the man wondered if his tireless Captain had somehow glimpsed a sail he had missed, and took a hasty glance all round the horizon. "Nothing in sight, sir."

Broke turned on his heel and wondered if his luck would ever change. He had a feeling that it would – one day. Many officers grew white in the service and retired without ever being granted a single opportunity for distinction, but he had a feeling that his own career would be otherwise. *Somewhere* there was a frigate fated to cross his path . . .

But it was only the fine weather which induced these thoughts, the sun and the breeze off those sparkling rollers from the Atlantic, sweeping in so clean-crested and blue, lifting the timbers beneath him, then surging white frothed to leeward as the *Shannon* settled in the trough – this weather and the sight of his taut frigate always had an effect on his pulses.

There were other days. There were hours of depression when he wondered if he was doomed to sail off the Black Rocks for the rest of his life while Louisa grew old and the children left home to go their own ways and hardly knew him. He would have missed both glory and his family then, fallen between the two and known neither.

When he lapsed into these moods he tried to console himself with the knowledge that his duty lay at sea, and it could not be otherwise until Bonaparte was overthrown. And then he threw himself into some practical work about the guns as a diversion.

But today on deck it was impossible to feel melancholy. There was a lift to the white sails and a kiss in the breeze under the sun which filled him with optimism – a foolish optimism perhaps, he thought, under the present conditions of sea warfare.

Presently the Marines were paraded on deck for musket drill. Their scarlet tunics made a bright splash of colour against the dull yellow of the lower masts and the paintwork of the boats stowed over the spare spars between the gangways. They stood in a single rank faced by the First Lieutenant of Marines and the Sergeant, with the two corporals opposite either end of the line. They held musquets and the sun glinted off the metal of the barrels and the rings of the bayonets hanging by their right sides.

The Sergeant began yelling the familiar ritual orders; the men responded briskly, every movement of the complicated loading drill long since worn into a groove of habit.

"Handle cartridges!"

The rank fell back with their right feet as one man, the crossed white belts shifting as they brought the musquets down beside them with both hands – a pause for a count of two and then their right hands moved from the barrels in unison to open their cartridge boxes and take out a cartridge – a movement of brown flesh upwards across the scarlet tunics and they were biting off the end of the cartridges with their teeth.

"Prime!"

The musquet barrels were allowed to drop to horizontal in their left hands, and they shook powder from the bitten cartridges into the open pan behind the flint-lock, afterwards returning the cartridges to their mouths, appearing to grin as they held the parchment cases in their teeth.

"Shut pans!"

Their right hands moved to the musquets again – a pause for a count of two and they clapped the steel shut – another pause for two and they siezed the musquets with their right hands and brought them straight up before them, at the same time bringing their right feet forward so that the heel came into the hollow of the left.

"About!"

The musquets twisted round and the butts dropped to the deck as

58

the rank took a step forward with their right legs, right knees bent a little.

"Enter cartridge!"

Broke watched the men snatch the cartridges from their mouths and twist them into the barrels of the musquets, bitten end first, a pause for two and they raised two forefingers, another pause and they clapped them over the muzzles. He always enjoyed the precision of the Marines' drill. He liked to think it was matched by his seamen gunners at the cannon, but although they could handle their pieces with incredible speed and agility by now, it was not the same kind of exercise at all. The great guns were unpredictable – any stiff, mechanical motions would end in several men being mown down under the jumping carriages each time the guns were fired. They had to be like monkeys . . .

He often wondered if some better design could not be worked out for the carriages. Their breeching ropes, working along a line below the axis of the metal, inevitably lifted them well clear of the deck at the end of the recoil. The square forward ends of the carriages made training forward or abaft the beam an unnecessarily difficult procedure, and after it had been accomplished the breeching ropes had to be very precisely middled or there was no telling where the gun would end up. As it was, one side or other of the rope took by far the greater strain whenever the guns were angled. But the apparatus had the great advantages of toughness and simplicity and adaptability – certainly they had stood the test of time.

Now the Sergeant of Marines, having brought his men to the present and fired a volley out over the waves to leeward, was ripping out his orders at speed, testing reflexes together with drill.

"Shoulder arms! Trail arms! Handle arms! Ground arms! Handle arms! Take up arms! Fix bayonets! Shoulder arms! Right face! . . ."

Broke continued his pacing, his thoughts punctuated by the sharp orders, the thump of the musquet stocks against the deck, the clicking steel of the bayonets, a music almost as soothing as the plash and hiss of the waves past the copper below. What more could he wish for on such a day? What more than his own lively frigate – except another to chase?

Afterwards he returned below for his dinner – solo on this occasion. A pity; he would have liked company in such fine, invigorating weather. He felt the ship leaning farther as the breeze freshened; his swords and pistols shifted to a greater angle on the pale green bulkhead.

When he had finished eating, he rose and walked to his rose bushes to sniff their fragrance once more. Then, desperate with the thoughts they conjured up, and unable to bear his solitude any longer, he continued on towards his companionway and up to the quarterdeck again. A perfect evening!

The evenings were the worst time – after the day's work was finished . . .

". . . I wish I was riding on a donkey at Dawlish. I hope you teach Philip to ride gracefully as well as boldly . . . I flatter myself the young ladies will soon ride as well as their mama used to do. May they continue all amusement and delight to my Loo and no anxiety – they all *multiply* my love for you, I won't say augment it because you will not believe me but whenever I meet pretty little children in your absence they are as bad to me as roses . . . God bless you all in healthy spirits and happiness for your affectionate, rose-bitten, simple, idle husband   P. B. V. Broke."

"June 28th off the Saints
". . . there are now so many bad books written expressly for the ladies, adhere to one rule in your selection – whenever you find an inclination in the author to make a vicious or weak character *amiable*, to be *pathetic* in *wickedness*, to spin out a deliberate tale of seduction and to appeal to the *feelings* of the polite reader without any reference to the immutable principles of religion and morality – shut up the book and let it not sully your toilette with its presence. There are abundance of such now, the Genlis, the Plunketts, the Mme de Staels etc. – mostly foreign but some, I grieve to say, native, whose works are an insult to Christian piety and female innocence . . . Oh dear, now I have preached – but the Loo will forgive me for not liking to see any she things painted but such as herself and my Swedish Queen, meek, gentle, patient, affectionate, innocent creatures, they are quite interesting enough for me, so God bless them all . . . Kiss little dear ones for me, adieu – your affectionate   P. B. V. Broke."

"July 8th
"I had only time today to write a short letter to my *Loo* before *Indefatigable* sailed – *not leisure* to tell her how much I loved her & how anxiously I was anticipating the expiration of our cruise but I put in all the hints & directions that suggested themselves to me, to secure our meeting on *Shannon*'s return to Plymouth where I hope to find you & all the little darlings in health & spirits . . .

"I expect Admiral Stopford here in a day or two on his way home & shall beg him he will remind *Lord Gambier* of the *Black Rock frigates* . . ."

"July 15th
". . . another tiresome, useless week! the only variety a little foul weather to tear our sails and make us swear at the wind . . . As the Roads have been bad for visiting we have each staid in our own houses and those houses have been much dispersed from each other . . . I should hardly have written at all but that my rose bush put forth a fresh blossom today which looked so mildly & tenderly at me that I could not help saying something . . .

"July 19th evening . . . I get every day more disloyal to old Neptune, but I must comfort myself that perhaps I shall get more ambitious as I grow older and think more of honours and distinctions instead of cooing with my gentle and playing with Loolins! But I don't feel any symptoms of that glorious reform at present . . .

"I have just got my beloved dear Loo's letters of 23rd and 29th and am charmed to hear so favourable an account of the dear children and so I put my rose by my side and sat down and kissed the letters and the roses and the Loo in imagination and felt very happy for a few minutes – till I began to reflect that the *real* Mme Loo was not there! but I hope yet to enjoy a more rational interview!

"Thursday Aug 2nd . . . a great, silly English ship has led me a chase today and disappointed me *grievously*. I shall console myself by making him convey my letters home."

"*Shannon* off Brest   Sept 9th
". . . we separated from *Poictiers* yesterday and have been all day teazed with a provoking chase after a schooner privateer, who now the wind is light, sails as fast as we do. We are of course all *very angry* . . . 9 o'clock: the little animal is escaped for *tonight* at least, but we have saved some ships who passed while we were hunting the vermin . . . Devilish sulky at not catching him! I shall comfort myself by talking to my gentle wife who is always my *retreat* & my *refuge* when I want to be *soothed*.

"13th. No *Poictiers* or *Seine*! . . . a hideous, roaring gale of wind to remind us of the season on Tuesday night – I think as a fresh ship it will have routed *Poictiers* . . . *Shannon* is all the better for it . . . we shall be very vigilant here now as the enemy have been moving and shamming a cruize just outside their harbour – the blowing season is approaching and they want to exercise their men

61

ready for a run. *Seine* is at Black Rocks and we shall join her there tonight."

"*Shannon* Ushant Sept 16th
". . . the dear Loo's lamentations make me moralize (and there's nothing worse for a sailor than thinking). I feel most confident that nothing but our being enabled to live together can secure our happiness and peace of mind for the few years allotted to us here – but now *publick duties, example, honour, character* all assert a peremptory call on me. I am so prone to reflection upon domestic comfort and the pleasures of social endearment that I *shun* it as a dangerous indulgence – as poor Don Quixote was obliged to eschew books of knight errantry. I could live in humble retirement with my soft Loo as happy as if in paradise – if impertinent people would be so good as to have no opinion concerning me. But it is a wicked and imperfect world we live in! And so I must set an example to my children of that sacrifice to the publick good which all men must make who do their duty to their country – of a good *patriot* to my boys, as my gentle Loo does of a kind and affectionate wife to her girls. I believe she will continue to act her part when I have much relaxed in mine, indeed I am very tired of all the varieties of the world and sometimes when weary and angry of this endless war wish myself obscurely tranquil in the shade of the Rookery, though I were the most unnoticed, homely farmer gentleman. But my lot is drawn – perhaps it may yet be compensated even in domestic life. We disappointed, baffled, anxious animals certainly enjoy ease and retirement more than those who have never felt the reverse . . ."

So yet another autumn and winter fastened on the *Shannon* as she rode her element stubbornly off Brest; her bilges were stale once more and dispersed their evil smells up through the berth decks where they were compounded with the odours of two hundred men living in close confinement, and farther up in the manger with the stench of the officers' supply of livestock; her exposed timbers, now so well salted, leaked the water in, her paintwork was dulled by constant buffetings, her copper buckled where she had occasionally taken the ground, and greening all over, hung with long weeds and clinkered with a knobbly crust of life so that in chase her speed, which had been such a pride to Broke, was annoyingly reduced. But of course there was little to chase. The French squadron remained idly in harbour – waiting for more severe gales perhaps.

The gales came, but the British ships crawled back to their stations

Blockade of Brest

One of Broke's
butchers' bills

we, by the mercy of heaven being born in christian countries, are easily instructed in this difference between good & evil, we know our duty both to God & man

224 THE DELUSIONS WHICH SEDUCE

ing of *an understanding heart, that he might discern between good and bad.*

THE World displays an extensive scene of temptation; not only to blind you to a sense of duty both moral and professional, but strives by every argument, which incredulity or blasphemy can devise, to silence the suggestions of honour, or the alarms of conscience. You are thus incited to acts of egotism and vanity, and to assume a more daring deportment; to spurn all sense of virtue, as the dream of dotage; and to trample on the Cross of your Redeemer, as the proof of an unfettered and philosophic mind.

IT has been a prevailing error of the present age, to render its religious Faith subservient to that fashion of the day, before which the multitude are at all times ready
                                to

A page from Broke's book of sermons with
deletions and additions in his own hand

computations of the
…gagements

Broke's letter to his wife written with his left
hand a few days after the *Shannon/Chesapeake*
action

Captain Broke standing on the Stars and Stripes

before the prisoners had a chance to escape, and hung there, flaunting their weather-faded ensigns, small, pitching symbols of the incredible determination of an island race.

"My dearest Looloo . . . I rejoice that I am not senior officer – having the *modesty* to think that I am in general *much too good* upon a blockade, so would rather be under a *less scrupulous director* than PBVB, you know *he* is a *fanciful particular* body . . ."

At the visits and dinners which the British Captains and officers exchanged when the weather permitted they talked hopefully over long glasses of claret of the chances of action; every small change in the weather became a subject of importance, each new sail a high excitement. The sailors, now as hard and resilient as the ships themselves, accepted the unremitting sea-life and the sharpness of the routine as a natural condition. They watched their wilder messmates bearing the 'cat' stoically whenever the gods, their officers, ordained it, knocked white maggots out of their biscuits, or tasted their cold fat on the tongue, rollicked at midday like children about the grog tub, heaved heartily or scurried aloft under the ever-present threat of the Boatswain's 'starters' about their shoulders – and in the evenings if the weather eased up they gathered on deck and sent haunting, romantic choruses in deep voice winging over the waters to the washed rocks and cliffs of France. Or to shut out the severity and monotony of their life in these brief periods of respite they yarned – long, spiced, embroidered tales, as well worn around their tongues as quids of tobacco, delivered with affection and craftsmanship, each berth-deck orator surrounded with as much convention as the sailmaker stitching his dull lengths of canvas into winged sails, or the old sailors laying up ornamental double Turk's heads in rope.

"Oct 10th

"My dearest Looloo . . . Mr. Bray admires Philip's *scholarship extremely*, but I don't think he yet reads anything for his own pleasure – I believe *my* early fondness for reading was excited by the habit of *listening* to *long stories* from Mrs. Orford etc till I took an interest in them & when people would tell me no more I thought it worth reading to *learn them* – I think our *nurse's heads* were rather *fuller stocked* with *red ridinghoods* & sleeping beauties than my wife's – but mother goose will help you out – till father goose comes home . . ."

In November the *Shannon*, which had suffered from a small outbreak of the dreaded smallpox, probably brought aboard by one of

63

the recently pressed sailors from an Indiaman, was released for a freshening-up period in Plymouth. But not for long. The following month she was despatched to Christmas at a new station in the Basque Roads.

"25th a happy Christmas to my beloved Looloo. I wish I was with her to make it a *merry one*. I suppose Master Philip claimed his whole mince pie upon the occasion – *Last* year we left this place on the *same day* we entered it *this* & kept Xmas just outside. My officers dined with me & I drank them the compliments of the Season in wholesome *cold water* – as they had no *coughs* they fared better – but I was *merry* and *wise* – vile weather all today but fortunately we are in a safe roadstead . . . heaven protect you all – *good night.*"

And soon 1811 came blustering in, the sixth year of *Shannon*'s commission, her fourth year on this desperate dull blockade work.

. . .

Meanwhile, as the two belligerents faced each other on their separate elements, the seafarers of the United States of America were writhing and twisting between them, not really wishing to go to war, but almost daily humiliated by acts of impressment or seizure of goods and even ships. On the one hand was Great Britain with her declaration of a blockade extending to all ports from which the British flag was excluded, and her demand that any vessels wishing to trade with such ports must first call in at a British port to pay dues on the cargo; on the other hand was Napoleon thundering in his Berlin Decree that "whoever deals on the Continent in British merchandise . . . becomes an accomplice (of Britain's)" and "all merchandise belonging to England or (even if neutral property) proceeding from its manufactories and colonies is lawful prize".

As both nations threatened and actually carried out confiscation of vessels caught violating these demands, life became as difficult for neutral ships as if they were engaged in the war. And as Britain possessed the greater presence at sea to compel her demands, and as the Royal Navy continued to impress any American sailors who could not prove their nationality to the satisfaction of the boarding officers, and as the *Chesapeake* and other incidents still rankled in American breasts, a great breach had opened between the United States and her former mother nation which was coming closer to war, it seemed, than the breach between America and France at the turn of the previous century.

British Naval officers were not much concerned. The inept

American Naval administration, instead of building ships of the line as originally proposed, or more frigates which would have compelled some respect, had squandered their timber and energies and time on a force of minute gunboats which fulfilled no useful tactical or strategic role, which were simply expressions of the American dream of pacifism and disassociation from the *sin* of the old world – useless products of idealism in a world at arms. They were regarded with scorn – and in practical terms, rightly so.

As for Broke, frustrated beyond measure by the inactivity of his French quarry and becoming intolerant on this account, he had even less sympathy with Americans and American complaints than before. Like many of his brother officers, who were increasingly recruited from the landed gentry, he considered 'Cousin Jonathan' to be a 'rude, unpolished colonial', a trader, who thought more of his profits than of the immutable principles of freedom for which Great Britain was fighting the war. To him it was self-evident that Napoleon was an *evil* tyrant, child of the 'Terror'. He had heard at first hand of the plunder, senseless slaughter, rape, eye-gouging, throat-slitting, child-spitting carnage among simple village folk that followed everywhere in the wake of Napoleon's armies – such horrific sights that even the brutalised British soldiery was shocked beyond measure. He was fighting so that such barbarism would never be seen in the pleasant countryside of England, that the leprous ideals of the revolution would not reach British peasantry or industrial workers, and that the ideals of liberty and justice for which his country stood should never be drowned under Bonaparte's Continental system. These were real and impelling ideals, deep-rooted and complementary to his love for his family and for his own land in Suffolk. But the Americans seemed unaware of the real issues. They played off one side against the other in the sole interest of their own profits. They professed a belief in the rights of man, but all they wanted were the rights of trade, and now they were openly siding with Bonaparte . . .

"Jan 31 Basque

". . . soon after *Spartan* in came a silly American, taking us for a *Frenchman* – he will go to Plymouth soon of course – and might have been a good little prize for *one* of us – *mars il en a trop*, he was either *sulky* or *ignorant* and so we got no news from him. The former was natural enough, poor man, on finding himself in such a den of thieves when he thought (by our colours) we were all honest Bonapartes. These obstinate, vicious, kicking Yankees will compel us to chasten them at last – they appear more insolent than ever by the late papers . . ."

65

America's latest demands were the culmination of a tortuous series of policy changes all designed to bring the belligerents to respect her neutral rights on the high seas without actually fighting for them. First they had passed the non-importation act to ban English and French manufactures from the American market, but this had proved difficult in application and they had followed it by banning American exports to Europe instead. When this, too, failed to seriously hurt the warring nations while virtually crippling their own shipping, they allowed free trade, but with this proviso: if either Britain or France revoked their obnoxious policies towards U.S. ships the President of the United States would 'declare' this revocation, whereupon the other belligerent would be expected to similarly concede U.S. rights within three months. If the other power failed to do so their ships and goods would be banned entry to the United States.

Napoleon, seizing on this immediately, had written a letter to his Foreign Minister announcing that his Berlin Decree was revoked – expecting therefore that the British would revoke their offending Orders in Council. The Americans took the letter at its face value. The British, more used to Bonaparte's subtleties, pointed out that there had been no *official* and public revocation, simply a letter, and that couched in ambiguous terms. The British were right. French policy continued unchanged, even to the extent of seizing and holding American vessels. But the deeply pacifist American President, Madison, nevertheless *wanted* to believe in the revocation as it suited his book, and did so. By the terms of his Act Britain now had three months to follow suit and repeal her policies of blockade or her exports would be banned.

So the misunderstandings, fed on British unimaginativeness and arrogance towards a nation with no ship-of-war larger than a frigate, led step by step to war.

The Royal Navy was largely unconcerned, even hopeful; a war with America would greatly increase the pickings for a few months until all their ships, like the French, were blockaded in their harbours. In the meantime they had their eyes on Wellington in Portugal, and the great line-of-battle ships building all around the ports of Napoleon's Continental Europe – and on the smaller craft which might be tempted out to provide diversion and some sorely needed prize money.

"Shannon off Aix   March 31

"... we are mousing here all day, but the vermin run into their holes and we never catch them. I get very weary and pray for peace heartily ..."

66

"*Shannon*   Basque Roads   April 9th

". . . the Frenchmen owe me now after guarding their coast so carefully these three weeks . . . indeed my gentle, dear Loo, I feel as much bound in duty to my people to give them their chance as if I had the disposal of the money they expect – we have taken *nothing* this year and our poor sailors would look quite dismal at their friends in harbour – as they have not all such kind, affectionate Loos as I have to make me indifferent to these worldly gains. If we could only get engaged in any great, brilliant action I should be happy to retire without any profit but honorable retreat – indeed I think about Nacton very often now . . ."

"April 21st

"Oh, what a dismal, stupid week we have passed! Fogs, calms and gales to pester us, but not a creature to chase or to give us the news . . . we have seen nothing – the winds have been rude and capricious, constantly changing and appear to be quarrelling amongst themselves, but always scolding us . . . the bad weather and the solitude makes me read and think much more than is good for sailors and I consider how long I have been serving in this war and whether I ought in conscience to retire or not before peace is obtained and I think I have settled that point in my favour, but when? And whether I am bound in duty, or only by vanity to wait some opportunity of retiring with *éclat*? It would relieve me from the necessity of showing myself so much in publick business at home, particularly in a *military way* – indeed I would give any of the French frigate Captains all the prize money I should obtain by taking him if he would only come out voluntarily to give me an opportunity of going home with honor . . . but I must stay by old *Shannon* so long as she will bear with me and perhaps she may be gracious enough to make me some return for my constancy – either in laurels or in lucre . . ."

CHAPTER FOUR

DURING May 1811 the American Navy had the revenge it sought for the *Chesapeake* affair. Commodore Rodgers, in the United States frigate *President*, sighted and gave chase to a British sloop-of-war, *Little Belt*, presumably to ascertain who she was. He caught up with her on a dark evening, and someone fired a gun. Afterwards both vessels accused the other of firing this first shot; whichever way it was there was no doubt of the temper of the Americans. A memorandum from the U.S. Secretary of the Navy had stated, "What has been perpetrated may be again attempted. It is therefore our duty to be prepared and determined at every hazard to vindicate the injured honor of our Navy . . ." Rodgers had added in his orders to his Captains, "I should consider the firing of a shot by a vessel of war of either nation . . . at one of our public vessels as a menace of the grossest order, and in amount an insult which it would be disgraceful not to resent by the return of two shot at least."

In the short engagement between the *President* and the *Little Belt*, minute beside her, the British vessel was badly knocked about and had nine men killed and more than twenty wounded.

An Anglo-American war moved a shade closer. My Lords of the Admiralty indicated their awareness of the situation by drafting orders for the Halifax, Nova Scotia squadron to be reinforced – by just two frigates. One of these was the *Shannon*.

On 1st June, Broke, unaware of the change of scenery proposed for him, brought his frigate thankfully into the familiar green harbour of Plymouth and feasted his eyes on the fields and green trees of Devon in early summer, the crowded white houses beyond the masts and spars and black- and yellow-chequered hulks sleeping on the Hamoaze – Drake's Island, the old batteries, menacing with their rows of dark embrasures, Mount Edgecumbe carpeted with smooth green and streaked and dotted with woods like solid masses of emerald cut in fretwork – and behind it the hills swept with light and cloud shade, variegated colours receding into the distance. He felt again that indefinable tearing at his heart which the sight of England always induced in him and, he knew, in all other long-exiled sea things. The water was calm in the shelter of the hills, sparkling into the numerous inlets and rippling at the rocks and sand and shingle beaches, changed into a placid friend again . . .

He delivered *Shannon* into dockyard hands to be re-coppered, re-fitted and reprovisioned and then escaped to Louisa and the children – and the wild flowers in the lanes, the scent of cut grass, the rich earth smelling warm under the sun or heavily fruitful after rain, the fresh new green in the trees and hedgerows all discovered tenfold after the sterility of wind and timber and moving water that was the greater part of his life.

Philip was a sturdy schoolboy now, eight years old and full of questions; the smaller ones chattered and somersaulted around their

68

own daddy at last, and the gloomy, despairing thoughts which had been afflicting him in *Shannon*'s great cabin fell away entirely as he threw himself into the delights of being a simple, real father.

The only shadows were occasioned by Louisa's questions. How long was he going to stay at sea? They had been married nine years now, and all they had seen of one another for the past five had been these brief, haunting holidays while *Shannon* was in port – how *long* would it have to be like this? Could he not even take a short rest from his command? There were a hundred and more Post Captains on half-pay just champing for employment – was he, Philip Broke, her *husband*, so indispensable to England? Had he no duties towards her – his family?

He cursed himself for making her unhappy. But which service wife was any more fortunate? He had to stay; others had served longer than him – indeed worn themselves out, and while the war lasted it was his duty – his duty, it needed repeating. Or was it simply ambition and this greed for distinction above his fellows that drove him?

He knew Louisa was ill-suited to be a sailor's wife. It was hard enough on all sailors' wives in these uncertain times, but harder on her than most; she was a shy, unassertive thing, the very stuff of gentle womanhood and not fitted for managing a household without a man's presence in the background – besides, her chief delight was in him, there was no doubting that. He put her questions off as best he could, but felt that his phrases were beginning to wear thin after constant use and his excuses for continuing a while longer, another cruise, another year, until he had achieved honour, were less convincing each time he used them – and did he really believe them himself?

These moments when they were alone together and he caught a glimpse of the anguish underlying her obvious joy in being with him again were the only dark times; for the rest it was walks and picnics and boating trips with her or the family, and in the lengthening evenings, dinners, theatres, musical evenings, concerts or simply promenading and exchanging greetings and civilities – optimistic service talk about the chances of action and distinction, discussion of the brilliant course of Lord Wellington's campaign in the Peninsula, speculation about a war with the Yankees – and how long would it take to find and whip their few frigates if they dared come out of their harbours? They were insolent enough to try!

But Broke's professional thoughts seldom strayed far from the main enemy – the 'little Emperor'.

"I love Boney's last speech to his Senate. He talks of coming to fight us fairly at sea in *four years* hence – but he must not be so unreasonable as to expect *I* am to wait all that time for him, after six years *dancing attendance* already! He then says, *perhaps* we may beat him in one – two – three – or even *four* battles, but at last he will beat us. By that time I shall be an old Captain in the line and shall have the honour of taking my thrashing in some large 74." He looked towards his wife, smiling admiringly up at him. "But it is to be hoped I may be spared for *part* of the interval without being thought an idler – by the by, I think his plan rather a *hazardous* one considering how little his Navy has profited by the lessons they have already taken!"

There was an air of life and gaiety about wartime Plymouth as the swaggering officers of His Britannic Majesty's unconquerable Navy drank their temporary freedom deep and renewed their spirits, like Broke's wearied from continual sea-keeping.

In July the *Shannon* was ordered to Portsmouth to complete for foreign service, and the shadow stole sharply across again. *Which* station would be a secret until she was well out at sea; not even Broke himself knew – nor how long he might be away. And there was always the possibility, never mentioned, indeed unmentionable, that he might not return at all. The last few days of this glorious summer holiday took on an added poignancy.

And then suddenly he was at sea again, and settling back into the old routine like a temporarily displaced halyard back around its sheave, moving smoothly in the well-worn groove. He convoyed a slow fleet of Indiamen through the privateer danger zone around the Western Approaches and then as far south as Cape St. Vincent before he took his leave and opened the Admiralty-sealed envelope.

> "*Shannon* off Lisbon   Aug 21st
> "I have discovered our destination my beloved Looloo but must not tell you as my orders are marked secret again . . . I shall not tell my officers till they find out by the way we steer . . . but you may enquire about a house in Suffolk as there is every possibility I shall be a *year away* and no particular likelihood of our touching at Plymouth in that time."

> "*Shannon* off Western Isles   Aug 26th
> " . . . we have spoken several Americans who all talk very peaceably – the trade in corn to Cadiz and Lisbon is so lucrative that their crops are sold before they are reaped . . . and those who profit by all this trade (with Lord Wellington) will by no means consent to

a war . . . our Shannons are quite disappointed with Jonathan's civility . . . I am not so good for foreign service as I thought for but hope our employ may be active to dissipate idle reflections and reveries . . . I am trying to amuse myself and kill thought as well as I can by attending to my wooden wife and her children – and the more I bustle the better I feel my health for it . . ."

Shannon soon found herself in a period of light winds and calms under a burning sky. The sails slatted against the masts, the helmsman, brim of his hat pulled down to protect his eyes from the glare, leaned easily on the lifeless wheel, the sailmaker's gang squatted on the fo'c'sle surrounded by the worn and greying canvas of torn stormsails, pushing their needles and twine with leather palms, the Marine sentinel, sweating away his scarlet hours of duty on the quarterdeck, watched a dolphin sporting lazily astern, glistening curves up from the long, easy blue swell of the Atlantic . . .

Broke ordered the lemonade to be served at midday, and the hands had some sport fishing with hooks and spears; one day, near an abandoned and derelict brig, they caught some fifty bonettas besides a few dolphins and a shark.

". . . we are now in 42 lat N and in 36 West – I expect soon to be in a *better fish country* . . ."

"Sept 11th   Lat 42 N, Long 42 West
". . . feel better at sea than I should do in sight of the land as it fills me with naughty thoughts to see trees and houses and land animals – whilst here amongst fish and sailors I see nothing to remind me of Loos and little dears, but the mischievous books. Kiss all your little trio for me, adieu, your affect^te   P. B. V. Broke."

By 22nd September the *Shannon* had reached Sable Island, and on the 24th she entered the spacious harbour of Halifax, base for the North American station. Here they found the Commander-in-Chief, Vice-Admiral Sawyer, flying his flag in the *Africa*, a slow tub of a vessel of 64 guns, smaller than a line-of-battle ship, larger than a frigate, lacking the best features of both – such was the Admiralty's estimate of the threat posed by the American Navy! With the *Africa* were four frigates, the *Spartan*, *Aeolus*, *Guerriere*, *Belvidera* and a number of sloops-of-war.

Broke soon became involved in the social life of the base, and enjoyed himself as Naval officers were wont on a foreign station. He took a snug little lodging house, sharing it with another frigate

Captain, dined in company every evening – starting with the Commissioner of the Navy Yard and working down through the Admiral to his brother Captains – went out after partridge through the great forests of birch and maple, pine, ash and spruce which clothed the country round about, shot snipe, entertained parties from ashore in his austere quarters aboard *Shannon*, gaily beflagged for the occasion, drank well and enjoyed the noisy inconsequence of good company after the disciplines and aloofness imposed upon him by his sea command.

He received letters from Louisa on arrival and seldom failed to chronicle his day's events for her in the evenings whenever his engagements permitted. Now that he had little time to himself to brood, his letters lost their gloomy and introspective note and became animated with detailed descriptions of his activities and of the countryside. As he confessed, the company "*now* suits me better than solitude and as it is the fashion to breakfast out in parties here as well as dine we are not much alone at home. So I act the bachelor as well as I can . . ."

On 7th October he was back at sea for a cruise and the thoughts returned.

"*Shannon* off Philadelphia   Oct 13

". . . we have hopes of benefitting by *Shannon*'s copper as she certainly is improved in speed and whether we have war or peace with the Americans, French traders will be good prizes. The meeting of Congress will perhaps determine our prospects. If anything brilliant present itself we are in readiness and may be useful to our country and ourselves too – and if no new struggle occurs I am perhaps wasting this remainder of my frigate service as profitably here as anywhere else (tho' not quite so happily). Whilst here (off Philadelphia and New York) we cruize chiefly for contraband Americans, but off Charleston I shall hope to seize some *slave ships* as a service in which I shall feel much more pleasure, it being the duty of every man of principle to crush that horrible trade – and in that we act in concert with the Americans. But I beg pardon and won't abuse them any more. Today at least, tho' they are polishing up their old gunboats and looking very impertinent the people we meet are all praying for peace . . . I am very idly inclined and constantly moralising upon my own obstinacy and folly in thus wasting my own youth and happiness and my poor Loo's too! We must have some brisker employ for our minds here or I shall get quite *desperate* . . . this fellow cruizer of mine, Captain Byng, is a poor comforter as he is just married and most wofully forlorn at leaving his young wife, so he comes and croaks to me to stir up my recollections . . ."

"Oct 20

"Oh what a dull week! till yesterday we have seen nothing but *Shannon* and *Goree*. I cannot think where all the people are all got to! At last we have met with two innocent Yankees from Portland . . . we have no great news by them, but from papers up to last week it appears that their government is determined to make a war with us, but the people in general are equally determined they will have peace – and I hope they will succeed – but there's a great discordancy of opinion between the Feds and the Demmies (as the Federalists and the Democrats call each other) tho' neither party seem yet to have looked beyond their own immediate interests in trade and agriculture and never with a generous impartiality to have considered which nation of two they are jarring with is engaged in the most moral and honorable course – and to which it is they owe their boasted freedom and their corn laws and every virtue which they have retained. I am really ashamed of the narrow, selfish light in which they have regarded the last struggle for liberty and morality in Europe – but our cousin Jonathan has no romantic fits of energy and acts only upon cool, solid calculation of a good market for rice or tobacco!"

"Off New York   Oct 27th

". . . I am only waiting for an opportunity of getting home to you – but don't tell this to anybody else. If there is an American war . . . our services will be brilliant for a short while and then there will be nothing but *blockade* and I may as well go home. I get very impatient . . . I shall persevere in keeping *Shannon* at sea to make my transportation as much like one long cruize as possible. I wish some Frenchman would let me chase him to the Lizard and take him there – but I kill thought and time, as I hope my Loo will do, with my books and my children – and my household affairs – tho' the latter don't afford me much amusement this rainy weather and without my chasing. God bless you all in health and cheerfulness – old and young – whichever you are – from your affect^te P. B. V. Broke."

"*Shannon*   Nov 3rd

". . . another Sunday already! You can't think how busy we have been doing nothing. Gales of wind and rain – then moderate – repair damage and dry sails – *encore*, wind and rain – repair again – Sun and Moon! and loose ourselves again till these pretty creatures

73

come out again to tell us where we are – and so we murder our time – in doing and undoing . . . I am very weary – if it was not for my boys and my books – and the sun, moon and stars I should be very miserable. But I make them divert me as much as possible for want of more active persuits. Perhaps the Congress may find some brisker work for us next month . . ."

In these letters, written in the evenings, Broke never alluded to his chief preoccupation with the great guns, lest it should start a morbid train of thought in Louisa's mind. But by day he never slackened his efforts to keep his people at a high pitch of gunnery efficiency, and he continued to devise novel exercises to prevent the drills degenerating into formality. One such for calm weather consisted in imitating the roll of the ship in heavy weather by swinging the barrel of the quarter-deck aiming cannon up and down manually. This was done by lashing two handspikes together in the form of a 'T', inserting the stem of the 'T' into the barrel and having two men at the cross of the 'T' swaying up and down. Meanwhile the captain of the gun, who was under instruction, gazed along the sights to a target rigged up on the fo'c'sle and thrust in his quoin to stop the motion when he was coming to a perfect aim on target.

Such imaginative instruction and continuous, grinding devotion to the fighting efficiency of the ship was becoming increasingly rare in the Service as a consequence, inevitable enough, of its unchallenged supremacy. Already there were signs of that concentration on paint-work and polishing and all manner of evolutions against the stopwatch which became such a feature of the Navy in the later part of the century. Already ships were beginning to glisten with ornament and prettification. Captains provided brass fittings and extra paint at their own expense and took immense pride in the yacht-like appearance of their vessels and the number of seconds in which their people could run up a t'gallant yard or put all canvas on from bare poles. This was entirely natural. There was precious little real fighting to be done; warships had, by merchant standards, enormous crews who had to be kept employed; idleness only bred thought and thought disaffection. The ships were pretty enough anyway, so what more natural than to further beautify their delightful curves and proud spars into gleaming symbols of perfection. Thus was the competitive spirit assuaged.

Broke kept a taut ship, but there were no frills. His frigate, like his person, was never artificially adorned. The breeching ropes for the guns were not whitened, nor painted; instead they and every hook and eye in their fastening was regularly tested in case the strain of a prac-

74

tice round might have produced a weak link somewhere; the shot were not painted nor arranged in ornamental patterns in satinwood cabinets, but were kept in strictly functional troughs around the hatchways for instant use at sea; the powder was frequently turned, and a machine was used to pump air into the damp magazines below the waterline whenever the weather was dry. Nothing was left undone to ensure that when the moment came, the moment for which all this agonising cruising was only a prelude, when that high moment arrived there would be nothing about the great guns, the small arms drill, the health or discipline of his people left to chance.

"The ship exhibited such a superiority in gunnery over her contemporaries as to render her conspicuous at the time and for several decades afterwards, the accepted model by which all such as care may measure themselves" (F. W. Robertson – *The Evolution of Naval Armament*).

Broke's quarters, like his ship, were strictly functional; they contained little which might hinder the carpenters when it came to stripping the timber partitions for action. The only ornaments were a few small, polished brass guns and two mahogany rudder head pieces, and his arms and maps on the bulkhead; for the rest he had a sofa to supplement the Admiralty settee which was fitted over lockers around his stern ports, a chest of drawers for his sleeping cabin, three mahogany tables, two swinging tables hung from the deckhead beams, and a set of stout dining chairs. On either side against the light green-painted timbers the great 18-pounders of the after quarters slept on their elm carriages, securely lashed against movement. In contrast, shelves above contained his books, their well-worn, faded calf covers a passport to those wider horizons which gave his imagination and intellect free play after the practicalities of the day. And at the extreme stern were the great windows following the upward camber of the deck through which he could listen to the sea bubbling around the rudder stock only a few feet below, or in heavy weather rising to within inches of him – and the scudding clouds and all the elemental grandeur of the open ocean.

"November 17th
". . . it has just cleared up and let us see the blue sky which makes me think of my Loo's eyes, and so I must pay her a visit at least in fancy . . .
"No prizes, 'tis sad, tiresome work cruizing here – quite, as Hamlet says, stale, flat, weary and unprofitable. And then, instead

of occupying all my time like a good officer, in arranging and criticising ropes and sails when there is no more important subject to employ my intellect I take up my book or think of my Loo . . ."

When his thoughts dwelled too nostalgically on that last, sweet holiday in Devon – how charmingly happy and healthy his children had looked riding their make-believe horses around the garden at Stonehouse on that last afternoon before he sailed, and Loo . . . when his thoughts lingered in England and there was no professional activity to divert him he found his books of sermons helpful. He read one every Sunday to his people during the service he conducted – first making such alterations as he thought would make the text more understandable to the rough, unlettered congregation. But probably the stern morality they conveyed had as much or more meaning for the Captain himself in his isolation.

"Among the principal errors of our imperfect nature are the false ideas we so continually form of human happiness. How often are we deceived respecting the real estimate of life; and with what an unremitting submission do we suffer the power of imagination to chase from our minds these important truths – that life itself is not given for perfect enjoyment; that the whole of our existence is divided between joy and sorrow; that a state of trial, which is the real character of life, cannot be a state of gratification; and that a being limited to a short period and that period uncertain in its duration, must look to happiness, not as the associate of time, but as the reward of eternity . . .

"Let no one then among us lament that he is obliged to practise the virtues of diligence and perseverance; let no one repine though it should be his allotment to get his bread with the peril of his life. Idleness is always attended with dishonour, and is productive of misery . . ."

On 29th November a man named Kingsbury fell to his death from the maintop, a fairly unusual event in the *Shannon* as Broke was not a stopwatch man except when it came to aiming the guns. Kingsbury's body, sewn in his hammock with two round shot at his feet, was committed to the deep.

A few days later the frigate sailed carefully through greening shoal water to an anchorage off St. John's, Bermuda. This was an important British Colony presided over by a Governor with many officials, and once again Broke was plunged into a whirl of social activity. By 9th December he was reporting it all back to Louisa, together with excited descriptions of rides over the islands taken during the day-time with another frigate Captain.

". . . the scenery throughout these islands is beautiful . . . the whole surface is covered with deep green cedar . . . they fringe the cliffs and shade every craggy rock that is not absolutely covered by the sea, and frequently in the shallow bays the mangroves rise out of the water itself and form floating groves. They have a dark, shining leaf . . . We were catching at every turn fresh prospects of the grand ocean on either side forming on the rocks, or come suddenly from some hollow, shadowy glen up the majestic lakes formed by the clustering isles – while the white houses and the vessels' sails were sparkling gaily through the crowded trees – and every bay is sprinkled with tufted islets, some affording a continuance of the prospect between their straggling trees and others breaking the splendour of the light in massy shades. The island lake called Harrington's Sound made me melancholy, the hollow, hanging cliffs scooped into dark grottoes or undermined and fallen with its green verdure into the still, clear lake and the woody mounts towering over it reminded me of that most beautiful shore under Mount Edgecumbe where I used to *creep* with my beloved Loo in the gig to enjoy the shade of the impending trees – and to steal for the woodbine. The tranquility of this scene buried in the woods left me leisure to be sad – the water was clear – but as green as the emerald and so calm that it reflected every charm upon its banks and every grey, rocky inlet on its surface with the wild foliage that crowned it – Oh, how I wished for my Looloo!"

"St. George's, Bermuda   Dec 14th
". . . my Loo told me when I was at home last that she was rather jealous of my attentions to the ladies! But indeed upon this station there is no danger of my being at all a gallant man – as I hardly meet any of these *dear creatures* and have not time to get acquainted with one . . . so much for my society . . . I have been sauntering in the woods to avoid the noon sun and have seen some fine wild aloes in bloom – one of the prettiest flowering shrubs here is the cotton plant . . .

"15th . . . I have walked almost all over the isles . . . every bold promontory or swelling mount affords a fine panorama of woody tracts indented by deep bays, white houses and green islands, rocks, ships and sailing boats appear in new positions from every hill – the vast ocean with its foaming breakers on the reef forming always the margin of the picture . . ."

77

The *Africa* and *Spartan* from his own station were now at anchor with the *Shannon*, and they were joined by several frigates from other commands, so that there was no shortage of Naval company ashore. Besides this, a former purser, who had been a shipmate of Broke in the *Southampton* frigate, kept a cheerful house in St. John's.

"... our club now are Bastard (*Africa*), Brenton (*Spartan*), Gardner and Senhouse and Mulcaster joined last night and we are a very sociable, noisy set of people..."

One of the group, Captain Brenton of the *Spartan*, was another of those comparatively rare Naval officers who carried a large library to sea with him and encouraged his officers and Midshipmen to borrow and learn from history and the classical authors. He afterwards wrote a history of the Royal Navy himself, in which he spoke of his intimate acquaintance with 'the gallant and excellent Captain Broke', gained on this station.

"The *Shannon* and the *Spartan* were sister ships; we were often much in company, and I had frequently observed the high state of discipline and training in which Captain Broke kept his ship; he was most exact in his exercises of the great guns, and to this particular branch of his duty he was, in great measure, indebted for his success."

Shortly before Christmas the *Shannon* was ordered to sail, but a high wind kept her in the anchorage. Broke champed at the inactivity. Now that his first delight in stretching his legs and discovering the beauties of the islands had been assuaged, he was growing bored with the social round, the games of whist and long, yarning drinking evenings that stood in for the more active stimuli he longed for.

"December 24th
"... I am much happiest at sea, where I have more persuits to engage my mind and nothing to make me think of *home* and *wives and children*. I shall soon be as bad as my officers and begin to pray heartily for an American war – not for profit, but for diversion from my own thoughts and for a chance of release by wooden wife's being disabled. Our prospects now are extremely blank, 'tis quite murdering the time without an object in view..."

But the gales were no respecter of feelings; they continued unabated and the *Shannon* hung and swung to her anchors through into the New Year. Meanwhile the First Lieutenant, James Bray, was offered command of a gun brig, a chance which he seized avidly, and Broke promoted another of his Lieutenants, a great bull of a man named Watt to the post.

". . . which I believe him very equal to – but it will give me much more work till he is used to it. But this is all in my favour – anything to *distract my mind from thinking*!

"I try to keep in company now I am in town and play cards or anything to divert my ideas. It is a sad loitering place for ships . . . I have been at one sociable family dance and unfortunately in the heighth of my politeness got engaged to the Lady who opened the exhibition – but having fortified myself with the Commodore's claret I danced through the service manfully. But my capering is over now for I will positively sail tomorrow . . .

"I went to the little Church this morning and prayed for my gentle wife and dear little ones. Adieu . . ."

It was at this time that Provo Wallis, later the incredibly long-lived Admiral of the Fleet, joined the *Shannon* as a young Lieutenant. Despite his youth he had already been in two frigate actions, first as a Midshipman of fourteen years when his ship, the *Cleopatra*, had been outgunned and taken by the French *Ville de Milan* – although later recaptured by a British 50-gun ship – and secondly in a victorious action only two years previously which had resulted in the destruction of two French frigates and the capture of shore batteries. Now, approaching his twenty-first birthday, he was a remarkably good-looking young man, tall and broad-shouldered with a pleasant disposition. He acquired an immediate respect, indeed admiration, for his outwardly cheerful, red-haired Captain, and an affection which was life-long grew up between them during his service in the frigate. Years afterwards he described his first impressions of Broke: "a fine, manly looking officer – a manner most courteous, and in command and on duty most decisive. At his table his society was very winning and agreeable. Little wonder is it that his officers and crew were ready to second such a leader to the last."

The Third Lieutenant was Charles Leslie Falkiner, son of a titled family, and described by Wallis as a fine officer and capital messmate. Now all the little band who were to share in their leader's triumph – some at the cost of their lives – were gathered together between the *Shannon*'s timbers – James Watt, Provo Wallis, Charles Falkiner, Lieutenants Johns and Law of the Marines, the purser, Aldham from Suffolk, Broke's clerk, Dunn, his Midshipmen, in whose education he took so much care, the gunner, Meehan, the Boatswain, Stevens, who

79

had fought with Rodney, Marine Sergeant Molyneaux – all moulded into a harmonious and expert fighting unit – all having the utmost faith in their commander.

Their story shortly came within inches of ending tragically. When the frigate finally sailed from the anchorage, the local pilot taking her out – said to be a very clever fellow – was unaccountably seized with confusion about his directions. Seeing the light green tell-tale of a reef through the water on his larboard bow, he called out, "Starboard!" The helmsman obeyed the order quickly, turning his wheel so that the tiller went to starboard correctly, the ship's head thus to port – towards the reef. Seeing this, the pilot lost his head altogether and started leaping about on the forward carronade slide, which he was using as an observation post, yelling, "Starboard! Starboard!" The wheel was put farther over and the *Shannon* turned nearer the reef. At the last moment the pilot suddenly came to himself and called out, "Port, I mean!"

It was too late by then; the *Shannon* drove her larboard bilge on to the coral with a terrible tearing, grating sound, heeling violently as she struck. She was travelling at about nine knots then under all plain sail and her momentum carried her right across the reef and into clear water the other side, luckily without any irreparable damage being caused. A few inches more to port and she might have become a total wreck. Broke, who had nearly been put on the rocks at Halifax by his gunner, who had professed to know the entrance well, took this narrow escape as another instance of the good fortune that sailed with him – and made a note to watch all pilots even more carefully in future. He set course northwards.

> "Jan 19th
>
> ". . . well, we are at sea and as was natural to expect have had gales of wind almost all the week. However I shall persevere. We are now close to the south end of the Newfoundland Bank but as our men have been well refreshed lately I shall not trouble the codfish now . . .
>
> "Next month may decide great points. The American government will make war if they *dare*, and are trying to persuade their people that the Prince Regent is a personal enemy of theirs. But there is no end to their spite and folly and no bound but the fear of their own people . . .
>
> "I make myself very busy all day with the ship – not to *think* of *better things*, my new lieutenant Watt goes on extremely well and is an able officer – a young lieutenant Wallis is appointed and with us. He belongs to Halifax and seems an amiable young man.

"Tuesday. The gale has just abated and we spoke a brig three months from Janeiro – no news whatever. He was bound to Cork, but I thought him too much of a *Paddy* to send a letter by. The weather looks finer, and we shall meet better postmen."

"Feb 2nd

"A new month! And a very ill-tempered one to judge by his entree. Incessant gales all the last week and no variety but storms of rain and lightning . . .

"The war party (American) are certainly a wicked and perverse set of men and are acting in downright enmity to the welfare of all free nations as well as to their natural allies – the mass of the party are sordid, grovelling men who would involve their country in a war for a shilling percent more profit on their particular trade and are perfectly indifferent whether they league themselves with honor or oppression – provided they get their *mammon*. Some of their leaders wish for a war only to get places, appointments and commands . . .

"March 1st . . . having found much occupation this week have hardly known how it passed. We have been putting *Shannon* to rights after all her buffettings and hope now for better weather. I have almost all day upon deck, and am always busy at some new *invention* or other . . ."

These inventions were mostly concerned with his guns. He was experimenting with his carronades on the non-recoil system – that is attaching their carriages to a post coming up through the deck so that their recoil was limited to the flexibility of the post. By cutting out all movement this speeded up the loading time considerably and allowed the piece to be manned by fewer hands. The system had been used at the end of the previous century, but had fallen out of favour because although the materials stood the strain under practice conditions, there was no telling how much powder or how many balls would be loaded in the fever of action – and if overloaded, the piece was liable to burst its mountings with dire consequences to all near by. Broke also experimented with a short recoil system, but found this completely unsatisfactory, even in practice.

Eventually he relegated the non-recoil principle to a standby in the event of both breeching ropes on a carronade breaking under the stress of close action. The crews were trained in this eventuality to lash their pieces to the non-recoil posts and continue firing with a reduced charge.

After cruising unsuccessfully down the trade route again, the

Shannon arrived back at Bermuda on 23rd March. Here she was joined by the *Guerriere*, an old frigate which concealed dangerous weaknesses in timber and gun fastenings under smart paintwork. Her Captain was a young and enthusiastic sprig of the aristocracy named Dacres, soon to have the dreadful shock of being the first British Captain to submit to a Yankee. Broke found him an amusing chatter-box.

"He is a good-natured fellow, but rather a rattle. He would amaze my Loo when in high spirits . . ."

While the two frigates lay at anchor reports came in of two French frigates which had been hovering about the West Indies, and were now sailing back for France. Broke immediately requested permission for the *Shannon* and *Guerriere* to chase and surprise them off the Western Isles (Azores) – the very opportunity he longed for. But the Admiral had his own station to consider. He ordered them up to cruise off Newfoundland instead, and Broke and Dacres, cursing the man's unimaginative nature – although Broke was very fond of the kindly Admiral – shortly weighed and set course northwards. However, they had not gone far before they spoke an American ship with very recent news of the two Frenchmen. Broke immediately put about.

Arriving back at St. George's, Bermuda, he sent Lieutenant Falkiner ashore with a letter to the Admiral requesting permission on the basis of his new intelligence for Dacres and himself to go after the Frenchmen. He gave Falkiner strict orders that if the Admiral was not in the town he was to waste no time enquiring for him, but was to repair on board immediately. As it happened, the Admiral was away. Falkiner soon returned on board, and the frigates weighed and set sail again – this time for the Western Isles.

"April 22nd
"A vile drizzling day . . . my beloved wife there is only this peevish American President who keeps me in suspense and he is so *shilly shally* that we know not what to expect of him. If he does not make a war this station will be not only dull and unprofitable, but even expensive to the officers – but I will come as soon as *honour* will let me, my Loo, and not go to sea again till the French are ready to fight us boldly with their fleets, and I think there will be time for repose before that arrives . . . I want to come home to see my little schoolboy. He was such a comfort in some of mama's sad letters as she seemed to have smiled away all her griefs whilst

talking of him and arch little Willie . . . I wrote a long letter to Philip in my best schoolmaster's hand that he might be able to read it himself and I sent him some learning too as a brother scholar. We shall talk Latin before the women and children when we have any *private discourse*, so the sooner you and Loolin can chatter French, the sooner you will be a match for us . . ."

Meanwhile, in the intervals of trying to read into his latest papers from America whether there would be a war or whether the mercantile and trading community would prevail over the Government, Broke was writing to his mother a long analysis of his feelings and conclusions about the life he was leading. He was a senior frigate Captain now, almost in line for a 74, and although well known for his gunnery innovations and marked in the Service as one of the most efficient young Captains on the list, he was otherwise undistinguished. He had also been unlucky in prizes, which would be even more difficult to come by in a line ship.

". . . As I am not under my gentle wife's spells I shall tell you more of my plans and prospects which you will consider as less influenced by her smiles and soft looks than when I was at Stonehouse. They are the result of many years reflection and consideration and I am now an old philosopher. Had the Admiral given me into a 74 at home or in the Mediterranean it was my intention to have resigned her in less than a year unless some hopes of brilliant service had arisen. Under my present circumstances and with the prospects of *war here* I shall continue to serve tho' I cannot tell how long . . .

"Now it is not civil to put ladies in mind of such circumstances but I am now, my dear mama, *thirty-five years old* and considering the age which my family have previously reached I can hardly look forward (indifferent of war) to twenty years to come *in this world*. Not two years of my life have I yet enjoyed as a domestic man or in a fixed home. The most of my time has been spent in service or seeking employment. I shall soon have completed a course of *seven years' banishment* for this war only – time which can never pass again, or its loss be atoned for . . .

"As a junior Captain of a 74 . . . I should drone away four years more sailings and in the line of some blockading fleet. If at home (as we call it) at intervals of seeing and grieving with my beloved wife and children that we must again speedily separate, and even at those short spaces we would be together living under constant

83

apprehension of a summons, and my time occupied in harbour duties . . .

"I have hitherto served on a (seat) of duty, considering myself as attached for the war, but times are changing and *war is life*. The conditions of service are of course altered. I am not a mere professional man attached to the service by necessity and having no other persuits or duties to consider. Having been, by favour of providence bound to the inheritance of an English gentleman it is my duty to fill that situation in a useful manner, both by example and influence amongst those I was born to preside over – it is true that such men should set an example of privation by serving in war, and it is a desirable thing in a political view that our officers, some of them, should be *independent men* and such as have an immediate interest in their country as well as in professional advancement – but let all take their time. *I have served my time fully* . . . I am now becoming anxious to share in the education of my little ones . . .

"My gentle Loo is one of those *daughters of Eve* who seem to have been formed as the helpmates of man but who *need his support*. She is equal to all the duties of wife and mother, but to leave her father's place also to fill is a cruel imposition . . ."

So the analysis, or self-justification, of his decision to retire shortly – so the agonised pages continued as his pen circled round and round the basic conflict between duty and family – eight long, closely written pages becoming more gloomy as the arguments were exhausted and repeated.

". . . I shall linger out four more years of my life in a ship, more irksome bondage and still more unprofitable than even I have already suffered – my wife miserable and my children strangers to me and I shall never become a happy domestic man, the *only character* in which I think life desirable unless when animated by the spur of ambition in the persuits of war. I shall be old without any pleasing recollections of past life to soothe my mind or prospects of tranquility before me, and with all this forelorn view I am to remember that *the path is of my own choosing* and that I drag one with me to share my wretchedness who cannot change but I do so and whose happiness is one of my most sacred duties . . . I have been a sad guardian of it!

"You will think these ideas gloomy. Indeed I feel them so bitterly whenever my mind, wearied of those studies or duties which I seek as dissipation, leaves me open to reflection."

In early May, having run across the Atlantic to the Western Isles, the two frigates fell in with the sloop-of-war *Niobe*, who told Broke that she had been shadowing the two Frenchmen he was after, but had lost them some two weeks back at night. She thought they had been heading to the south-east.

"My beloved Looloo ... What a plague these Frenchmen are to run three or four thousand miles after them and *be jilted* at last and go home empty handed ..."

But this was not his intention if it could be helped and, expecting that they had gone south to do some mischief to the outward-bound trade at Madeira, he ran down after them before a stirring gale.

"We, *Shannon* and *Guerriere*, fear nobody – we are Lords of the Manor, so woe be to M. Crapaud if he comes our way ..."

Alas, the French frigates were caught and destroyed by one of his late Black Rocks companions, Henry Hotham in the 74-gun *Northumberland*. Broke returned to explain his cruise to the Admiral at Bermuda with nothing but a few prizes to show for it.

But by this time the more urgent affair of the impending war with America was engaging everyone's attention. President Madison had turned with all the force of a thwarted idealist towards the use of arms. The incredible economic manoeuvres he had been indulging in had failed; his war party had their eyes hungrily on the colonial territories of Canada, especially the Eastern seaboard, and it seemed evident that Britain, with all her energies concentrated on the death-struggle with Napoleon, would be unable to put up effective resistance – at least on land.

The British Government, for their part, were unable to believe that America would go to war. The protests of, especially, the New England trading community and the farmers and shippers who were supplying Wellington's armies in the Peninsula were sufficiently loud to suggest that the President would not risk dividing his young and shaky federation of states simply for the *principles* he made such noise about – notably free trade and freedom from impressment. Besides, with the laughable Naval force at his disposal against Britain's thousand sail, what could he hope to gain? The British Government failed to comprehend the anger which had been aroused over a decade by the sheer arrogance of the Royal Navy; Naval boarding officers had been leaving American ships dangerously undermanned since long before the Orders in Council of 1807 had further wounded American pride by forcing the ships themselves into American ports.

Britain, thinking of the *practical* considerations, failed to appreciate the emotional ones.

Their attitude to the President's latest ultimatum that the Orders in Council must be revoked now that Napoleon had repealed his Decrees remained as it had been from the first: His Majesty's Government did not believe that Napoleon *had* revoked – but ". . . if at any time the Berlin and Milan Decrees should be absolutely and unconditionally repealed by some authentic act of the French government publicly promulgated, then the Orders in Council . . . shall without any further order be wholly and absolutely revoked".

The wily Napoleon thereupon produced such a document, said to have been made but not published on 28th April 1812. Britain accepted it in late June, and a message was despatched to President Madison declaring that the Orders in Council he complained of stood repealed from 1st August. By then it was too late. Communications across the seas were too slow. Already, on 1st June, Madison had delivered a belligerent message to Congress reciting all the American grievances – impressment, British regulation of all trade by sea, British violation of American territorial waters, resulting in the *Chesapeake* and *Little Belt* affairs . . .

On 18th June war was declared.

The tiny U.S. Navy now had a profound strategical problem; whether to take the offensive against British trade or whether to attempt the protection of returning American trade against British depredations. And whichever was decided, whether to do it as small units or as a combined squadron of all available ships of force. Fortunately for the senior Commodore, Rodgers, the Government's orders, which were entirely defensive, did not reach him with the news of war and so he was able to reach his own decision; this was offensive and – overruling his junior Commodores, Bainbridge and Decatur – based on concentration of force. Rodgers knew that a large British convoy had sailed homeward from Jamaica on 20th May, and without wasting any time he put to sea in chase with the frigates *President*, *United States*, *Congress*, the sloop-of-war *Hornet* and the brig *Argus*.

Two days later, at first light on the morning of 23rd June, he came upon the lone British frigate, *Belvidera*, way on the north-east horizon. Her Captain, Richard Byron, was unaware of the declaration of war, although fully aware of the extraordinary delicacy of the position with America, and, like all British Captains on the station, under orders not to take any action which might be construed as provocative. Directly he saw the strange sail to the south-west he

86

steered down to investigate. Rodgers, meanwhile, took in his stud-ding sails in great haste and hauled up towards him, whereupon Byron made the private signal. Rodgers, naturally, left it unanswered. Byron tacked away. The chase was on.

They continued under a moderate breeze through the morning and it soon became apparent that the American frigates, which were much larger than the lone Britisher, were gaining appreciably. In the lead was Rodgers himself in the *President*, drawing away from the rest of the squadron. By noon he was less than three miles astern, and Byron, watching him closely through his long glass, observed his bow-chasing guns being trained. The *President* had already hoisted the Stars and Stripes in reply to the *Belvidera*'s British colours. and there was now no doubt left in Byron's mind; this was war. He cleared ship for action.

The *President* closed the distance steadily; about four o'clock in the afternoon she fired three shots from her bow-chasers which were aimed with such extraordinary accuracy that all took effect, two enter-ing Byron's cabin just below where he stood, and one entering the gunroom below that. A sailor at the larboard stern-chaser was killed instantly and six others wounded, one mortally. Five minutes later the *Belvidera* had reorganised the guns' crews and returned the fire. The wind was light and she also made excellent and methodical practice, first carrying away a studding sail and then putting her shot among the guns' crews.

But the Americans shortly suffered a far more serious, self-inflicted wound. One of *President*'s bow-chasers exploded with awful results to the closely bunched men around, and also to the Commodore him-self, who was cheering them on the fo'c'sle. Rodgers was carried away wounded. This was the decisive point in the chase, for after-wards, with part of his fo'c'sle and the maindeck below shattered, Rodgers gave orders for the helm to be put over to bring the broad-side guns to bear, first one side then the other. The accuracy of his fire immediately fell away, as nearly always happened when gunners were expected to take aim while the ship swung – but of far more consequence, he lost precious ground. Not heeding this lesson, per-haps because of his wound, Rodgers continued these tactics and lost more ground each time without doing the *Belvidera* any serious damage. Byron for his part kept up a steady and harassing fire with-out deviating from his course. And giving orders to start the drinking water and pitch all spare spars, boats and movable weights including his anchors overboard, he so lightened the ship that he was able to in-crease his lead and eventually escape during the dark hours that night.

G

The round undoubtedly went to the British; for the Royal Navy it was just another proof of their superiority by divine right.

Broke heard of the abortive chase on 30th June when he arrived off Halifax after a short cruise of five days from Bermuda.

"My beloved Looloo . . . a most honorable action between *Belvidera* and almost all the American Navy in which they were so disgracefully foiled that I think their *mob* will punish their commander severely; for King *Mob* is the supreme court there. Their conduct indeed was dastardly, and we suspect in consequence that their loss has been great – as Byron made a steady retreat and with a constant sharp fire on them for three hours whilst they might *at once* have crushed him by closer battle. But they had not spirit to run him alongside . . ."

Running in to anchor inside the harbour on the following day, Broke heard official confirmation of the American declaration of war. Like his officers he was overjoyed. He was senior Captain on the station; he would have an opportunity with *frigates* to search out and destroy Rodgers in equal combat before any reinforcements in the shape of 74s might be sent to Halifax – if indeed the Admiralty considered the Americans deserved such a compliment to their warlike skill. Here at last was the opportunity he had been preparing himself and *Shannon* for; long years of frustration dropped away – he was in the right place at the right time. Fortune had provided him a chance of that brilliant service which would send his name ringing through England.

The *Shannon* could do it. She was as perfect in every detail as constant drill, considerable invention and the attentions of his shipwrights and armourers and gunners could make her. There wasn't a frigate to touch her. Not that he would have been so ill-mannered as to mention it.

"July 2nd

". . . we shall probably sail in a few days, but with such a force as will *sweep the seas* clear of all enemies and shall then reap our harvest. I grieve at this war as a patriot, my Loo, but as a naval officer must rejoice at it – England has borne much insult from these graceless people and latterly has tried every service to soothe them but they are determined to throw themselves into the arms of France and one way or another will be punished as they deserve. We are all sanguine in our expectations of soon sweeping their Navy into our ports and sending (or rather bringing) home a convoy of good prizes . . ."

Three days later, on 5th July, Broke led his squadron out of Halifax. Copies of his orders had gone to each Captain. The order of sailing was *Shannon* as sole ship in the weather line, the lee line to be led by the gallant Byron in *Belvidera*, next *Guerriere*, when she joined, *Aeolus*, and bringing up the rear, as she would in any case, the slow 50-gun *Africa*. The order of battle was *Shannon*, *Guerriere*, *Belvidera*, *Aeolus*, *Africa*.

Broke was thirty-five years old. He sailed as Commodore with a light heart. This was such a chance as Nelson would have dreamed – to destroy the American Navy before it had a chance to accomplish anything.

Shannon would lead the line.

CHAPTER FIVE

BROKE led his squadron southwards to seek for news of his opponent. On the first day out he came upon an American merchant brig, *Minerva*, returning home after carrying supplies to Wellington's army in the Peninsula. Broke had her Captain sent aboard the *Shannon* and, finding that the man was ignorant of the outbreak of war between their two countries, questioned him at some length for information of Commodore Rodgers and the U.S. Navy.

To the *Shannon*'s officers, observing the interview from a discreet distance, it was obvious that their Captain was not enjoying the deception forced upon him. But the most painful moment was yet to come. When he had extracted all the news he could, and after struggling for the best way of putting it, he forced out at last, "Well, Captain – I must burn your ship."

The American, who had been friendly and unreserved until then, was struck dumb for a moment.

"Burn her?" he faltered.

"Indeed I must."

"Burn her – for what? Will money not save her? She is all my own – all the property I have in the world." He paused, realising the truth from Broke's expression. "It is war then?"

"Yes."

"War between America and England?"

"Yes. It is war between America and England. Your country declared it and three of your frigates fired upon one of ours before we had notice. England has not yet declared war in return, but I have orders to act as if she had done so."

The American turned to gaze at his brig, lying daintily on the water nearby, and Broke put his arm up to the man's shoulder in silent sympathy. The officers noticed that both men's eyes glistened with tears.

After burning *Minerva* Broke continued southwards and three days later burnt another returning American, *Brutus*, while *Belvidera* destroyed a schooner; the next day *Shannon* burnt a schooner and the following day a ship called the *Mechanic* and the day after that the *Gracie*. So it went. The course of the squadron was marked by a trail of charred wreckage, and the berth decks of the British ships filled with American prisoners. In the first two weeks no less than forty craft were destroyed. Broke, in company with everyone else in the squadron, was not pleased at all this easy prize money going up in smoke, but he put his duty higher than financial reward, and his duty as he saw it was to keep his ships fully manned for the decisive encounter with Rodgers. Had he yielded to the temptations of prizes a good proportion of his sailors would by now be on their way to Halifax with the captured ships.

As it happened, it would scarcely have mattered because Rodgers was thousands of miles away and sailing in the opposite direction, following a trail of floating refuse behind the homeward West Indian convoy. As the Americans neared the Western Approaches to the English Channel the English squadron bore up towards Sandy Hook just south of New York. Broke sailed easterly along Long Island in morning fogs and then, ordering his ships to heave to, he hoisted the Stars and Stripes over *Shannon* and sailed alone close in to Montauk Point to seek information.

The small craft there avoided him at first, rightly suspicious, but when he made no attempt to fire or chase they gained courage and sailed nearer. Then two fishermen, apparently satisfied with the American flag, came up the side and offered their services as pilots. Broke, playing the spider again, welcomed them aboard. This was the good ship *Congress* – the sail in the offing, he explained throwing his arm wide, were the rest of Rodgers' squadron. The fishermen were fully taken in and congratulated him on the *Belvidera* engagement – believing wrongly that the Britisher had been taken – and talked freely of several other privateer encounters in the news. Broke, listening to them, formed the impression that Rodgers must have been making for the Grand Banks to harass the Halifax and West Indian trade. And as soon as he had learned all he could he put the friendly people back in their boats and tacked out to rejoin his squadron.

The following day was squally and he only burnt one schooner, which tried to escape by flying Spanish colours. But the next morning brought several craft including the U.S. brig-of-war *Nautilus* of 16 guns, which was chased and soon taken by *Shannon* outsailing her consorts as she usually did. Papers captured aboard her seemed to confirm Broke's suspicion that Rodgers was making for the Grand Banks, and he thereupon decided to pursue him up there rather than haunt New York in a too literal interpretation of his orders.

"July 21st

"To Commander in Chief, Halifax

". . . as every information by the *Nautilus* and other captures confirms the account of the enemy's squadron being on the Banks I shall now proceed that way. At least we are sure of protecting our outward bound supplies and as Rodgers will now probably get notice of our having been off the Hook, he will run for some other port, and our continuance off New York could only enable us to destroy some scattered merchant ships, whilst our West India and Halifax convoys would remain exposed to the enemy's squadron to be destroyed *en masse* . . ."

Again in this decision duty triumphed over any desire for prize money. He was deliberately leaving the richest hunting-ground off New York and Boston, where there was bound to be a continuing stream of returning merchantmen, and sailing instead for the British trade routes. In military terms this was undoubtedly correct. Surmising that a British convoy was Commodore Rodgers' 'grand object', it merely remained for him to find the same convoy and, as he put it in his despatch, "their presence may lead to a meeting of our squadrons".

Meanwhile a lone U.S. frigate was also seeking a meeting with Rodgers. This was *Constitution*, Commodore Isaac Hull, who, anxious to escape a possible British blockade, had sailed from the Chesapeake to join forces with his brother frigate commanders. Instead he came upon Broke.

The meeting took place off Egg Harbor, New Jersey, on the evening of the *Nautilus* capture, 16th July; Hull sighted four sail, actually *Shannon*, *Belvidera*, *Aeolus* and *Africa*, and while closing cautiously in the hope that they might be Rodgers' squadron, saw another sail to seaward, which was in fact *Guerriere* rejoining after a chase. As the

Constitution and *Guerriere*, both making for the squadron to leeward, closed each other during the night, Hull made private lantern signals to which the English Captain, Dacres, made no reply; he simply kept in touch, expecting an action at dawn. Meanwhile Broke and his squadron stood to quarters all night, watching the two frigates' slow approach, but, being downwind, quite unable to do anything but wait.

At 3.15 a.m., as the first grey light crept over the horizon, Dacres, who was now very close to the squadron, made the night signal to the nearest ship, *Belvidera*. This was reported to Captain Byron on the quarterdeck.

"From the haziness of the morning I was not satisfactorily convinced it was the real night signal. I rather thought it was the signal to distinguish British ships from the enemy when going into or in action, and I had mine hanging at the gaff ready for showing all night."

So Byron did not reply. There was another reason too; the *Constitution* was now so close to him, barely a mile away and close hauled to starboard, that he didn't wish to frighten her off with strange signals; as it was coming up to daylight he hoisted the day signal instead. However, all this was not apparent to Captain Dacres, and suspecting from the absence of any reply to his lantern signals that he might be running right into Rodgers' entire squadron, which the other lone frigate was rejoining, he immediately put about and ran. Hull realised his own mistake soon afterwards as the early light revealed Broke's ships and he also put about, cutting away his taffrail and mounting long stern-chasers. Broke set off after him.

There followed a chase more agonising even than the *Belvidera* incident earlier. At dawn the *Shannon* was a bare four miles from the *Constitution*, and appeared at first to be gradually overhauling her in the light, fluky airs that came with the sun – certainly *Shannon* was soon leading the rest of the British squadron.

But what breeze there was soon died away, and both chased and chasers put boats overside with the most stalwart members of their crew at the oars to tow them over the oily surface. After a while Broke signalled for all the boats of his squadron to leave their respective ships and harness on to the *Shannon*; directly this was done, he began to creep up on the lone American. Hull countered, on the advice of one of his Lieutenants, Charles Morris, by 'cadging' (kedging).

Two lines, each nearly a mile in length, were formed by joining all available spare hawsers and ropes together, and each was attached to an anchor, one of which was then rowed ahead of the ship to its full extent and dropped. The men at the capstan walked round merrily and heaved the ship over the ground by main strength. The boats with the second anchor were meanwhile pulling ahead, and as the first was tripped from the bottom the second was dropped and another team manned the capstan. So it went, anchor by anchor. It was gruelling work. Although American ships were used to the evolution in shallow water and could reach three knots in favourable conditions, it says much for the seamanship and steadiness of the *Constitution*'s crew, only five days out in their first commission, that in this deeper water the 'cadging' went on without a hitch, and the big frigate walked steadily away from the *Shannon* and her boats. Had there been just one false move to foul up the anchors the Americans would have been in a parlous position.

The *Shannon* could not reply in like manner because, had she managed to close the distance, her boats with the kedge anchors way out ahead would have been exposed to a steady fire from the *Constitution*'s stern-chasers.

By noon the slow procession had moved some thirty miles to seaward. Afterwards a chance breeze blew *Belvidera* up into the lead and she exchanged a few shots with the American, but they all dropped short. The breeze soon died and she fell back.

The evening came with the vessels in much the same relative positions, and so it continued throughout the night, with the men not at work sleeping exhausted at their posts. Next morning the *Constitution* was still there, hauntingly just out of gunshot ahead. Now a southerly breeze got up and the boats were taken in, all sails set, and the crews put to work hoisting tubs of water to the masthead and dousing the sails with water to stretch them and make them hold the wind better. Again the crew of the American frigate showed impeccable and nerveless seamanship although they were under greater pressure than the British sailors. The *Constitution* continued to increase her lead.

Now all the high art of sailing the ships for maximum speed came into play. The canvas was set to balance itself as nearly as possible so that the movement of the rudder would not retard progress through the water, the yards and sheets were trimmed afresh for each change of wind, however small, different combinations and permutations of square and fore and aft sails on the fore and main were tried as the quarry veered this way and that, seeking her best point of sailing advantage. It was all to no avail. The wind increased and steadied through the afternoon, and the *Constitution*, longer on the waterline than any of her pursuers, walked away steadily.

As night settled again on the straggling line of ships it was obvious that she was far enough ahead to lose the British during the dark hours. Broke, who had scarcely slept for two days and nights, went up to the fo'c'sle and gazed out through red-rimmed eyes to where she had been. There was only the night now, and he knew that his first real chance had escaped him. The wind was fresh and the *Shannon* was racing through the sea, tumbling it away from the stem just below; the same wind would be benefiting his quarry more.

He turned and looked back – curving shapes of canvas against the dark sky. The lower studding sails stretched out far beyond the deck either side, above them the topmast studding sails, then the t'gallants, all tapering up towards the royal studding sails flying like two pale kites way above – all so perfectly stretched that they were motionless as if carved and polished in marble, and from below here so beautifully rounded, such exquisite partners to the wind, their mistress. It was nights like this that amply repaid him for all the frustrations and deprivations of cruising – these nights when he could see God in the boundless black waves and in the stars breaking through above, feel Him in the cool breeze against his cheek and know Him perfectly through this lovely structure of timber and hemp and white canvas that His creatures had built and sailed to do His service on the oceans.

He was keyed up to a high pitch of awareness after the tension of the past few days, and he stood a long while in silence glorying in the spirit of his ship, the way she leaned and surged to the wind. The people were quiet at their stations or asleep beside their arms and the only sounds in the darkness came from the urgent plash and hiss of the water around the bow. He felt humbled in the presence of his Maker; He had given him further disappointment to add to his years of endurance and striving – as atonement perhaps for the pride which afflicted him in his Captain's uniform, his hunger for distinction above his fellow men.

But he knew his day would come. He could feel himself a part, a most insignificant part to be sure against the vast bowl of the heavens and the wide waters and teeming continents beyond, but a part of the grand design, and his labours *would* be rewarded.

The following morning the horizon ahead was empty. The *Constitution* had gone. Broke reduced to easy canvas and lay to, to await the rest of the squadron.

Undoubtedly the round had gone to the Americans. Although the *Constitution* was a larger ship and a faster sailer than any of the British frigates, her escape had been equally due to superb seamanship. The British, cheated of what they had thought was easy game, were bitterly angry with themselves – from the officers down to the youngest boys. During the morning all the Captains were called to exchange explanations in *Shannon*'s great cabin.

The two ships on whom most doubt fell were the *Guerriere* and *Belvidera* because of their signals muddle and their extreme proximity to the American during the first night. Captain Byron of the *Belvidera* felt the loss most heavily.

"Nothing can exceed my mortification from the extraordinary escape of the American frigate. I really did not think, from the Squadron's position in the evening, the *Guerriere* would take the *Belvidera* and *Aeolus* to be *American* frigates. I considered the rockets and guns of the *Guerriere* to be announcing an enemy in view but whether one or more ships the daylight immediately coming on would inform us. I am now very sorry I did not answer her signal, but it was *so near* daylight. Whatever I did was from the most anxious intention to secure the enemy . . ."

No one doubted this, and after thrashing the circumstances out again and again no one could suggest how, after the initial mistakes of identification had been made, the swifter American could have been brought to action. The meeting broke up without recrimination, and after waiting for the sluggardly *Africa* and the prize, *Nautilus*, to catch up the squadron set course for the Grand Banks before a steady breeze.

Broke's opinion of his adversaries was now undergoing a sea change.

"July 21st

"My dear, beloved Loo, so constantly since we left Halifax have my moments been occupied in Service that I could never find one of quiet leisure to write to you, *even* to my gentle wife. I am sent in pursuit of an active and artful enemy, who will, if he can, do vast mischief to our trade, and perhaps (God forbid) evade after all the vengeance we intend to wreak on him. Dark, foggy weather and calms have almost neutralised war proceedings and we have just learned that my *particular object*, Rodgers and his squadron, are far away from where I was sent to look for them. However my Admiral has given me liberal scope to do all we can and we yet hope that is much – although we have been in a *fever of anxiety* since we sailed.

"An American frigate escaped us by her rapid sailing last week. We will have her yet. Prizes I don't count on. We burn all we meet, but vessels of war. One of their Navy brigs went to Halifax yesterday, but these are *poor triumphs*. These wretches have declared war in a most insulting and ungenerous manner, but I trust will repent and also trust it will restore me sooner to my beloved Loo . . ."

"July 26th

". . . we have had no success but destroying a few more ships. But we have *done good*, for we released thirty prisoners – poor Americans taken in merchant ships and as most of them were settled family men I think it was *charity* and we have little merit as we were glad to be rid of them. We have just discovered that the West India convoy under Byam (in *Thetis*) is somewhere very near us. They are the pray Commodore Rodgers came to lie wait for, so we hope, by following the game to meet the *poachers* . . ."

Broke fell in with the convoy four days later and after sending another one hundred and twenty of his American prisoners to their homes in a captured brig – first making them sign an undertaking not to serve in arms against Great Britain until they were officially exchanged for British prisoners – he joined his own squadron to the lone British escort.

That evening, 30th July, he had Captain Byam, the escort Captain, aboard to dinner, and they talked enthusiastically of the chances of surprising Rodgers. He continued the conversation after Byam had gone with his wife.

"My beloved Looloo . . . I hope we are to take the American squadron as a splendid compensation for our lack of prizes in a mercantile way. It seems settled, my Loo, that I should never be enriched by war. Our outset here afforded a fine prospect, but the imperious call of publick duty has turned our attention from the *destruction* of the enemy's trade to the *protection* of our own and in a few weeks the harvest will be over and nothing but iron war remain. 'Tis more honorable than golden emolument I own and therefore hope we shall have a proud show in it to soothe our disappointments. Honor and peace with my Loo will content *me*. God grant them soon."

Alas, Rodgers was still a thousand miles ahead of him, and this soon became apparent from intelligence gathered as they proceeded eastwards.

"To Commander in Chief Halifax

"We have escorted *Thetis* and her valuable convoy safe beyond
the limits of this station, but American squadron has evaded our
pursuit by proceeding onwards towards Europe . . . I shall return
off their harbours with a view to intercepting them on the passage
home."

In case Rodgers might still be waiting in mid-Atlantic he sent the
Africa on with the convoy, instructing her to escort them as far as
45° West longitude, and telling Byam to take them on a detour to
52° North latitude directly *Africa* left him. That done, he despatched
Guerriere to Halifax for much-needed repairs, while he led his two
remaining frigates back towards New York.

Meanwhile Isaac Hull in the *Constitution* had been plundering
British trade around Cape Race, Newfoundland, until, hearing of
Broke's presence in the vicinity, he decided to make off southwards
towards Bermuda. Thus it was by strange chance in the early afternoon of 19th August his course crossed that of the lone *Guerriere*'s
some three hundred miles south-eastward of Sable Island.

The day was cloudy, the wind fresh from the north-west, and the
Constitution, driving before it, immediately crowded on all canvas to
investigate the strange sail. Dacres in the *Guerriere* watched her coming down on his beam from windward and held on south-westwards
under easy sail. By three o'clock he realised that she was a large
frigate, and hostile, and beat to quarters, hauling up his courses and
backing his main topsail flat against the mast, and awaited her
approach with satisfaction. Fortune had favoured him with the first
chance to thrash a Yankee in equal combat! He issued his men with
a ration of grog and exhorted them to do their duty like Britons – at
the same time sportingly allowing seven Americans in his crew to go
below out of the coming conflict.

The *Constitution* creamed towards them. Some three miles off, just
outside extreme gunshot, she wore and headed easterly for a while to
reduce to fighting canvas, hauling up her courses, taking in the flying
jib and staysails and t'gallants, and taking a second reef in the topsails. The drum beat to quarters and the American crew gave three
enthusiastic cheers which carried easily downwind to the Britishers
waiting by the guns of the starboard battery as the *Guerriere*, making
bare headway, rolled her muzzles in slow arcs. Three British ensigns
fluttered bravely from the masts above.

Did Isaac Hull have any qualms as he pointed his frigate, trimmed for action, at the *Guerriere*'s starboard quarter? Certainly none that showed. There was no hesitation, no disinclination for close combat. And yet, however much he might have rationalised his own *matériel* superiority, he would have been more than human if those three British ensigns symbolising absolute supremacy and ferocity in sea warfare caused him no twinges of unease.

And what of Dacres? Did he realise the hopeless material disadvantage he was facing? Probably not. British victories were a habit, and nothing that had happened in the war so far had given reason to suppose that the Americans would be any different from the French or Spanish. Besides, the condition of his frigate was fair evidence that, like many of the younger British Captains, he regarded his nation's sea supremacy as due by right rather than forethought or warlike preparation. Some of the breeching ropes of his cannon were perished, the bolts and eyes holding them rusted, the timbers they passed through rotten. There was little he could have done about other defects such as the sprung bowsprit and the rotten core of the foremast, but his guns might have received better care.

Not that it would have made much difference. He was outmatched in every department. The big American warships, *Constitution*, *United States*, *President*, although nominally frigates, were far larger than any other vessels of that class in the world. Commenting on this increased size during their construction, the American Secretary at War had expected that "they would possess in an eminent degree, the advantage of sailing, that separately they would be superior to any European frigate of the usual dimensions; that if assailed by numbers they would always be able to lead ahead; that they could never be obliged to go into action but on their own terms, except in a calm; and that in heavy weather they would be capable of engaging double decked ships".

Thus the *Constitution*, 175 feet between perpendiculars, had an advantage over the *Guerriere* of 17 feet in length, nearly 5 feet in beam, some 5 inches in thickness of topside planking, 7 inches in diameter of mainmast. Below the maindeck gunport sills her sides had the scantlings of a British 74-gun ship. Her 15 long guns on each side were 24-pounders, the *Guerriere*'s 14 were 18-pounders; above this main battery the *Constitution* had 12 32-pounder carronades each side against the *Guerriere*'s 8 – a total advantage in weight of shot of nearly 3 to 2. She had a similar advantage in tonnage, 1,500 against 1,100, and carried nearly double the men, 463 against 244 at quarters in the *Guerriere*.

Against such force, and against the methodical gunnery training which the American Navy, as the weaker force, paid such attention to, only the most extraordinary luck could have saved the *Guerriere* or any comparable ship.

Dacres, unaware of the impossible odds, watched the American heading to cross his stern and rake the length of his decks. Directly he judged his own starboard battery within range, he ordered them to fire, then quickly wore ship to protect his stern and presented his port battery. The guns roared, and he wore again to point the starboard guns a second time. Hull, meanwhile, untroubled by the shot which all fell short – possibly because of damp powder after the *Guerriere*'s long cruising – made slight alterations of course, both to bring his own foremost guns to bear and to prevent Dacres getting across his bows to rake him. So the waltz continued downwind until, finding he could obtain no advantage, Dacres bore up and ran on a steady course under topsails and jib with the wind astern. Hull set his main t'gallant sail to catch him and soon came up on the port quarter, running in to less than a hundred yards and discharging his starboard guns double-shotted with round and grape. The American training and weight of metal began to tell almost at once. Within a quarter of an hour the *Guerriere*'s mainyard had fallen in the slings and then the mizzen-mast crashed over the starboard quarter and, dragging in the water, slewed her bows to starboard. The *Constitution* had been overhauling all the time; now she forged ahead, and putting her wheel over, came across the *Guerriere*'s bow and raked with her starboard battery. Then, seeing that the wallowing Britisher was still moving slowly forward, Hull ordered the helm up to prevent her coming across his stern and raking in her turn. Most of the *Constitution*'s braces had been shot away by this time, and as she answered more slowly than usual, the *Guerriere*'s bowsprit, still moving ahead and to starboard, caught in his port mizzen rigging and held. The two ships locked together.

Both Commanders immediately called away the boarders, but Dacres, seeing the army of men opposed to him, contented himself with defending his own deck. The Americans for their part could not get aboard the *Guerriere* because of the swell which was lifting and dropping the ships erratically. So, while the *Guerriere*'s forward maindeck guns brought havoc and fire to Hull's cabin just below the quarterdeck, the boarders above fought a spirited musquetry battle across the swinging bowsprit.

Dacres, whatever his shortcomings of preparation before the fight, was a mettlesome and courageous leader in the best traditions of the British service. He stood on the starboard hammock nettings up on the fo'c'sle, cheering his men enthusiastically until he was struck by a musket ball. Even then he remained on deck, refusing to be carried below while he had breath to encourage his people.

The wind was swinging the ships back to port all the time, and soon the *Constitution* broke free of the British vessel. Almost immediately afterwards both the *Guerriere*'s remaining masts crashed over the starboard side without another shot fired, and she lay a wallowing and unmanageable wreck to the waves. While heroic efforts were made to rig a jury spritsail and cut away the tangle of spars hanging to starboard, the *Constitution* made off a short distance to repair her own damages, which, although not in any way comparable to the *Guerriere*'s, were substantial about the rigging.

The American company, however, was almost unharmed. Despite the fact that the *Guerriere* had started the action two hours before, and had been closely engaged for the past thirty minutes, the *Constitution* had suffered only seven dead and seven seriously wounded, and most of these casualties had occurred during the musquetry engagement. Her gun deck and hull were generally untouched except for the Commodore's cabin, which had been locked up against the muzzles of the British forward guns while the ships had been drifting together; it had been impossible to miss. With all allowance for the sea running at the time, the *Guerriere*'s fire had been deplorable. The rolling ship, the damp powder and the inferior calibre of her main battery would have made long hits extremely difficult, but once the *Constitution* came fairly alongside, had the British guns been well laid for horizontal fire and their captains trained for rolling conditions they must have done far more damage before the superior weight of the American shot began to compound itself. In fact most of the British shot must have flown high, as the *Constitution* was considerably wounded in her lower masts and her rigging was cut to pieces.

By comparison the *Guerriere* had at least 30 round shot in her hull, 15 men killed, 63 wounded, several mortally, and many of her cannon unshipped – although many of these probably had defective fittings.

The *Constitution* spent some thirty minutes repairing her rigging and then returned in high spirit to take her prize. Dacres, seeing her approaching, called his officers about him on the quarterdeck; the *Guerriere* was unmanageable still and helpless in the trough of the sea, the maindeck gunports were rolling wildly right under the waves, and in any case could not be brought to bear while the American took up the raking position she was obviously heading for. Nearly a third of the ship's company was dead or wounded – obviously further resistance would be a needless waste of life. It was decided to strike.

The wounded were taken aboard the *Constitution*, and efforts made to repair the shattered hulk of the British vessel and pump her bilges during the evening. But by daylight the following morning the water had gained to such an extent that she was given up. All hands were evacuated to the American frigate, and she was put to the match. The unfortunate Dacres, weak from his wound, and mortified by the disaster of having to strike to one of the despised Yankees, watched her blow up as Isaac Hull set course for Boston.

The moral results of this unequal contest were, as always at the start of a war, wildly disproportionate to the actual effect. The Americans crowed with triumph. So far as the public were concerned, a U.S. *frigate* had taken a British *frigate* – and who was going to point out the enormous disparity in force? Hull and the Constitutions were heroes overnight, and fêted and toasted throughout the breadth of the country. They had accomplished first time off what all the European Navies had consistently failed to do; they had lowered the arrogant Union flag in equal contest.

The British reaction was equally extreme. The extraordinary shock and depression which the news produced can only be explained by the public faith that their ships were unbeatable. As *The Times* put it in an article forecasting a train of gloomy circumstances following on this disaster, the 'spell of victory' had been broken. The *Naval Chronicle* remarked, "An English frigate rated 38 guns should undoubtedly, barring extraordinary accidents, cope successfully with a 44-gun ship of any other nation."

Poor Dacres! He was the first to be humbled. He must have wondered what had hit him. Even the French apparently took heart, and not long afterwards *L'Arethusa* frigate, Captain Bouvet, lying off the African coast, *waited* for the British *Amelia* to attack her, and then fought with such spirit that the encounter became the most bloody that had been seen for years. They lay side by side almost touching one another on a calm, moonlit night and pounded away for three and a half hours until every officer on both sides had been killed or wounded and both ships riven with shot. When at last they separated in a drawn contest the British frigate had 141 killed and wounded, *L'Arethusa* scarcely less.

The Times commented, "It is long since we have seen anything like these persevering and slaughtering efforts on the part of French seamen. Is it not obvious that they are stimulated to them by the late triumph of the American Navy?"

Broke heard of the *Guerriere*'s loss towards the end of September while beating in to Halifax Harbour with some prizes he had permitted himself.

"We are all very angry at hearing that the American frigate *Constitution*, whom our squadron *hunted* so lately has taken one of our frigates and burned her. However this will all forward the chance of *Shannon*'s making an *honorable game* of it as the enemy will be *saucy now*."

A correct estimation.

Rodgers, meanwhile, had returned from his cruise across the Atlantic and slipped back into Boston without meeting any British men-of-war. He had only seven prizes to show for the long haul, a lamentable average per ship when compared with the damage done to British trade by the scores of American privateers which had been hurriedly fitted out all along the eastern seaboard. Rodgers was Broke's grand objective none the less, and he was in a fever of impatience to complete with stores and rejoin the rest of his squadron, which he had left off New York. There was talk of an armistice in the air; the New England traders especially were unsympathetic to the war, and if they prevailed upon their Government the chances of glory would vanish in a moment. There wasn't a day to be lost.

"Halifax, Sept 22nd

". . . we find here all depression at the unfortunate loss of the *Guerriere*, poor Dacres! He did his best, but *fortune* ran against him. We expect him every day. He is wounded but not seriously – we are all eager for an opportunity of *convincing* the *Yankees* how much they are indebted to chance for their success in this contest. Their force is superior in ship and metal and number of men, but not in *skill* or *courage* equal. We cannot rest here. I am hurrying out and in a few days shall rejoin the squadron off New York to do all we can for the splendour of the *proud old flag* . . ."

Before he could do so Admiral Sir John Borlase Warren arrived with two 74s to take over command of a combined West Indies and Halifax station. He was a courtly old man, sent out by the British Government as much for his diplomatic as his sailor-like qualities, for they still hoped that the Americans might see reason now that the objectionable Orders in Council had been rescinded. Warren was empowered to make peace either with the central government or, if that was not possible, then with independent states' governments – a policy of division.

Warren also brought with him good news of the war in Spain. While Napoleon was pressing towards what everyone believed was inevitable victory in Moscow, Lord Wellington had routed his creature, Marmont, at Salamanca. On 28th September every British warship in Halifax Harbour fired a 21-gun salute in honour of the victory. For Broke the guns were charged with special significance: his brother, Major Charles Broke, who was very close to him, was serving with Wellington's army.

Afterwards he made his number with the Admiral.

". . . a consultation with the Admiral and we are to go off Boston directly, but he does not decide very quick and so all our zeal and hurry of last week is wasted. But *Shannon* is all ready to start and seek reperation for our disappointments last cruise. We shall have a squadron of six fine frigates and shall *strut about* the Yankee ports in great pride . . ."

Captain Dacres and the surviving crew of the *Guerriere* arrived in the city the following day as exchange for repatriated Americans, and several of the men were drafted into the *Shannon*. Broke took the first opportunity to visit Dacres, listening eagerly to his account of the action, and pressing him with questions about the American frigate, her organisation, guns and the practice she had made with them. Dacres convinced him that the decisive fact in the action had not been weight of metal or better aim, but simply the early loss of his own mizzen-mast rendering his ship unmanageable. But for that . . .

They went on to talk indignantly of the British sailors among the crew of the American frigate. Broke, too, had found deserters in the U.S.S. *Nautilus*, and other captures. He had pleaded for their pardon in a letter of 20th September – just before arriving at Halifax and hearing of the *Guerriere*'s loss – on the grounds that 'no blood had yet been shed in the war". He was not so sure he would do the same again, especially as Dacres seemed convinced that it was the British-ers among the Constitutions who had been foremost in the attempts to board.

That night Broke recorded his interview in a letter to Louisa.

"Sept 29th

". . . Dacres arrived this morning with all the remainder of his brave crew. He is almost well and in excellent spirits, wishing only another frigate to go to *take his revenge*. The citizens of America (Boston) were very kind and polite to him and his officers. The

H

American officers too rude a lot of animals for gentlemen to associate with."

Dacres' court martial followed on 2nd October, and as expected, he was "unanimously and honourably acquitted of all blame on account of her capture". The same day there came news of the wreck of a British vessel called *Barbadoes* on Sable Island, and Broke, thoroughly tired of the social round of Halifax, took *Shannon* out in a westerly gale to save those of her crew who had managed to get ashore. This accomplished he returned to Halifax, only to find that in the 'phoney war' which was being conducted in an effort not to antagonise the New England states, rather to play them off against Washington, he was to kick his heels ashore for a further period. There was, however, some talk of the Admiral leaving for warmer climes – in which case Broke would be senior Captain.

> "Halifax   Oct 15th
> ". . . if so I shall rout them all out to sea with me . . . I don't mean to be a harbour commodore! . . . our cannon must tame these malicious and ignorant people who think they can manage the world. But severe chastisement awaits them, and I flatter myself that when convinced that Britain can control their spiteful frenzy they may cool and perceive that their true interests lie only in brotherly love and union with their natural relations, and they the only true and virtuous nation left on earth. But they must be *whipped* out of their *conceit* and frowardness and perhaps like some other naughty children they may *love us for it afterwards* . . ."

At last he received the orders he had been waiting for, and on 18th October, sailed from Halifax with *Tenedos*, *Nymphe* and *Curlew* in company. On the same morning the 'naughty children', their tails well up, gave mother England the first of several more sharp lessons.

Captain Whinyates, escorting a homeward bound convoy from the West Indies in the sloop-of-war *Frolic*, had reached some two hundred and fifty miles north of Bermuda, and was repairing severe storm damages received on the previous night, when a sail was observed bearing down towards him from westward. He sent the convoy on and waited, meanwhile lashing his damaged mainyard to the deck, clearing for action and hoisting Spanish colours.

The strange sail proved to be the U.S. sloop-of-war *Wasp*, Captain Jacob Jones. She had lost her bowsprit in the same storm, and in other respects they were very equally matched, both mounting 8 carronades, 32-pounders, on each broadside besides one or two small-calibre long guns of little value. The complement of H.M.S. *Frolic* was 109 men and boys, of U.S.S. *Wasp*, 138; the *Frolic* was 100 feet in length, the *Wasp* only 5 feet longer. In Admiral Mahan's words, the ensuing fight was "as nearly equal as it is given to such affairs to be".

It was a wild day, with a strong wind from the westward and a high swell left over from three days of gales. The *Wasp* approached without any hesitation from windward and hailed; for answer Captain Whinyates lowered his Spanish ensign, hoisted British colours and gave him a broadside and a volley of musquetry. Whereupon the *Wasp* ran close in and the battle commenced broadside to broadside.

Accurate aim was extremely difficult from the tossing decks of the small craft; the British sloop, firing rather more rapidly than the American and aiming on the up-roll, was sending her shot generally flying high so that the *Wasp*'s maintopmast fell within four minutes and her mizzen t'gallant and spanker soon afterwards. The Americans on the other hand, firing on the down-roll, were placing their shot lower and often hulling the *Frolic* and cutting her masts and rigging closer to the deck. Of course they had the advantage of the weather gage and were not facing an incoming sea each time they fired.

Whatever their actual superiority with the great guns, the fight, like the previous engagement, was won when the *Frolic* lost her jury mainsail and was rendered unmanageable. The *Wasp* then shot ahead and took up a raking position on her bow, so close that when the Americans pushed their rammer handles out of the gunports they were striking their opponent's timbers. It was a tempestuous scene. The vessels shuddered together as the swell dropped them, the sea burst up between and over the decks and lower rigging as the 32-pounders roared and smashed everything before them. Musquets and rifles popped from point blank over the bulwarks.

Despite their impossible position the men of the *Frolic* kept up a spirited resistance with those forward guns which would bear, cheering and cheering again as they loaded and fired – but fewer each time the carronades swept the length of their deck with grape and splinters. Meanwhile the Americans, led by one Jack Laing who had formerly suffered impressment under the British flag, were bunching by the *Frolic*'s bowsprit, eagerly awaiting the order to run across it. When at last they went without orders they found only four men on their feet on the upper deck – the man at the wheel, Captain Whinyates and two officers with him aft. Whinyates himself was so badly wounded he could only stand with support, and as the Americans ran aft over decks slippery with blood and salt water and littered with bodies under a tangle of rigging, the officers dropped their swords. The engagement had lasted nearly three quarters of an hour at point blank.

As the vessels drifted apart, both the *Frolic*'s masts went, the fore-mast 15 feet above the deck and the main close to the deck. The American casualties were trifling, 5 dead, of whom 3 were in the tops and 5 seriously wounded; the British casualties totalled over half her complement, 58 killed and wounded at the most conservative estimate. Nevertheless Whinyates had saved the convoy, and the Americans never reaped the reward of their victory as the *Wasp*, with her sails in ribbons from the engagement was almost immediately afterwards captured by the British 74, *Poictiers* – one of Broke's former companions at the Black Rocks.

These things went unheeded by the public. For them the *contest* was the object. The Americans had another round of coast-to-coast jubilation, and the British felt the loss as yet another vital blow to their Naval prestige.

But even before the news reached across the Atlantic the United States Navy had struck again. As with the *Guerriere* and *Constitution* it was frigate versus frigate, and like that time the similar *class* of vessel concealed the actual disparity in force. The *United States*, Commodore Stephen Decatur, was a powerful ship with the same dimensions as the *Constitution*; below the gun-deck ports her sides were a mass of timber to a depth of 22 inches. She mounted 15 long 24-pounders either side of the gun deck and 8 carronades, no less than 42-pounders either side of the spar deck above, with a smaller calibre carronade at the gangway ports.

His Britannic Majesty's frigate *Macedonian*, 154 feet between perpendiculars and carrying 14 18-pounders each side of her gun deck, and 9 carronades, 32-pounders, each side above, was hopelessly outmatched. In weight of metal on the broadside her inferiority was roughly 550 pounds to 850 pounds; in men 290 to 478, in tonnage 1,100 to 1,500 – overall an inferiority in force of nearly a third.

The Captain of the *Macedonian*, John Carden, was a comparatively elderly man for a frigate, but an experienced fighting sailor. He had been a Midshipman in the *Marlborough* in the thick of the fighting during Howe's victory of the Glorious First of June, 1794, and later as First Lieutenant of the *Fishguard* frigate he had been commended for steady, good conduct when the French *L'Immortalité* was taken in single combat. Since then he had been in a number of less glamorous encounters in India and around the coast of Spain.

He had taken over the *Macedonian* a year previously after the former Captain had been court martialled for tyranny and oppression; according to one young volunteer in the frigate, Carden was little better.

"His arrival excited a transitory hope of a brighter lot, as he was an older man than the others, and as we vainly trusted a kinder one . . . Here, however, we were mistaken; he was like all the others, the same unfeeling, heartless lover of whip discipline."

This young man, Samuel Leech, later deserted to the American service and it is interesting to note that he recounts many more instances of brutality from Captain Porter of the U.S. brig-of-war *Boxer* than he does of Carden. Probably Carden was no worse than many other hard-case British officers, indeed from between the lines of Leech's account, considerably better; he often excused men for drunkenness, a sin that even the enlightened Broke punished with the 'cat'. Carden delighted in a smart crew and an outward show, and he actually encouraged any sailors whom he thought inferior to desert, sending them ashore on some pretext with a broad hint that he did not expect to see them again! He paraded his company every Sunday dressed in a uniform which varied according to the weather or his whim. One week it might be blue jackets and white trousers, the next scarlet vests, blue trousers, but always the brass buttons on their vests or jackets had to be shining and the flat black hats clean and glossy; each one had the name of the ship painted around the brim. Another of his peculiarities was his band composed of French, Germans and Italians, who used to play to him during the dinner hour and when he honoured the wardroom with his presence every Sunday; they also made stirring music whenever the ship entered or left port. All in all Carden seems a good deal less of an ogre than he has so frequently been made out.

Nevertheless the *Macedonian* was less happy than many ships, and for this the blame probably lies with the First Lieutenant, John Hope, who was, according to Leech, sadistic, cat-happy and typical of the worst type of Naval officer – although he did have the saving virtue of courage.

The brutalised crew of this unfortunate vessel seem seldom, if ever, to have been practised at a mark, and as for organisation for battle, Leech records that the First Lieutenant issued them with cutlasses and pistols as they stood to quarters for the fatal action, at the same time "telling them how to proceed should it be necessary for them to board the enemy". The inference is that the men had no prior knowledge of their duties in this respect. Such last-minute preparation would have been unnecessary, even confusing, in a vessel like the *Shannon* where every man knew his duty in every forseeable contingency. It seems likely that the *Macedonian*, despite Carden's familiarity with action, or perhaps because of it, had yielded to the current Royal Naval concern with smartness – indeed she was known as a 'crack' ship – to the exclusion of warlike organisation and meaningful gun drill.

The young United States Navy, on the other hand, with no invincible legend behind them, and deeply conscious of their hopeless numerical inferiority, naturally devoted themselves to the things that mattered most. They exercised the great guns at a mark, even in harbour, they supplied the Marines with rifled guns instead of muskets, they trained them in sharp-shooting, and the crew were constantly at cutlass and small-arms drill or competing at singlestick. They were hungry; the Royal Navy had grown fat and in some cases complacent.

Sunday, 25th October; the *Macedonian* was cruising in the Atlantic after leaving an East Indiaman she had been convoying. The hands were just finishing breakfast and about to don their fancy uniforms for the Captain when there was a cry of "Sail ho!" from the masthead. Carden rushed on deck. "Where away is the sail? What does she look like?"

"A square-rigged vessel, sir," the lookout replied, and a few moments later, "A large ship, sir, standing towards us."

All hands were gripped in excited speculation. A Yankee? They had heard of the declaration of war, but not of the loss of either the *Guerriere* or the *Frolic*, and according to Leech they were contemptuous of the small American Navy and confident, as always, of victory. Presently discussion was stilled as Carden pointed the frigate up for the strange sail and ordered the decks cleared for action.

There was a stiff breeze from the south-eastward, and the *Macedonian* leant over as she brought it on her starboard quarter and paced northerly towards the American ship. When all preparations for action were complete and the men were standing quietly to their guns Carden sent some of the Midshipmen down to the berth deck with orders given loudly for the benefit of the crew to shoot any man who attempted to run below from his quarters. The Lieutenants stood on the gun deck with drawn swords for the same purpose.

There were several Americans among the sailors and one of these, John Card, now presented himself to Carden as he paced the quarterdeck with his telescope beneath his arm, and asked to be excused the fighting against his own countrymen. Unlike Dacres, Carden refused angrily and, taking a pistol from the belt of one of the boarders near-by, levelled it at Card and ordered him to his quarters on pain of death. None of the Americans ventured to ask again, but whether they fought with full spirit is another matter.

The two frigates closed fast. The American was bright with ensigns from the main and mizzen-mastheads and the gaff, and from the foremasthead she flew the American Jack, fifteen white stars on a blue ground. Carden recognised his opponent as the *United States*. He had visited her in Norfolk, Virginia, the previous year and ex-changed hospitalities with Decatur. He must have known her size and her stout timbers and the exceptional calibre of her spar deck armament. He must have known that this was a tough opponent – just how tough was mercifully concealed: he had not heard of the British defeats and he could not have known that the First Lieuten-ant, William Henry Allen, the same who had fired a *Chesapeake* gun at the *Leopard* with a burning coal, had trained his guns' crews to extreme efficiency and accuracy.

As they came together on almost opposite courses Carden held a council with his First Lieutenant and Sailing Master on the quarter-deck. The Master advised trying to pass close under her stern and then hauling up to leeward of her, David Hope thought that they ought to stand on across the American's bows and bring her to close action that way. But Carden, apparently anxious to preserve the weather gage, which was considered of great importance, rejected both courses and instead hauled away from her a couple of points so as to pass at a distance and then wear round and come upon her from astern – still to windward. This ran counter to the bold tactics which the British always used against their European opponents, and must have been caused, at least in part, by the respect Carden felt for the powerful batteries of the *United States*. Thus, as in the *Guerriere* contest, it was the *British* who chose to start a manoeuvring fight – the worst possible choice under the circumstances of their inferior calibre guns – and the Americans who were enabled to open the duel at comparatively long range to their own best advantage.

After some manoeuvring in which Decatur of the *United States* was apparently seeking to gain the weather gage from Carden, they passed on opposite courses at about a mile, and the *United States* opened with her port broadside. Three of the *Macedonian*'s maindeck guns replied, but the order immediately came down to cease fire, "You are throwing your shot away." Soon afterwards Carden wore his frigate and the guns' crews stood to the starboard batteries as the *Macedonian* closed the American from her port quarter – still to windward. Decatur hauled up to bring his broadside to bear; the main action commenced.

Samuel Leech, powder boy at the fifth maindeck gun from forward, heard the crash as the *United States* opened fire, and a strange noise like the tearing of sails overhead as the balls winged by. Those of the *Macedonian*'s forward guns which bore answered them and the ship began to shake with the discharges and the pounding of the carriages. Most of the British shot went high, but the Americans soon found the *Macedonian*'s hull timbers and kept up a merciless rate of fire, estimated by some witnesses as two to every one from the Britisher. Her hull appeared to be on fire from the continued rapid discharges.

As Carden, suddenly aware of his mistake, tried to close more rapidly and so threw all but his bow guns off target, the weight, accuracy and sheer volume of the American metal turned his decks into a shambles. So accurate was the concentration from the *United States* that the midships section of the *Macedonian*'s maindeck received by far the greater proportion of the shot; it became 'the slaughterhouse'.

In the midst of the butchery was Samuel Leech, carrying cartridges from the magazine hatch to his gunners.

"It was like some awfully tremendous thunder storm whose deafening roar is attended by incessant streaks of lightning, carrying death in every flash and strewing the ground with the victims of its wrath; only in our case the scene was rendered more horrible than that by the presence of torrents of blood which dyed our decks . . ."

One after another the carronades, and then two maindeck guns, were unshipped by hits from the enemy; the grape flew in at the ports, scouring men in bunches, and interspersed with it great judders as solid balls crashed in through the side, showering timber splinters like darts across the crimson decks. Limbs flew like straws in the wind. The surviving gunners, in a frenzy of excitement, tore off their jackets and shirts and sponged and loaded like tigers, cheering continuously so that the cries and groans of the mutilated were drowned for brief periods.

Still the *Macedonian* closed. Leech, with his cartridge, saw blood spurt suddenly from the arm of one of the tackle numbers although there had been no visible cause. The next moment a man named Aldrich had a hand taken off, and almost in the same instant another shot tore his lower trunk open. As he fell two of his companions caught him and pushed his still living carcase through a port into the sea; he couldn't have survived the terrible wound.

The First Lieutenant was a tower of strength, encouraging the men continuously through the din until he was struck by a flying piece of iron and had to be carried below to the sick bay. The Boatswain, trying to fasten a stopper on a back stay which had been carried away, had his head smashed in by a ball, and another sailor following him at the task was also struck down.

One by one the *Macedonian*'s guns fell silent. The First Lieutenant appeared again from below with a bandage around his wound, still shouting hoarsely to the men to fight on. Leech observed a man named John being carried past him to the sick-bay ladder and heard, above the thunder, the large drops of his blood, pat-pat-pat along the deck. He found himself repeating the Lord's Prayer over and over to himself.

And now, as the British frigate still closed, the 42-pounder carronades of the *United States* came within range and added their devastating weight to the carnage; by contrast only three or four of the *Macedonian*'s 32-pounders remained on their carriages to reply. In addition her mizzen-mast had fallen forward into the maintop, the mainyard and maintopsail were shot away and the standing rigging cut to pieces. Carden, a tall and erect figure amidst the wreck of his quarterdeck, surveyed the apparently untouched American frigate, and felt the awful pangs of defeat.

"It is not in the power of my pen or dictate to express my feelings on this unfortunate occasion, fighting an enemy whom I soon found was of too overwhelming a force to conquer – observing my comparatively small masts and yards cut in short pieces by the very superior size and weight of the enemy's guns and seeing my brave but comparatively small crew falling about me in appalling numbers. In the midst of this more than desperate situation I decided on the only possible chance left to me, to board the enemy . . ."

He ordered the foresheet to be hauled aft. But as the breeze filled the sail and the frigate began to pay off towards the American again a shot took the sheet away and she came slowly back. The last, impossible chance faded and she lay helpless while the American gunners completed her destruction.

The British, encouraged by the demonic Hope, filled the gaps in their numbers by doing the work of two or three on the tackles. Sweat trickled down their bare, smoke-blackened bodies, their boots or bare feet were slippery with the blood of their former comrades. In brief intervals when the smoke dispersed, the morning light came in through new, jagged gaps in the timbers and pointed up unreal details of dismembered flesh and bone and splintered debris like some crazed scene from hell.

Leech was still carrying his powder through it all, cheering with the rest, and doing his duty – there was nothing else to do.

"That men are without thought when they stand amid the dying and the dead is too absurd an idea to be entertained for a moment. We all appeared cheerful, but I know that many a serious thought ran through my mind . . . every groan, every falling man told me that the next instant I might be before the Judge of all the earth . . ."

And on the exposed quarterdeck Carden stood hopeless and helpless, defying the American rifles across the water, wondering perhaps how long he could or should continue.

When all but two of the *Macedonian*'s carronades were silent and her fore- and maintopmasts had fallen, the *United States* ceased firing and stood away to repair damages to her rigging, which had been badly, although not vitally, cut about. Her hull, by contrast, had received only two or three balls, and her loss in killed and seriously wounded was trifling, twelve men all told. The shattered wreck she left held sixty-eight wounded receiving coarse attentions from the surgeon and there were thirty-six already in the sea.

When the *United States* came back an hour later David Hope was still swearing defiance at her and all Americans, and counselling Carden to fight on and sink his frigate alongside. But he was alone in his madness.

Carden ordered the colours to be struck.

Then he was pulled across to the big American frigate and climbed wearily up her side. He was greeted at the top by Stephen Decatur in a plain suit topped by an old straw hat. This farmer's rig could not, however, conceal the American's commanding presence, and his handsome eyes were alight with excitement.

Carden proffered his sword, but it was declined.

"Sir, I cannot receive the sword of a man who has so bravely defended his ship. But I will receive your hand," whereupon Decatur conducted him down to his cabin and ordered refreshments to be served.

". . . One half of the satisfaction arising from the victory is destroyed in seeing the distress of poor Carden, who deserved success as much as we did, who had the good fortune to obtain it. I do all I can to console him . . ." (Decatur to his wife – a charming note laying a 'small sprig of laurel' at her feet.)

Down below in the British frigate the surgeon and his assistants, splashed liberally with blood from head to foot, moved up a deck to use the wardroom as an overflow operating theatre; dulled of emotion, they starting sawing and probing at their writhing patients. Those wounded who had not been attended lay or sat in rows, swearing or groaning involuntarily, some praying. Forward of these a pig had escaped unharmed and was shuffling around by the main hatchway, routing pieces of human flesh and brain sticking in the ringbolts. Its skin was smeared all over in gore. Two able-bodied sailors picked it up and threw it, squealing, overboard.

It was Sunday. After the hymn Broke read the sermon he had prepared from one of his books to the Shannons assembled quietly between the lashed cannon.

"When the arm of hostile nations is stretched forth, when the happiness, the honor, nay, the very existence of an whole people is threatened it is the duty of every man to arm himself in defence of his country. But to meet the tempest at a distance and to keep the horrors of war from our own shores recourse must be had to the whole profession of the sword, whose arm is clothed in thunder, whose glory is found in the conflict of the battle, and who so sensibly feel it an honor that they get their bread in this service of their country, though it be with the peril of their lives . . ."

· · ·

Broke, unaware of the two latest disasters to the Service he was so proud of, cruised off the American coast without great success. He took a privateer or two, and continued to burn merchantmen, but they were becoming rarer every day. And his main target, Rodgers, had vanished. In fact, after the comparative failure of his first cruise, Rodgers had done what his junior Commodores had wished for all along and split his force into three squadrons, all acting separately.

"Nov 2nd

". . . Mr. Rodgers made me burn most of our captures last time and *now* they are scarce. I wish we had a frigate to take and I would soon be home with my Loo. But perhaps the Admiral will be *tired* of me in *Shannon* and pack me off sooner – for a 74 is no object to *me* – particularly here where such a ship could meet no creditable match . . ."

113

Towards the end of November the *Shannon* returned to port.

"24th. Arrived in Halifax and dined with Admiral Warren. Another week of *severe* dinner service."

The week turned into nearly a fortnight without a single evening free of social engagements. He kept up his conversation with Louisa despite it all, as if he were still at sea.

"Halifax   Nov 26th

"The Admiral had arranged to leave me to command all the divisions hereabouts and chiefly to remain in port to administer others. But I cannot endure *port Admiral's* duty at Halifax when all that makes social life dear to me is on the *other side of the Atlantic*! *Whilst cruizing* I hope every day will bring some event to hasten my return to you. But to remain in harbour here would be a cruel and hopeless waste of time indeed! notwithstanding all the civilities which *my dignity* would attract to me in the Admiral's absence, I would not stay here for all the *salaries* and honors of all their governors and chiefs put together . . . I consider every excursion as a chance for my passport home to England. You know I never meant to quit my frigate but had not the American war occurred I should have broken that *resolution* if they had not given me a chance by offering me a ship of the line. But now the unlucky events of *Guerriere's* and *Frolic's* actions bind us all to the service till we have restored the splendour of our flag. If they send me a 74 I can acquire no honor by any conflict with the enemy's *frigates* my views are so brilliant and the call of honor so imperious that my only chance of release from the charge is by continued and active pursuit of our enemy, and I trust our next cruise will be a successful one . . ."

"Halifax, Dec 4th

"We have no intelligence, except about some little privateer up on the coast – nothing from the States or Europe. These last five days have been a Nova Scotia winter – a white world glazed with frost. The air has been chill and piercing . . . the frost has pinched our Admiral and he talks of sailing on Sunday with his division for Bermuda. We hope to move on Tuesday for a cruize I hope much from."

He sailed on 12th December with the *Nymphe, Tenedos* and *Curlew* and a small homeward convoy.

"Dec 14th . . . we are prowling about, half convoying and half cruizing and very angry at our want of success. I hope to dismiss our merchantmen in a week or ten days and shall then *stride* about more freely . . ."

"Dec 21st . . . I hope you are pleasantly quartered at Bath. I dare say you will meet the mother of one of our Lieutenants there, Lady Falkiner and you may say the boy is well and a fine, brisk, chattering fellow."

"Dec 25th . . . I shall send my letters and dismiss the convoy to-day *halfway to you* my lovely Looloo! I had hoped to have passed this Christmas in domestic happiness – heaven grant we may soon meet to forget all our griefs, for my thoughts never rest but on my gentle, smiling Loo. Love and merry Christmas to all our dear friends round you. I hope they keep you cheerful – be happy my Loo for *my sake* and trust I shall soon be with you. We shall now go south for better weather and better fortune . . ."

Meanwhile the news of the *Frolic* and *Macedonian* disasters reached England and were received with alarm. The Admiralty issued an order forbidding British 18-pounder frigates to engage American 24-pounder ships in single combat. Even Lord Wellington, entrenched in the heart of Spain, but becoming concerned about the preservation of his ocean supply-routes, wondered when the Navy would reassert itself. Only the *Naval Chronicle* seemed to have no doubts that it would. In their Naval Poetry section they carried a remarkable prophecy under the title, *The Retort Courteous.*

> *And as the War they did provoke,*
> *We'll pay them with our cannon.*
> *The first to do it will be Broke*
> *In his gallant ship, the* Shannon.

CHAPTER SIX

COMMODORE BAINBRIDGE had relieved Isaac Hull in command of the *Constitution*. Together with the sloop-of-war *Hornet* he had been blockading the British sloop-of-war *Bonne Citoyenne* in San Salvador, Brazil, since 13th December. On 26th December, perhaps thinking to entice the British vessel to single combat with the *Hornet*, perhaps simply on the lookout for prizes, he left for a short cruise offshore and three days later in the early morning sighted two sail in company to windward.

These were His Majesty's frigate *Java* and an American prize of hers, the *William*. Directly Captain Lambert of the *Java* saw the sails of the *Constitution* he directed his prize to run for San Salvador, while he set off in chase. Bainbridge ran, both to separate him from the other sail and to ensure that the fight would be far from neutral Brazilian waters.

The Chase continued throughout the morning with the *Java*, until recently a French ship, creaming before the wind at ten knots or more, all studding sails pulling. The breeze was freshening and after midday dinner the royals were furled. Still she gained on her larger quarry. At 1.30 Bainbridge hoisted the 'Stars and Stripes', and some twenty minutes later luffed up to the wind and shortened sail to his t'gallants, jib and spanker, and cleared for action. Lambert had not received the Admiralty order forbidding his class of frigate to engage an American 24-pounder; he hoisted the British colours, shortened sail and cleared ship, bearing straight down to intercept the American frigate at close range. He did not repeat Carden's mistake. At about half a mile distant the *Constitution* opened her broadside at him, but Lambert held his own fire for some two or three minutes until he had closed to pistol shot on the American's port bow – then he gave the order.

When the smoke cleared away he found that Bainbridge had worn ship to prevent him crossing ahead and raking; he was going away before the wind. Lambert followed. They luffed up with the *Java* still to windward and exchanged their opposite broadsides for some ten minutes until Lambert wore under the *Constitution*'s stern, raking her as he went past, but giving Bainbridge the advantage of the weather gage if he chose to take it. Bainbridge declined; he ran off before the wind again. Lambert luffed up to give him his starboard guns, then followed him. Bainbridge shortened sail and the *Java* caught up and engaged, still from to windward, with her starboard broadside opposed to the American port guns. After only a few minutes the *Constitution* wore again in the smoke, this time unperceived until she was almost around. As the *Java* had just lost her jib-boom and part of her bowsprit, which left her without a jib to push her around from the wind, Lambert decided to tack. He had not way enough though, and the frigate hung in stays as the *Constitution* came round under her stern and delivered a heavy raking fire from about 400 yards. Eventually the British ship got round and brought her port guns to bear – upon which Bainbridge wore again. Again Lambert followed him round.

But by now the weight and accuracy of the American shot was beginning to tell; the *Java* was badly wounded in the lower masts and rigging, hulled several times between wind and water, and her gun deck was beginning to resemble the slaughterhouse of the *Macedonian*. Lambert decided, as Carden had before him, that the only way to retrieve a hopeless situation was by boarding. He instructed his First Lieutenant, Chads, to lay the frigate alongside.

As they were approaching closely in obedience to the order, with the British Marines drawn up ready to leap aboard by the American main chains, the foremast fell and they lost way. So instead of closing her amidships the stump of the *Java*'s bowsprit caught in her opponent's mizzen-rigging and she was carried up into the wind until they disengaged without any chance of the Marines going over. Whereupon Bainbridge wore and raked her from across the bows, then luffed up to come under her starboard quarter. The *Java* was now a helpless wreck; her maintopmast had fallen, her mizzen was about to go, she could not manoeuvre, and Bainbridge lay just off her quarter pouring in shot from his full broadside while she had only two or three guns that would bear. The *Constitution*'s marksmen were also sending a hail of bullets from the tops, and presently they found Captain Lambert with a shot that lodged in his spine. He was carried below and the command devolved upon Lieutenant Chads.

Lambert had fought an aggressive battle, always seeking to close the range and bring his adversary fairly alongside. His gunners had severely wounded the *Constitution*'s masts and rigging and shot away her wheel, but the stouter timbers of the American had resisted better and her greater broadside weight accurately aimed had proved irresistible. The British continued to fight back fiercely as the Macedonians had done, but while the *Java* lay unable to manoeuvre, the rest of the action was a one-sided slaughter. After the British mizzen- and maintopmasts went, the *Constitution* filled and retired out of gunshot to repair her rigging. When she came back again and took up a raking position Lieutenant Chads had no sensible option but to hail that he was striking.

The British lost 24 dead, 100 wounded, the Americans probably 10 dead and 44 severely wounded, including Bainbridge, although their official report only mentioned 34 killed and wounded. Captain Lambert's gunners, although they had practised with powder on only one occasion since leaving England six weeks before, had done better than Carden's – but not well enough to offset the superior American force and training. As for Lambert, he died a few days later after being relieved of regular quantities of precious blood by the British doctor; the *Java*, being a shattered hulk, was burned like the *Guerriere*, and the *Constitution*, after putting in to Bahia and landing the prisoners on parole, set sail for Boston to convey the latest stirring tidings to the American people.

Lieutenant Chads wrote the official report of the action for the Admiralty, concluding with his grateful acknowledgement of "the generous treatment Captain Lambert and his officers have experienced from our gallant enemy, Commodore Bainbridge and his officers". For his part Bainbridge wrote, "The *Java* was exceedingly well handled and bravely fought. Poor Captain Lambert was a distinguished and gallant officer and a most worthy man whose death I sincerely regret."

Gallantry, however, was little sop for the British public. The full facts of the disparity in size and force which the British frigates were seeking to overcome had not sunk in, and *The Times* expressed opinion accurately when the news burst.

"The public will learn with sentiments which we shall not presume to anticipate that a *third* British frigate has struck to an American . . . *Five hundred merchantmen* (reported as taken by U.S. men-of-war and privateers) *and three frigates*: Can these statements be true, and can the British people hear them unmoved? Anyone who had predicted such a result of an American war this time last year would have been treated as a madman or a traitor . . ."

Correspondents to the *Naval Chronicle*, having recovered from the first shock of the American successes, began to take a more objective view. "The first and *grand* cause is that the American seamen have been more exercised at firing at a mark than ours – their government having given their commanders leave to exercise whenever they think proper and to fire away as much ammunition as they please." Another correspondent made the strong point that the American ships were manned by real seamen, which was "necessarily the consequence of any commercial nation after a long peace. Look at our ships how they are manned at the breaking out of a war and compare them with the generality of ships now commissioned . . . a very small proportion of able seamen and the remainder filled up with good, bad and indifferent, viz, ordinary seamen, landsmen, *foreigners*, the sweepings of *Newgate*, from the *hulks* and almost all the prisons in the country . . ."

But whatever might be said about these fatal contests, the British had never been found wanting in courage.

. . . .

Broke and his squadron were still hunting easterly through the wide Atlantic after Rodgers' elusive ships. In January they stood southwards towards milder weather about the Azores, where Broke hoped to meet with some recent intelligence of the Americans.

"Jan 3rd. Heaven bless my Loo with many happier New Year's days than has ushered this in. On the 1st we chased a little sly-looking schooner, but had not breeze enough to get hold of him, we suppose an American privateer; and this is the only break on our solitude since we left our convoy . . . We are all well – wonderfully so indeed – thank God! but all impatient to be less idly employed . . .

"Jan 8th.   off St. Michael's Island, Azores.
We have met *Jalouse* after a dreary, solitary week. We hear the French are annihilated in Russia. God send it to be true. *Macedonian* must be avenged, or the Americans will be *quite too saucy* . . .

"Jan 10th . . . We got some scattered papers of December, up to the 12th, but not the grand victory over the French in Russia . . . I fear *Macedonian*'s misfortunes will be more felt at home than all our allies' successes. We must catch one of these great American ships with our squadron, to send her home for a show, that people may *see what a great creature it is*, and that our frigates have fought very well, though so unlucky. But we begin to doubt that all our rivals of Rodgers' and the other squadron are gone home, and we shall have no chance of a meeting for this cruise. I am in great hopes *Macedonian* is retaken by Beresford or Sir J. Warren, as they both lay in her way. We can't allow the 74s to take the American frigates, as *that is our concern*. But we are now a month out and no prize. That vile convoy wasted us three weeks . . .

"I suppose you at Bath, and like to persuade myself that you have so many of your dearest friends round you that they will occupy and amuse your ideas and keep you cheerful. I think of nothing but making my escape from service, and hope every day for some event which will enable me. Kiss little dears for me, and believe me coming. We are, thank God! remarkably healthy, not a sick man amongst our whole family of more than 300 people."

I

During these weeks of abortive cruising Broke's training routine was carried on without interruption:

"12th: Seamen at target.
"13th: Swivel men at target.
"15th: Mids at target and carronade.
"16th: Swivels in maintop . . ."

He made it a rule never to disturb the watch below for these routine exercises. Each gun's crew was formed out of the members of *one* watch; thus the even-numbered guns were manned from the starboard watch, the odd numbers from the larboard. In this way those men who would fight together were trained together. The weekly routine at sea was for the watch on deck to be exercised at the great guns on Monday and Tuesday forenoons, and in the afternoons the first division of the watch was exercised at small arms. Wednesday and Thursday forenoons saw the watch on deck at the carronades, and in the afternoons the second division of the watch at small arms. Friday was reserved for the Midshipmen – great guns in the morning, small arms in the afternoon. Thus each man had one morning at the 18-pounders, one morning at the carronades and two afternoons with musquets in every week. Saturdays were reserved for washing clothes and scrubbing the berth deck in the afternoon. Sunday, apart from Church service and any necessary evolutions with the sails, was free.

In addition to this routine, which was very familiar to the people after their years of service in the *Shannon*, there were field days when all hands were drummed to quarters and Broke devised different hypothetical situations which had to be met. There were also surprise attacks at night, or in the daytime when a beef-cask target was thrown overboard without warning and two guns' crews suddenly detailed to clear for action and fire. To complete the fitness of the crew for the day of battle, they were constantly brought together at singlestick. This was a game employing roughly similar thrusts and parries as were used with the cutlass, but as it was played with blunt sticks, hits, although painful, were not often dangerous. It soon developed quickness of eye and wrist.

From the Azores Broke cruised back westerly in balmy weather towards Bermuda, still without definite news of his quarry.

"Jan 17th . . . I am very tired my beloved Looloo, very weary indeed of this cruel banishment. But I dare not think of home, and can only try to hasten my return to you by persevering in the search of our enemy. We deserve some success after hunting for them so incessantly . . .

"Jan 20th . . . *Bad luck cannot last for ever*; so we hope to mend our fortunes every day, and that some happy *rencontre* may send me home to my gentle wife. Heaven bless you and all around you . . .

"Feb 4th. I have not been idle, my beloved Loo, though I did not begin another letter before now. We have been amazingly busy in our chases and exercises to make ourselves clever people, and had no opportunity of sending letters.

"Feb 14th . . . On Tuesday we met Sir Thomas Hardy (Commodore) off Bermuda with *Acasta, Martin* and *Doterel* . . . Hardy told me some of the news. No Lady H. came out with him. *What a sad man!* Beresford and Lady are at Bermuda well; he has been lucky and in company with Kerr, Captain of *Acasta*, taken a rich Bourdeaux ship, worth more than all the prizes I ever took in my life. But I am glad so generous a fellow as Beresford is the man . . .

"Our luck is certainly all to come. I am sure we have all been diligent and patient enough. My chief horror is the idea of *Shannon*'s craziness keeping me in port to refit during the bad weather, which is slow, stupid work; but I hope to steal another cruise before we are obliged to lay by at all. Whilst the *Shannon* moves I am alive, but when she sleeps I feel hopeless of any happy event to finish my campaign with.

". . . My being poor is no disappointment to me. To return without any success to prove how we have been exerting ourselves in so long and tiresome a pursuit, and which we feel conscious of deserving *is* mortifying. But my Loo must comfort me when I come to her. Indeed you can't imagine the pains I have bestowed on this *graceless wooden wife* of mine, particularly since she ran away with me here; and perhaps I shall have to leave some other person to reap all the credit of her beautiful play, unless we have someone to *open a concert* with very soon. But when tempted to think of home, I am constantly reminded that naval success will be my speediest liberation from exile.

"So then I turn to *Shannon* to see if she is perfection. I think she will do me credit if she finds an opportunity, and I am sure the other wife will make me happy if I quit this *game of honor*; so I must make the best of it and pray God to let us soon meet in joy and security."

.   .   .

As Broke penned these words the Americans gained their fifth successive victory in single-ship combat – and their easiest.

The victor was the little sloop-of-war *Hornet*, which we left outside San Salvador blockading the British *Bonne Citoyenne* while the *Constitution* returned to Boston with the news of her second triumph. In command of the *Hornet* was Master Commandant James Lawrence. He was a young man, just thirty-one, and like Philip Broke, whom he was shortly to be cast opposite in the cataclysmic action that was the longed-for climax to both their careers, he burned with ambition for glory in action. Like Broke also, he trained his people for that action consistently at the great guns, and again like Broke he was a strict disciplinarian without ever crossing the border to needless brutality or sadism; indeed he commanded the same respect from his people and affection bordering on hero-worship from some of his Midshipmen that Broke had from his Shannons. But whereas Broke was calm, easy-tempered and good-humoured almost to the point of phlegm, Lawrence was impulsive and passionate. Whereas Broke made it a point that a senior officer was always right, Lawrence frequently took the opposite view and said so without mincing his words or looking for favours.

His ancestors were of English stock, but his immediate forebears were American citizens of some prominence in Burlington, New Jersey, where he was born in October 1781 in a pleasant house at the corner of Main and Library Streets. Like Broke, he early showed a desire to go to sea despite his parents' endeavours to put him to the law, and eventually he had his way, attended a three months' course in theoretical navigation and entered the United States Navy as a Midshipman in 1798, one month short of his seventeenth birthday.

While Broke, as Third Lieutenant of the *Amelia* frigate, Captain the Hon. C. Herbert, was watching a French squadron in Brest, Lawrence began to learn his trade aboard the U.S.S. *Ganges*, a former East Indiaman converted to a 24-gun frigate.

He made some mark as a Midshipman, for after three years he was selected as Acting Third Lieutenant in the *Adams* frigate. But America shortly signed peace with France, with all the usual results for the fighting services, and he did not receive his commission as a full Lieutenant until in 1802 war was declared against the Barbary powers of North Africa, who had long been preying on American merchantmen. He was sent as First Lieutenant to the little topsail schooner *Enterprise*, mounting twelve 12-pounders, and served in her in the Mediterranean first under Isaac Hull and then under Stephen Decatur, both Naval officers of the first order. It was here that he had his baptism of hand-to-hand fighting, and was praised for his courage by David Porter, another future star of the U.S. Navy.

But the high point of his service in the *Enterprise* was undoubtedly the burning of the *Philadelphia*. This escapade, led by the dashing Stephen Decatur to very precise instructions from his Commander-in-Chief, compares with any of those which made Lord Cochrane's name a byword for impudence against odds. The *Philadelphia* was a U.S. frigate which had run hard on a shoal while chasing a corsair, and had subsequently been taken by a force of enemy gunboats. They had towed her off and refitted her, and when the Americans under Decatur came to destroy her one dark night in February 1804 she was lying fully manned under the guns of Tripoli. Decatur's party approached in a small ketch of 70 tons, and when hailed by the sentry on board the *Philadelphia* the pilot replied that they were Maltese and had lost both anchors in a gale the previous night – could they make fast to the frigate until morning? Permission being granted, Lawrence, disguised as a Maltese, went away in charge of a boat to take a line to the frigate. This passed off well enough, but when they started warping the little ketch alongside, the enemy suddenly realised what they were up to and raised the alarm, "*Americanos!*" It was too late. The ketch bumped against the frigate, the Americans rose from where they had been hiding and swarmed aboard with sabres and tomahawks, killing and driving all before them. When they had possession they put the frigate to the match.

For this notable exploit Stephen Decatur was promoted Post Captain, but the other officers who had taken part were only voted two months' extra pay, a reward which the high-spirited Lawrence chose to regard as a slight, and refused.

Returning home shortly afterwards, he obtained his first command. He was then twenty-four years old. She was a new 71-foot gunboat called prosaically *No. 6*, and she mounted two long 32-pounders, one right forward, one right aft. Despite dubious thoughts about her sea-keeping qualities he successfully navigated her across the Atlantic – to the astonishment of one British Naval Captain met the other side – and was steering for the Mediterranean when he fell in with a British squadron under Vice-Admiral Collingwood blockading Cadiz. He was brought to by the *Tenedos* frigate. A boat was sent across and, greeting it, Lawrence invited the boarding officers down to his minute cabin.

"While I was below with the officers, three of my men who had been very unruly during the passage, finding some of their old shipmates in the boat, declared themselves English subjects and demanded protection . . ."

This startling reversal of the usual procedure was accepted by the British with satisfaction, but Lawrence, naturally indignant, demanded the men back, first taking his case to the Captain of Collingwood's flagship, the *Dreadnought*, and then up to the Vice-Admiral himself – with complete lack of success. Afterwards he returned, fuming, aboard his little craft. Still very young and possessed of high temperament, he felt the insult deeply; whatever *No. 6* gunboat might appear to be – and she was at one time taken for a half-submerged wreck – she was nevertheless a U.S. man-of-war, and he her commander!

The remainder of his time in *No. 6* continued without notable incident and presented no opportunities for gaining distinction. He took her back across the Atlantic and had a brief spell ashore during which he was able to add to his own first-hand knowledge of the Royal Navy's flagrant insults to the American Naval flag when appointed to serve on the court martial of Commodore Barron of the *Chesapeake* for his part in the *Leopard* affair. In the event Barron was acquitted of the major charges against him, but found guilty of "neglecting, on the probability of an engagement, to clear his ship for action".

In this same year, 1808, Lawrence married Julia Montaudevert, the daughter of a French sea Captain who had been lost with his ship off the Scilly Islands. Soon after the marriage he was appointed First Lieutenant of the *Constitution*, and after only seven months, still a Lieutenant, to his first sizable command, the 12-gun brig-of-war *Vixen*. His moves were rapid at this period for some reason which has never been explained, and he hardly had time to work up his vessel before he was sent to command the 18-gun ship-rigged sloop-of-war *Wasp*. It was perhaps to discuss this exchange that he asked permission in April 1810 to go to Washington to see the Secretary of the Navy. He wrote to his wife just before the interview:

"Baltimore, May 5th
"My dearest Julia . . . I this morning left the brig in my new boat and arrived here after a pleasant passage of $5\frac{1}{2}$ hours, intending to leave early in the morning for Washington, but on attempting to dress for the purpose of making one or two calls, you can better judge than I describe my disappointment on overhauling my trunk to find that in place of my new coat, my d——d Pourtagee *steward*

had packed up an old storm staysail that has been condemned these two years. You will scarcely credit me when I assure you I bore it like a philosopher, imputed it to accident on his part, did not *utter an oath* ! ! ! !, set down and eat a hearty supper, felt much more *comfortable* than if I had got into a violent passion, and finally determined to send Mr. Cooper back for my coat and await his return with patience . . ."

He ended with a reference to their first child:

"I believe our darling is a year old today, kiss her affectionately for me. That she may experience many many happy returns of the day is the fervent prayer of her doting father . . ."

Whatever the outcome of his talk with the Secretary, he soon took over the *Wasp*, but had only been in her a few weeks before he was again transferred, this time to the brig *Argus* of 18 guns.

"U.S. Ship, *Wasp*
"New York, June 19th, 1810

"To the Secretary of the Navy
". . . As Commander of the *Wasp* I have been at considerable trouble in procuring, disciplining and obtaining a knowledge of my crew as absolute essentials for carrying into effect such orders as might be committed to me, and after having secured these objects by the most unremitted care and anxiety, I must confess my feelings would be wounded by a causeless removal from a command which I had considered such an honour . . ."

But the Secretary was adamant and Lawrence again changed ships. He was made happier shortly afterwards by receiving his commission as Master Commandant – roughly equivalent to the present-day Commander. Notwithstanding this, he soon had occasion to write another of his plain-speaking letters to the Secretary of the Navy, this time about a Marine detachment which had been sent to his brig; he objected to them on the grounds that they were no use aloft, and he found his guard of Sergeants quite adequate for the duties assigned them.

From the *Argus* – complete with Marines – Master Commandant James Lawrence went in October 1811 to her sister, *Hornet*, which had been re-rigged as a ship-sloop. By this time he and many others in the United States Navy looked forward to war with the British, and eight months later he heard his men's cheers at the announcement of hostilities with satisfaction and great enthusiasm for the opportunities for distinction which must now present themselves. The *Hornet* sailed almost immediately with Rodgers' squadron.

On his return from this rather unsatisfactory cruise Lawrence learned that Lieutenant Morris, first of the *Constitution* during her victorious action with the *Guerriere,* had been jumped up to Post Captain for his services, thus overleaping all the Master Commandants. It was felt by many officers that a step as far as Master Commandant would have been quite sufficient reward, and Lawrence especially felt this keenly as it still hurt that his own services during the *Philadelphia* affair had been insufficiently recognised. Once again he took up his pen to the Navy Department and guided it with passion.

"... After devoting nearly fifteen years of the prime of my life faithfully to the service of my country, without a furlough (excepting for six weeks) you must not think hard of my having remonstrated thus plainly on Lt. Morris's promotion over me. I assure you I should regret extremely leaving the Service at any period, particularly at this, but if outranked by an officer who has no greater claim than myself to promotion, I have no alternative ..."

The Secretary of the Navy could scarcely have wasted less time over his reply.

"... if (without cause) you leave the service of your country, there will still remain heroes and patriots to support the honor of its flag ..."

Lawrence was restrained from resigning by his friends and almost certainly by the opportunities for glory that were sure to present themselves in the war. Instead he sailed the *Hornet* in company with his friend Bainbridge in the *Constitution* southwards for prizes. So they came to San Salvador and, it seemed, the chance that Lawrence sought so eagerly. H.M. sloop-of-war *Bonne Citoyenne* lay inside, a very fair match for the *Hornet.* Lawrence sent in a verbal challenge to her Captain, Greene, *via* the American Consul, assuring him that neither the *Constitution* nor any other American vessel would interfere if the *Bonne Citoyenne* would come out to fight the *Hornet.* This achieved no result so he followed it up by standing in to the harbour, sailing around the shipping and out again, which aroused some fluttering in the British community, but no response from Captain Greene. Lawrence then sent a formal letter of challenge, and Bainbridge pledged his honour that he would stand aside from the contest. But Captain Pitt Burnaby Greene, who was carrying a valuable cargo of specie, declined this invitation to single and equal combat with a

Captain Broke assailed by three Americans on the deck of *Chesapeake*

Shannon, attributed to Captain King (as are the other watercolours on these pages)

The cannonade, yardarm to yardarm

Chesapeake luffs up out of control

Shannon leading *Chesapeake* into Halifax

Broke in old age, by W. C. Ross, acknowledged by Broke as "an excellent likeness"

Captain James Lawrence, engraved by T. Williamson

somewhat tactless letter, doubting that Bainbridge would so far swerve from the duty he owed his country as to become an "inactive spectator and see a ship belonging to the very squadron under his orders fall into the hands of an enemy . . ."

Lawrence wrote a note to the American Consul:

"Jan 1st, 1812

". . . I am astonished that he (Captain Greene) should in any shape doubt the word of Commodore Bainbridge. I trust, however, by keeping a good lookout to bring him to action and although he feels so confident of success I will pledge myself to give a good account of him . . ."

And on 2nd January he ended a request to the Consul for 3,000 gallons of water and as much bread as he could procure, "If you can persuade Captain Greene to come out I will save you the trouble, and endeavour to help myself from his ship."

But that action was not to be. After remaining several more weeks and taunting the British sailors, the blockaders *par excellence*, with her single presence, the *Hornet* was eventually forced by the appearance of a British 74 to sneak away by night.

Lawrence headed southwards. On 14th February he took the British brig *Resolution*, and after relieving her of twenty-three thousand dollars in specie, set her alight and chased another sail to the mouth of the Demerara River – then he forgot all about her. For there at anchor outside the bar was another British man-of-war, a brig and just about his own weight. The frustration attendant on the *Bonne Citoyenne* affair dropped away. This was his day – at last.

The *Hornet* beat around the Caroband Bank to reach the anchored brig. Lawrence paced his small quarterdeck impatiently, frequently stopping and resting his long glass against a shroud to observe any movement aboard the Britisher. We can see him through the eyes of the former Commander-in-Chief of the American Squadron in the Mediterranean, "tall, a little under six feet, with a handsome, manly face and dark hair with side whiskers combed up and shaved under his ears as was then the style. His proportions were good and his movements graceful, and he carried himself as one born to command, and in fact he was a man made up and finished such as we like to look upon." He was also a bit of a dandy in dress, and before an action attired himself in full uniform.

There could scarcely have been a greater contrast between ships and commanders than that between the *Hornet* and her anchored prey, *L'Espiegle*. The British Captain was one John Taylor, "a fat, pursy fellow with shifting eyes" and a foul mouth, who had brutalised and terrorised his company with the 'cat', driven the carpenter to idiocy and had even been known to 'start' sick men with a rope's end. His sailors were in such a state that no 'bumboats' were allowed alongside for fear of mass desertion. Even the officers were sullen. The First Lieutenant was repeatedly insulted before the men and on one occasion had been locked in his cabin with a Marine on guard outside. Of course the vessel's fighting efficiency was negligible, especially as the men were scarcely ever exercised at the guns.

On this occasion the loutish Captain was ashore, and as much of her rigging was dismantled there could have been no doubt about the result. Fortunately for her, before Lawrence got fairly on his approach he observed another British man-of-war bearing down on him from his weather quarter. He immediately revised his intention of attacking *L'Espiegle* and stood up to try and weather the newcomer.

The new sail was the brig-of-war *Peacock*, a consort of the vessel at anchor, and although not brutalised, certainly just as unpractised at the guns. Indeed this was the rule on the West Indies station, where the climate, the continued lack of warlike activity now that the French had been practically driven out and also perhaps the prevailing fevers all combined to make it easy for officers and ships to go rotten.

The *Peacock*'s malaise was not apparent on the surface. Her appearance was brilliant. Her Captain, Peake, took immense pride in his paintwork and in the tasteful arrangements on deck; the shot lockers had been moved to provide a clear expanse of holystoned planking, the breechings of the small carronades – 24-pounders against the *Hornet*'s 32-pounders – were all bound with spotless white canvas, and the traversing bars and screws glistened with high polish.

Admiralty Regulations, 1813: "*Elevating screws of carronades . . .* on board many ships where not only the screw but the shark and crop lever of it are kept bright and polished and files as also emery used for that purpose, the thread very soon becomes so much reduced as to run through the box, or female screw, & becomes useless.

"*Swords:* The guard and shield of the hilts being of plate iron, varnished black, is not sufficiently thick to allow being filed bright, without making very weak in the first instance, and to keep them so . . . they soon become no thicker in substance than tin.

"*Pikes:* By filing and polishing the ironwork it soon becomes weak, & gives way; & by scraping the woodwork with pieces of glass bottle etc . . . the staves become so much reduced as to be unfit for weapons . . ."

The *Peacock* was known on the station as 'The Yacht'; she drew cries of admiration from visitors as she toured the islands, bright as burnish. Alas, she had been little prepared to fight.

Lawrence discovered her at 3.30 in the afternoon; by 5.10 he found he could obtain the weather gage and tacked to meet her. At 5.25 they passed on opposite courses and exchanged broadsides. The *Peacock* wore immediately afterwards to parallel the *Hornet*'s course, upon which Lawrence came down from to windward, placed himself close alongside her starboard quarter and proceeded to cut her to pieces with his superior weight of carronade served by his expert gunners. It was all over in less than fifteen minutes from the first broadside. The British, having lost 5 dead including the Captain, and 29 wounded, 3 mortally, and with water flooding in through shot holes about her copper, hoisted the ensign union downwards. Lawrence's loss was 1 killed and 2 wounded; his vessel was little hurt.

Expecting that *L'Espiegle*, in plain sight from the masts, would beat out to engage them, the Hornets hurried to remove the prisoners from 'The Yacht' and plug up the shot holes in her riven hull. But fast as they worked, the water gained and she shortly sank beneath them, carrying down 9 of her wounded and 3 of the *Hornet*'s men who were attempting to save them. *L'Espiegle* made no move.

It was an infinitely sad day for the Royal Navy. And, as one British officer subsequently described the contest, "If the *Peacock* had been moored for the purpose of experiment she could not have sunk sooner." Lawrence remarked to an acquaintance that his Clerk had reported the time of the action as eleven minutes, "but I thought fifteen minutes was short enough so I made it that in my report". This remark, if truly recollected, is a remarkable coincidence – as will appear.

Lawrence immediately became the latest in the growing line of U.S. Naval heroes. Bainbridge wrote to him from Boston, "The news of your glorious victory reached the Theatre here last evening, when the walls of it *really rung* with acclamations of applause . . ." And when the *Hornet* reached New York Lawrence was presented with the freedom of the City, and together with his officers and crew was guest of honour at a public dinner; he was made an honorary member of the Cincinnati Society and showered with invitations, eulogies and letters of congratulation.

One of the letters he prized was from the surviving officers of the

Peacock, grateful for the kindness and hospitality they had experienced from him: ". . . we cannot better express our feelings than by saying, 'we ceased to consider ourselves prisoners' and everything that friendship could dictate was adopted by you and the officers of the *Hornet* . . ."

Broke's strictures on the manners of American officers were not all borne out.

.   .   .

Broke's squadron meanwhile, trying to get a look into Boston harbour to see what their opponents were about, found themselves running short of water and gripped in a severe period of freezing weather and adverse winds. Broke decided to make for Halifax to replenish his ships for what he was coming to realise might be the *Shannon*'s last cruise before an extensive refit. Her speed, which had been such a pride to him in the early days on the station after her new coppering was failing, and her masts and timbers were beginning to show signs of her long vigil.

They were held up for a while by strong north-easterly gales, but eventually, with rigging cased in ice, sails as brittle and unmanageable as *Shannon*'s had been on her Arctic cruise, and with the people heavily clad in worsted beneath their outer wear, and mittens on their nerveless hands, the frigates beat into Halifax on 23rd February.

Here Broke heard of some old brass 6-pounder long guns which had been landed from another vessel, and immediately put in a requisition for them to the dockyard storekeeper. He was told that the issue of brass guns was not permitted by the Honourable Board of Ordnance, but if he would put his reasons in writing to clear the storekeeper's yardarm . . .

"To Storekeeper . . . The superiority of the enemy's frigates over ours in number of guns and weight of metal induces me to wish that in addition to the two carronades (32 pdr.) just issued to the frigates, you will supply one of the old fashioned brass guns, lately returned from the *Hunter*, to the *Shannon* and the other to the *Nymphe*. That our frigates should carry every gun which can possibly be brought into service in action must appear obvious to you . . . it's being desirable that by every means we should put ourselves as nearly as possible on an equality in point of strength with the enemy frigates will, I think, justify you in departing from the Board's orders . . ."

In private, he was telling his officers, "Our only remedy for the disadvantage is to *get alongside them* as soon as possible, and so stop all *distant, scientific practice* and hammer them *'more marjorum'*!"

The extra guns were aboard before his letter went off. *Shannon* also had a new topmast fitted, which induced the sailors to think that her luck would be changed for the better. They, and indeed some of the officers in the squadron, had been getting increasingly restive with the comparative shortage of prizes and particularly with Broke's distressing habit of burning those they did take.

A Midshipman, one of Broke's sea children, wrote, "Prizes were useless, they were burned . . . and the great object for which they were given up not presenting itself, disappointment was natural, and some words of discontent were too common in ranks that should have been more patriotic. Still all were sound *at heart*. The Captain was adored (as the expression goes); the men well knew what they could do . . ."

Broke lived ashore in the house of a brother Captain, the Hon. Philip Wodehouse, Commissioner of H.M. Dockyard, during this stay in Halifax while the work went ahead and the frigates completed with stores. Progress was frequently delayed by the weather, which became so bitter for days on end that nothing could be done. However, Broke found himself continually occupied with details of administration, reading and writing reports – and in the evenings dining out in his capacity as senior Naval officer while the Admiral was warming himself in Bermuda. The company he enjoyed as always, but the desk work bored him. "I hope some senior will arrive soon to relieve me from this irksome part of my duties."

At last, by 20th March, the *Shannon* and another frigate, *Tenedos*, were ready, and wasting no time he handed over his administrative duties and took them out on the following day. They stood from the harbour in a snow storm, and had no sooner cleared Sambro Light than Broke's former wish for a senior was granted.

"My dearest Looloo . . . I was deposed from my supremacy as soon as we got out of harbour, meeting two old 74's who came to dwell in our country – *Valiant* (Captain Oliver) and Capel in *La Hogue*. They gladdened me with letters from my Loo. The one December 28th was delightfully cheering by the accounts it gave of all the dear children, and Hotham wrote and told me how well you were looking when he left you at Plymouth . . ."

"Bermuda, March 7th 1813

From Captain Henry Hotham:

"My dear Broke . . . I have the pleasure of sending you perfectly good accounts of Mrs. Broke, as I saw her at Plymouth in the end of December, where I arrived from the old station off Brest with my poor *Northumberland* in bad repair . . . I had however the pleasure of walking with her and she said she and the children were all well; we spoke of the probability of your return to England which I shall hope may arrive as soon as you wish it may, but shall regret it very much on my own account . . ." (Hotham being on his way to join Broke on the North American station.)

"I have been made very happy my dear Broke by hearing of your success since the commencement of the war, and I have always longed to hear of *your* having an opportunity of trying, more fairly than it has yet been tried, how far our frigates are equal to cope with those of the Americans for my knowledge of the perfect state of the training and experience of your ship's company, and the complete preparedness, taking into account also the consummate skill of her Commander, gives me, and has always enabled me to feel a degree of confidence in the *Shannon* which I confess I can only feel in the same proportion in a very few."

Unbeknown to either Hotham or Broke, a term had already been set to the *Shannon*'s time on the station. On its way with the next batch of mail across the Atlantic was a letter from Broke's friend and former Captain, now Admiral Sir George Hope, a Lord of the Admiralty.

"Feb. 13th, 1813

"My dear Broke, I inclose you a letter from your wife it was Lord Melville's intention to have sent out a new line of battle ship for you, but in consequence of what Admiral Sawyer told me of your wishes to come home in the *Shannon* I shall take care you are not removed & Sir John Warren's attention has been called to the state of the *Shannon* in order that he may send her home in the course of the Summer – which I hope will meet your wishes.

"Why don't you get a look at these Yankees and not allow them to bully us in this way."

Although Broke was unaware of the orders on their way to his Commander-in-Chief, he knew that *Shannon* could not last much longer without a major refit. He knew this must be her last cruise in these opening stages of the war while the chances of brilliant action still remained, because very soon it would be simple blockade work. Not even the big American frigates would stand up and fight the ships of the line which were on their way out and they must soon be locked in their harbours with little chance of escape, and the station deteriorated into a copy of the Black Rocks. Even now it might be too late.

Oliver and Capel were not the shorebound sort of seniors he had looked for, and he attached *Shannon* and *Tenedos* to their flag, Commodore no longer. However, the following day a fortunate squall blew up, obscuring the other vessels, and by the next morning he found himself again alone on the ocean.

Apr 3rd

"To Robert Dudley Oliver, Esq., Captain of H.M.S. *Valiant*

Having parted company from the squadron under your orders on the 22nd . . . owing to thick, rainy weather which caused us to mistake some signal that was made in the night, and seeing no ships when the squalls cleared away I presumed you had wore and did so accordingly in the hope of rejoining at daylight . . .

"From Robert Dudley Oliver, Apr 8th

Dear Broke, I have received your letter by Capel which is perfectly satisfactory. The night you parted we neither moved sheet nor tack after ten o'clock when we took in the main topsail, and continued on the same tack till nine the next morning . . ."

The *Tenedos* had also lost herself during the night but somehow met up with the *Shannon* running south-westwards the following evening. Broke ordered her Captain, Hyde Parker, to keep company and continued on his course to reconnoitre Boston. They were delayed by variable winds for a while, but arrived off the Capes of Boston at the end of March and on 3rd April were enabled to stand right in to the Roads and survey the harbour.

Aprl 3rd

"To Robert Dudley Oliver, Esq., Captain of H.M.S. *Valiant*

". . . lying close to the town ready for sea one large frigate said to be *Congress*, her sails set. Lying higher up by the dockyard two other large frigates . . . apparently nearly ready for sea (said to be the *President* and *Constitution*) . . ."

Five days later, still hovering off the port and gaining intelligence from pilots and coasters, he wrote to Oliver again, surmising that, "if two of us show off Boston for a few days, *President* and *Congress* will *turn out*, provided no 74's are seen from the Capes or pilot boats".

By strange chance, as he ran eastwards to deliver this message, the frigate he was destined to meet eventually, the *Chesapeake*, returned from a disappointing cruise and went into Boston for a refit. They missed by hours. When Broke and Hyde Parker returned on 11th April and stood in to the Roads again for reconnaisance they saw the newcomer undergoing repairs to her masts, and the *Constitution* still stripped down – but of far greater import, both the *President* and *Congress* ready for sea.

Broke now felt confident that the day he had been awaiting so long must be nearly upon him. Both the frigates ready for sea were larger than either *Shannon* or *Tenedos*, and in any case the Americans were openly boastful after their string of successes that one of their ships could lick any Britisher afloat. If Rodgers engaged, he would be close to his own harbour and could easily get back inside to repair damages afterwards; also it was well known that the Americans exercised their crews thoroughly at the great guns, small arms and cutlass in harbour before going to sea – there would be no fear of inexperience on that count. Surely they *must* turn out.

The next day he noted in his diary, "Enemy's frigates in Boston loosed sails." As the *Shannon* stood out to sea again after the reconnaissance he donned his cocked hat and sword to witness the first punishment aboard his ship for three weeks; Thomas McCue, a Marine, received twenty-four lashes for insolence.

For a week *Shannon* and *Tenedos* haunted the Capes together, keyed to a high pitch of efficiency, exercising whenever the weather permitted and very conscious that the reputation of the flag would hang upon their performance. They chased returning coasters and privateers, but *Shannon*'s fouling copper often permitted the larger ones to escape. The smaller ones he left; he neither wished to antagonise the pacific New Englanders nor to bleed his ships of men before the struggle which he confidently expected. Besides, these small craft were useful for sending in the taunts and challenges with which he hoped to draw Rodgers out. Whenever he caught up with one he made a point of giving the skipper details of the force of *Shannon* and *Tenedos* down to the last boy and boat gun, and asking him to tell or send message to Commodore Rodgers that they would be happy to meet the *President* and *Congress* anywhere he might choose to try the honour of their flags.

"I will send any other vessels – should they be so discourteous as to interrupt us – outside the power of interfering. You understand, sir? Equal combat is my one wish – that we may try whether your papers are correct in saying that the English have forgotten how to fight!"

"My beloved Looloo, having at last been favoured with such a boisterous, rainy day that I can find nothing to employ myself about for the good of His Majesty's service, I determined to seize the opportunity of having a chat with you. I am so eternally occupied that such chance is not to be lost. Keeping now close to the land, we are constantly chasing or reconnoitring our enemy, or exercising ourselves in readiness *to play our part well* when he meets us. *Tenedos* is our comrade here, and has been our companion for some time. Whilst we went by order to report our reconnaisance of Boston one of their frigates, *Chesapeake*, got safe in; this is mortifying, but fortune must change in time.

"The prizes taken by our squadron in our absence have been very considerable, but we must comfort ourselves that we were doing our duty, and deserve equal success in our turn. Oliver has been very fortunate for his short stay here. I wish much, for my people's sake, to make some good capture, for they have had hard cruising. I shall at any time feel contented with the attainment of my only object when I first embarked – an opportunity of retiring honorably, and with the consciousness of having done my duty as an Englishman. Eight years of my youth and all my plans of rural quiet and domestic happiness have faded away or been cruelly interrupted by this imperious call of honor. But surely no man deserves to enjoy an estate in England who will not sacrifice some of his prospects to his country's wellfare, either by actual service, if capable, or at least by the example of zeal and voluntary privation in her cause. If I find my beloved wife and dear little children in health and comfort when I return, I shall feel as rich as when I left them, and as happy as I can imagine myself being . . .

"I hope *Shannon*'s campaign will soon be honorably terminated, though perhaps, the fear of our friends in the offing (*La Hogue* and *Valiant*) may render our antagonists cautious of meeting us. Indeed my wooden wife is very weak and crazy, and must soon be sent home. I could not think, my gentle Loo, of asking Admiral Hope for a 74, because if I ask for one I must serve. If *they* move me into one I feel acquitted. To wear out a new frigate is quite enough for one term of service for any man . . .

"I long to see our little George, (born 26th April the previous year) whilst you say he is such a pretty infant, and to witness the improvement in the others. Tell Philip to write to me sometimes from home as well as from Ottery. I hope when you took the

Martins home with them you made a merry Christmas party of it. I suppose Willy is now stout enough to make a good playfellow for Loolins. She may teach him to dance and make up a reel with you and Philip when he comes home. Do try and make her teach him reading; it will do her much service. You know I am very anxious about their being learned at their age, so that their minds only are *improving* and they are cheerful and happy with one another . . ."

Towards the end of April there was a spell of squally weather and the two big American frigates put to sea on a change of wind while *Shannon* and *Tenedos* were keeping an offing from the lee shore. Broke took it calmly at first, expecting that Rodgers was simply working his ships' companies up for a meeting, and would shortly return to try his force. As the days passed and there was still no sight of them, he gave up hope.

". . . We have had a furious gale of wind and been rudely buffetted these three days, but I hope more seasonable weather is now returning. Last night we missed our constant companion, *Tenedos*, in a rainy storm, but I doubt not I shall see her as soon as it clears for fogs have succeeded the gales and we are all in the *smoke*. I fear our intended adversary, Rodgers, and his comrade *Congress*, did not come out to visit us. They started studdenly on a change of wind, and must now be far away. I hope *La Hogue* has seen them to beat them soundly for disappointing us.

"We have now little hope but of meeting *Chesapeake* who is nearly ready, or *Essex* on her return. I feel much mortified by *President* escaping us after watching so long and anxiously for him. God send us better fortune to finish our campaign creditably. The day those rogues sailed it was thick weather. We must have been very close to them; but they did not *seek* us . . ."

Rodgers' decision to avoid an encounter with the British frigates which had been waiting for him and flaunting their colours in full view of the people of Boston and the nearby coastal towns must have been a painful one. Probably, as Broke and the renowned American historian Admiral Mahan later surmised, he was put off by the thought of the 74s which he must have known were somewhere in the offing although out of sight. Perhaps he simply considered that his orders to dislocate British trade were more important than the destruction of two frigates, perhaps he considered his ships' companies needed to be worked up before engaging enemy men-of-war; perhaps he simply missed them by chance. But if it was a *decision* not to fight it was a surprising one, because Rodgers and Captain John Smith of the *Congress* had not yet won the distinction in action achieved by other senior commanders, Hull, Bainbridge, Decatur or even juniors like Lawrence and Jacob Jones.

Broke, deprived of what he had considered to be a certain encounter, continued his paper conversation home.

"My Sunday devotions bear me home to my Loo; I wish I could pray by her side. Alas! I shall see *no primroses* this May to remind me of my gentle Looloo. When shall I read to her again whilst she ties up the violets? Poor Nacton! 'tis far away. I must not think of it till I am on my return. I hope the dear little children all go on as happily as when you last wrote, as I feel how much my dear Loo's happiness depends on theirs . . .

"I must close up this and attend to my wooden mistress, she is a *great tyrant*! Give my love to the dear little cherubs round you and heaven protect you all!"

.   .   .

James Lawrence had brought the *Hornet* safely home, and was enjoying some weeks ashore with his wife and small daughter. This was almost the first spell of leave since his marriage and it was made doubly happy by his late triumph which had brought, besides enthusiastic public recognition, a step up to Post Captain, and compliments from the Secretary of the Navy which were so different from the sharp note received just before he sailed as might have caused him to wonder if they were addressed to the same person. Of course they weren't. From being an ambitious but quite unknown young sloop commander, he had suddenly become 'Captain Jim', the toast of the Eastern Seaboard, whose *Hornet* had stung the *Peacock* to death in less time than any previous engagement in the war.

Far from satisfying his restless ambition, this success had whetted his appetite for more. Soon after arriving in port he had written to the Navy Department suggesting that he did not want to leave the *Hornet*; for good measure he had detailed two possible routes which he might follow on his next cruise, expecting that if he did so in company with the *Argus* the "enemy's trade would be much cut up, & her fishery for the year destroyed". He had ended, "Should the above plans not meet with your approbation, I trust you will excuse the liberty I have taken, and attribute it to my zeal for the Service and my ardent wish to be employed at sea."

But he now had 'too much rank' for a sloop, and he was appointed to command the New York Navy Yard. Then it began to appear as if he might go to the *Constitution* instead, for his friend and former Commodore, William Bainbridge, had been appointed Commandant of Boston, a shore post which left the great frigate without a Captain, and Bainbridge was recommending him. Directly this opportunity opened up, Lawrence set his heart upon it. Alas, it was not to be. What happened between the speculation and the final result is impossible to determine – jealousy, internal politics or a simple matter of seniority, we shall never know. Captain Stewart was appointed to the big ship, and Lawrence to the smaller *Chesapeake*. The orders which had been addressed to Captain Evans, who had commanded *Chesapeake* on her last cruise but was now to be removed on account of ill health, were forwarded to Lawrence instead.

"Navy Department   May 6, 1813
"Captain James Lawrence United States Navy
    "Sir – My last of the 4th instant will have informed you of my intention to have ordered you to the *Constitution* without reservation & the enclosed copy of a letter, this moment received after I had sealed the enclosed letter to Captain Evans, will explain to you the cause of the indispensable change of that determination. (This letter has not been found.)
    "Knowing your ardent desire for Active Service I feel a pleasure in gratifying your laudable zeal, and therefore desire that you will proceed immediately to Boston, take command of the frigate *Chesapeake* and proceed in conformity with the original instructions which you will consider as if originally addressed to yourself. If in the course of your cruise you should derive such information of the force of the enemy, or other sufficient cause, as to render a strict adherence to my instructions prejudicial to the public Service, you are at liberty to exercise your own judgement and persue such other course as may, in your opinion be best calculated to accomplish the important objectives of your cruise . . ."

Lawrence replied that he was honoured by the appointment, and would proceed direct to Boston as soon as he had handed over the *Hornet* – but then asked if he might try and make another arrangement.

    "When I requested permission to go again in the *Hornet* I conceived that I could with propriety leave my family, but have since found that Mrs. Lawrence's health is so *delicate* & her situation at this time so very critical that I am induced to request your permission to remain until the *Constitution* is ready, provided I can make the arrangement with Captain Stewart, who I understand is ordered to her, but who, I understand is extremely anxious to get to sea."

Having thus unburdened himself of some part of his disappointment, Lawrence handed over his late sloop to her new Captain and travelled overland to Boston, where he arrived on 18th May. He reported to Bainbridge, and two days later went aboard the *Chesapeake* to take over formerly from Captain Evans. At six bells on the same day he had the hands beat to quarters and exercised at the great guns which were loaded throughout with round and grape. That evening he wrote to the Navy Department to inform them that he had taken command.

"I found her ready for sea with the exception of some provisions and slops ... and a few men now on their way from Portland.

"In consequence of the *Chesapeake* being under sailing orders, Commodore Bainbridge has ordered Purser Chew to her. He will request a few days to arrange his accounts at the Navy Yard.

"By that time I shall have time to see everything arranged to my satisfaction & shall proceed to sea with the first favourable chance, as I am induced to believe from a conversation I have had last evening with my friend Commodore Bainbridge, that I have little chance of an exchange of ships between Captain Stewart and myself. At all events I should have put to sea the moment the *Chesapeake* was ready ..."

Whatever Lawrence's disappointment at having been baulked of the great frigate, his new command was not one to be despised. She was an exceedingly handsome craft and was known to be very fast. She had been laid down in Norfolk, Virginia, originally to the same specification as the big ships, *Constitution*, *President* and *United States*, but afterwards the plans were reduced to "the largest size frigates in the British Navy ... with a prospect of finishing the ship in half the time it would take to complete her on the former scale, with half the expense". This memo provides proof, if any is needed, of the vastly superior construction of the big American frigates to even the largest in the British service: "half the time ... half the expense".

The *Chesapeake* was completed thus economically and largely by slave labour to new plans provided by Josiah Fox, probably the most talented designer of Naval craft in the United States at the time. He specialised in sharper bottom sections than were usual, and both

Lawrence's previous commands, *Wasp* and *Hornet*, had been extremely fast vessels to his sharp design.

The *Chesapeake* was launched in June 1799, and got away to sea the same year. She was thus seven years older than the *Shannon*, but in all other respects she was as equal a match as could be found anywhere. Instead of being 145 feet on the keel as originally planned, she was 127 feet 5 inches, and her length between perpendiculars (English measurement) was 151 feet; the *Shannon* was 150 feet 1½ inches. The *Chesapeake* had a moulded beam of 40 feet 4 inches, the *Shannon* 39 feet 3 inches. The *Chesapeake* carried 14 long 18-pounder cannon each side of her maindeck; so did the *Shannon*. The *Chesapeake* carried 10 carronades, 32-pounders either side of her spar deck, with one long 18-pounder which could be shifted to whichever broadside was required; the *Shannon* on her present cruise fought 8 carronades, 32-pounders, each side on the upper deck (six on the quarterdeck and two on the fo'c'sle), and in addition she had 2 long 9-pounders; these were mounted at the after end of the fo'c'sle and the forward end of the quarterdeck on special swivel brackets raised high above the deck to have a clear fire overall and with facility of elevation to 33°, especially for use against either the enemy's tops or to dismantle the wheel. Broke had also fitted a launch carronade 12-pounder in the starboard entry port, and the brass 6-pounder that had been put aboard lately at Halifax to port. Thus both ships had a broadside of 14 long guns on the maindeck and 11 carronades and others on the upper deck, although the *Chesapeake* had a small advantage in weight of shot from the upper deck.

So much for the physical comparisons. But, as every sailor knows, there is more to a ship than the material she is built with; every vessel is a character in her own right. And it is undoubtedly true that the *Chesapeake*'s character was bad and she exerted a singularly baleful influence over a number of personalities in the United States Navy. Leaving aside the loss of lives at her launching and subsequently which had caused the sailors to label her as 'unlucky', she had already been a party to Commodore Barron's humiliation from the *Leopard* and subsequent suspension for five years from the United States Navy, and this same incident was to be revived by Barron some years afterwards as an excuse to challenge to a duel and kill one of the most gifted and attractive of all American Naval heroes, Stephen Decatur.

On 20th May 1813 the *Chesapeake* cast her spell on James Lawrence. He had no inkling of it.

The following day the hands were employed taking in stores, and early in the morning of 22nd May they unmoored and dropped down off Long Wharf. On Sunday, 23rd May, they were mustered and Lawrence, splendid in his new Captain's uniform, read the Articles of War, afterwards producing a bugle and asking who among the men could blow it. A mulatto named William Brown, a slow, dull-witted man who had been loblolly boy, or surgeon's assistant, on the preceding cruise under Evans, stepped forward. Lawrence tossed the bugle to him and told him to practise. "And let any others who are disposed to do so, practice as well."

But of all the men who tried, only William Brown – who had never in fact blown a bugle in his life – could make a noise. He was appointed bugler. Henceforth his sole duty at quarters would be to stand by on the quarterdeck and call the boarders away by sounding his instrument when ordered.

After the muster Lawrence had the men exercised at the great guns for the second time since he had taken command four days previously; he walked both gun decks personally supervising the drill – 'Captain Jim', a name to be conjured with. During this exercise William Brown succeeded in making sufficient noise with his shining new bugle to rouse the boarders up from the farthest parts of the ship.

Not far off, out in Massachusetts Bay, Broke was reading his Sunday morning sermon to the assembled Shannons. Some time later, after church service had ended, *Tenedos* and the lately joined British brig-of-war *Curlew*, who had been chasing, returned with a fine American privateer as prize, and after extracting all the information he could, Broke sent *Curlew* and the prize to Halifax. The following morning a schooner sneaked out from Salem, but while trying to evade the British in the mist, ran right into them; American papers aboard confirmed Broke's hopes that the *Chesapeake* was almost ready for sea. They also told him that Lawrence had been appointed to her.

This was good news on both counts. It was good that she was nearly ready to come out because the *Shannon*, having haunted Boston for no less than fifty-six days, could not stay much longer unless she replenished her stores, particularly water; it was good that Lawrence was in command because he was a young man, likely to be confident after his walkover with the *Peacock* and spoiling for another chance of glory. Rumour had it that he was a hot-headed fellow. Besides he was well known, not only for his latest victory but also for the challenge he had sent in to the Captain of the *Bonne Citoyenne*, which had received wide publicity both sides of the Atlantic. Broke suspected that if he flaunted *Shannon* alone and in easy view before Boston it would prove too much for the challenger of the *Bonne Citoyenne* to resist. He called Hyde Parker over from *Tenedos* and explained his intentions, afterwards drafting an official letter.

"His Majesty's Ship, *Shannon* off Boston   25th May, 1813.
"To Hyde Parker, Esq., Captain of H.M. Ship *Tenedos*
    "Sir, Having every reason to believe that the American frigate *Chesapeake* will sail from Boston in a few days, and thinking there is more chance of her being intercepted by our frigates cruising separately than if they keep together, I have to direct that during the absence of the Hon. Captain Capel, the senior officer, you will proceed to and cruise upon the range lately occupied by *La Hogue*, viz from Cape Sable to the latitude of 42 10N to watch for the *Chesapeake* should she pass the *Shannon* in night time or thick weather. You are to take an opportunity, in such winds as you think least likely to favour the enemy's escape, to procure water enough to last out your provisions at Shelburne, or any other port you may find most convenient, joining the *Shannon* off Boston on the 14th June, unless otherwise ordered by the senior officer.
    "I am, Sir, Your very obedient, humble servant,
                            "P. B. V. Broke."

Fifteen tons of fresh water and various casks of provisions were taken from the *Tenedos* into the *Shannon*, then they parted company. The *Tenedos* made easterly while the *Shannon* wafted easily northwards as the wind shifted into the south-east and gusted up to gale force, bringing rain and a heavy swell.

While Broke had been making his preparations, Lawrence had been bending all his energies to ensure that *his* frigate would be fit in every respect for the difficult business of dodging the British blockade. Besides paying attention to her *matériel*, he found it necessary to give his First Lieutenant indefinite leave of absence as he was a disruptive element on board and "at variance with every officer in his mess". The former juniors were all stepped up, Page to First, Ludlow and Budd Second and Third, while one of his own protégés, Cox, who was the son of his brother-in-law's business partner, was stepped up from Midshipman to acting Fourth Lieutenant. By now Lawrence was reconciled to having missed his opportunity of the *Constitution*, and he was fully determined to take the *Chesapeake* out at the first opportunity that Broke might allow him. On 27th May he wrote in this vein to the Captain of the *Hornet*, who was to meet him if possible off Cape Breton for a cruise in company.

"I shall sail on Sunday (May 30th), provided I have a chance of getting out clear of the *Shannon* and *Tenedos* who are on the lookout. My intention is to pass out by Cape Sable and then run out West (presumably meaning East) until I get into the stream, then haul in . . ."

On the following day the new Second Lieutenant, Augustus Ludlow, wrote to his brother Charles with the news.

"May 28th
"There are only three frigates now, cruising off Boston Bay; they send in no prizes but burn them all. Commodore Broke says he does not intend to weaken his crew by manning prizes . . . There is a report we shall go to sea on Sunday, but I cannot believe it. I hardly think we shall go out in such fine weather when there are three frigates off. The ship is in better order for battle than ever I saw before. Page is a-going out our First Lieutenant. Lt. Pierce has left the ship . . ."

Ludlow's reference to *three* frigates was probably due to mistaken identification of the *Curlew*. But of course the *Shannon* was now quite alone. And as the high winds dropped and a fog rolled up over the swell they had left Broke started a letter home.

"*Shannon* off Boston   May 28th, 1813
"My dearest Looloo, We still haunt this tiresome place without any success to reward us; indeed I have been so particularly anxious to watch the great ships that it has thrown us much out of the way of the smaller though richer prizes. Since Rodgers escaped we have rarely hunted our game far from his den, which still contains another wild beast. If all the nobler prey elude us we must chase the vermin, but have great hopes of *an honorable encounter*. Indeed my beloved Looloo I feel very naughty in not having written you a few lines last week by *Curlew*, whom we sent to Halifax with prisoners; but you must forgive me. I have been so anxious and unsettled from our hopes and disappointments here that I could never compose myself to write even to my gentle Loo . . .
"My constant comrade, Parker, I detached two days ago on a separate range, that we might show an even more inviting appearance to our enemy, now a single frigate of our own size; we shall do a grand service if we can get hold of him, preventing all the mischief he would do if he escaped out; and I trust in God and our brave crew in brightening up the honor of our flag and soothing the

feelings of our countrymen for their late mortifications. I think I shall soon be home again with my Loo . . .

"You will imagine that I am even here, frequently awakened to sorrowful recollections when the ships we meet are from Ipswich, Harwich or Plymouth; indeed English and mostly Suffolk names are frequent on this coast. Dedham and Cambridge are very near me, and Marshfield, a small coasting town, reminds me often how long we were detained at its namesake going to Clifton. I have not yet been severe with any of these half-countrymen of ours, but fear I must begin to pester them now as their President's troops are at last invading Canada . . ."

The following day, 29th May, was still foggy in the morning with light variable winds. Broke made some corrections to the sights of his dismantling service 9-pounders and the men were exercised at a target with muskets. At four in the afternoon *Shannon* fell in with the Liverpool privateer *Sir John Sherbrooke* in company with her latest prize, the notorious American privateer *General Plumer*, captured two days previously. The American's hold was full of booty from a three months' cruise and she carried 54 prisoners, some 40 of whom were Irish, many of them servants who had been travelling as passengers from Waterford to Newfoundland in a little brig called the *Duck*. Most of these couldn't speak English, but Broke, anxious to keep *Shannon*'s strength up as he had recently sent some fourteen men away in two prizes for Halifax, called for volunteers. The Irish, 'all aisy lads', stepped forward, whereupon Broke selected 22 of the youngest and toughest and put them on his books. They were exercised at small arms at a target during the next two days while *Shannon* hovered in shifting fogs and rain squalls never far from Cape Ann.

On Monday, 31st May, Broke decided to pay Lawrence off in his own coin, and started drafting a careful letter challenging him to single combat. He took infinite pains. The impression it might make on Lawrence could mean the difference between action or evasion, between a glorious termination to his command of *Shannon* or seven years of rigorous cruising and training signifying – nothing.

"Sir, As the *Chesapeake* appears now ready for sea, I request that you will do me the favour to meet the *Shannon* with her, ship to ship, to try the fortune of our respective flags. To an officer of your character, it requires some apology to proceed to further particulars. Be assured, sir, that it is not from any doubt I can entertain of your wishing to close with my proposal, but merely to provide an answer to any objection which might be made, and very reasonably, upon the chance of our receiving unfair support. After the diligent attention which we had paid to Commodore Rodgers, the pains I took to detach all force but the *Shannon* and *Tenedos* to such a distance that they could not possibly join in any action fought in sight of the Capes, and the various verbal messages which had been sent into Boston to that effect, we were much disappointed to find the Commodore had eluded us by sailing on the first change, after the prevailing easterly winds had obliged us to keep an offing from the coast. He, perhaps, wished for some stronger assurance of a fair meeting. I am therefore induced to address you more particularly, and to assure you that what I write, I pledge my honor to perform to the utmost of my power. The *Shannon* mounts twenty-four guns upon her broadside and one light boat gun – eighteen pounders upon her maindeck, and thirty two pound carronades on her quarterdeck and forecastle, and is manned with a complement of 300 men and boys (a large proportion of the latter), besides thirty seamen, boys and passengers who were taken out of recaptured vessels lately. I am thus minute because a report has prevailed in some of the Boston papers that we had 150 men additional lent us from *La Hogue*, which really never was the case. *La Hogue* is now gone to Halifax for provisions, and I will send all other ships beyond the power of interfering with us, and meet you wherever it is most agreeable to you, within the limits of the undermentioned rendezvous, viz. from six to ten leagues East of Cape Cod lighthouse; from eight to ten leagues East of Cape Ann's Light; on Cashe's ledge, in latitude 43 North; at any bearing and distance you please to fix, off the South breakers of Nantucket, or the shoal on St. George's Bank.

"If you will favor me with any plan of signals or telegraph, I will warn you (if sailing under this promise) should any of my friends be too nigh, or anywhere in sight, until I can detach them out of my way; or I would sail with you under a flag of truce, to any place you think safest from our cruisers, hauling it down when fair to begin hostilities.

"You must, sir, be aware that my proposals are highly advantageous to you, as you cannot proceed to sea singly in the *Chesapeake* without imminent risk of being crushed by the superior force of the numerous British squadrons which are now abroad, where all your efforts, in case of a *rencontre*, would, however gallant, be perfectly hopeless. I entreat you, sir, not to imagine that I am urged by mere personal vanity to the wish of meeting the

Chesapeake, or that I depend only upon your personal ambition for your acceding to this invitation; we both have nobler motives.

"You will feel it as a compliment if I say that the result of our meeting may be the most grateful service I can render to my country; and, I doubt not, that you, equally confident of success, will feel that it is only by repeated triumphs, in *even combats*, that your little navy can now hope to console your country for the loss of that trade it can no longer protect. Favour me with a speedy reply.

"We are short of provisions and water, and cannot stay long here.
"I have the honor to be, etc."

He added a note:

"N.B. For the general service of watching your coast it is requisite for me to keep another ship in company to support me with her guns and boats, when employed near the land, and particularly to aid each other if either ship, in chase, should get on shore. You must be aware that I cannot, consistent with my duty, waive so great an advantage for this general service by detaching my consort without an assurance on your part of meeting me directly, and that you will neither seek nor admit aid from any other of your armed vessels if I despatch mine expressly for the sake of meeting you.

"Should any special order restrain you from thus answering a formal challenge, you may yet oblige me by keeping my proposal a secret, and appointing any place you like to meet us (within 300 miles of Boston) in a given number of days after you sail; as unless you agree to an interview, I may be busied on some other service, and perhaps be at a distance from Boston when you get to sea.

"Choose your terms, but let us meet."

This famous challenge has been called by Colonel (later President) Roosevelt, "a model of courtesy, manliness and candour". After a second or third reading the 'courtesy' can be seen, as it was by the celebrated Naval historian Admiral Mahan, as that "of a French duellist, nervously anxious lest he should misplace an accent in the name of a man whom he intended to force into a fight and kill. It was provocative to the last degree . . ."

.   .   .

That evening the *Shannon* discovered a little fishing vessel and ran her alongside to seek intelligence. The skipper of the boat, a wild fellow named Eben Slocum, hurled imprecations up instead, and when he saw Broke shook his fist and shouted that if he had a ship of force he would drive him off the coast or carry him in to Boston – furthermore, as soon as he returned to Boston there would be a ship sent out to bring Broke in. He continued hurling abuse in this vein until Broke tired of it and ordered him to be gagged, put in irons and taken below. Then, instead of sending the little craft back to its home as he always did with such comparatively worthless vessels, he ordered it to be burned. The voluble Slocum had, however, revealed what the previous days' fogs had kept hidden.

He returned to his cabin and wrote a brief note to Louisa which ended, "*Chesapeake is not gone*. Adieu! God bless you all in health and happiness."

CHAPTER SEVEN

THE morning of 1st June broke splendidly. The damp fogs and rain of the last few days had given way to blue sky with puffy clouds over the land. The sun rose brilliantly and shone and sparked off the gently heaving ocean, its surface creased with a cool, invigorating breeze from northwards. Broke tapped his glass and noted it still rising. Promise of a fair summer's day. But more than that if he had judged Lawrence aright – much more . . .

He went on deck and acknowledged his First Lieutenant's salute. Watt, too, had been lifted by the sun. The big man's face was animated and there was a glint in his eye which entirely matched Broke's mood. No need to express it; on such a morning words were superfluous.

Today?

The *Shannon* slid easily through the now friendly blue water southwards towards Boston. Cape Ann receded gradually on the quarter; stretching round as far as the eye could see to starboard lay the green and peaceful countryside of New England with its tall beeches and pines clustering thickly down to the dry, pinkish rock by the shore. Smoke curled lazily from the chimneys of timber 'frame houses', small fishing boats were putting out from the coastal towns – snuggling roofs and narrow, twisting streets like the West Country of England – and beyond lay all the English names, Bradford, Georgetown, Broke's own Ipswich and Haverhill, the same distance away as the Suffolk Haverhill from the Suffolk Ipswich – Andover, Gloucester, Weymouth, Braintree, Abington, Bridgewater, Kingston, Plymouth,

Wareham, Sandwich – and Boston itself. Strange to be fighting these half-countrymen of theirs . . .

Presently, beyond the spur of Nahant and the cluster of fishing craft after cod and halibut, perch, haddock just south of Pea Island, the far view of the city presented itself clear in the morning light. The clustering masts and spars of scores of blockaded vessels marked the outline of wharves stretching down to Boston Neck and Dorchester, and behind them the houses and public buildings rose to Beacon Hill, bright sun glinting off paintwork and windows and white stone, monuments to a wealthy mercantile community.

Then, as the *Shannon* slipped nearer and opened the view into President's Roads between the trees on Deer Island and Long Island, they saw her – a sleek frigate showing gunports along her side and a fresh, bright band of yellow paint below them extending right up in the bows to her fiddlehead, her masts standing tall, rigging set taut, royal yards crossed and her furled white sails stopped with rope yarns ready to drop on the instant.

There she lay!

Broke's heart pounded. Up until that moment there had always been the chance that she might somehow have slipped out unnoticed and unreported. But there she was – *Chesapeake* – and ready for sea. He hadn't realised quite how much he depended upon her – his ticket home, his passport to glory, above all his *release* in action for all the warlike tension built up over seven years of gunnery thought and improvements and drill, drill – like a spring wound full stretch, his company demanded release. And so did he. He shuddered at the violence of his feelings.

He stood *Shannon* closer in towards the lighthouse, close-hauled to the light breeze which was backing ever more westerly, until within about two miles he luffed up and fired a gun. Could *Chesapeake* resist this challenge?

Here was a British frigate entirely alone, her weathered sides streaked down from the gunports and chains with the signs of long cruising, flaunting a faded blue ensign at the very mouth of the U.S. Navy base, firing a single, teasing gun. What American commander could submit to this in the present mood of the Navy and the country? What young, ardent spirit – what *Lawrence*?

Of course Lawrence had no option. His fiery spirit demanded that he accept this plain challenge; the confidence inspired by his recent easy victory and all the American frigate successes to date left no room for doubts, his own ambition left no time for hesitation.

That is – if the *Shannon* were truly alone. So long as this was not just a trick to draw him out on this fine westerly breeze and into the arms of one or two of the *Shannon*'s consorts ready to appear from the offing.

Lawrence's attention had first been called to the strange sail between 8 and 9 o'clock that morning. Lieutenant Budd, the officer of the deck, had sent a Midshipman down to report, as he supposed, a frigate. Lawrence had gone up on deck and then ascended the main shrouds for a better view, soon coming to the conclusion that she was a large frigate. Returning to the deck, he had hailed a passing pilot boat and directed her to reconnoitre outside the harbour and report back to him if the strange frigate was alone, meanwhile ordering all hands to prepare the ship for sailing and to heave short on the anchor cable. Afterwards he had gone below to his cabin and written a short letter to the Secretary of the Navy to acquaint him with his decision.

"Since I had the honour of addressing you last, I have been detained for want of men. I am now getting under way to carry into execution the instructions you have honoured me with. An English frigate is now in plain sight from my deck; I have sent a pilot boat out to reconnoitre & should she be alone I am in hopes to give a good account of her before night. My crew appear to be in fine spirits, & I trust will do their duty.

"Lieutenant Page is so ill as to be unable to go to sea in the ship . . . Commodore Bainbridge has ordered midshipmen Cox and Ballard to act until your pleasure is known. They are both fine young men, and I am confident from their long service, will do everything that can be expected from any commissioned lieutenant."

Then he wrote a short note to his brother-in-law about prize money due for captures during the last cruise, ending:

". . . An English frigate is close in with the lighthouse, & we are now clearing ship for action. Should I be so unfortunate as to be taken off, I leave my wife and children to your care, and feel confident you will behave to them the same as if they were your own. Remember me affectionately to your good mother, Mary and Cox and believe me,

"Sincerely yours,
"J. Lawrence

"P.S. 10 am. the frigate is in plain sight from our deck and we are now getting under way."

As the *Shannon* fired her gun Lawrence ordered one of his own to reply, and had the foretopsail loosed so that it hung shivering in the breeze. One of the sailors hoisted a white flag bearing the words FREE TRADE AND SAILOR'S RIGHTS to the fore royal masthead. Then they waited for the pilot boat to return.

Certainly Lawrence could have rationalised his decision: the British blockade was tightening every day; now that the British Government had realised that the war was more than a simple misunderstanding, and the Admiralty had woken to the need for more ships of force to contain the U.S. Navy and the scores of privateers preying on trade, it was only a matter of time before it would be impossible to break their blockade in fair weather. That might mean waiting for the winter gales before he could get out. His orders, which left him great freedom to exercise his own judgement, were to proceed to the mouth of the St. Lawrence and attack the troop convoys and supplies going to the relief of the British Army in Canada; they contained the unarguable assertion, "It is impossible to conceive a naval service of a higher order in a national point of view than the destruction of the enemy's vessels with supplies for his army in Canada and his fleets on this station." But if he had to await the gales he would probably be too late. The supplies and reinforcements would have arrived. And what was the alternative? Simply to go out now while the wind and the opportunity favoured, bring in this insolent British frigate while she lay unsupported, quickly make good whatever damage was sustained in the process and then sail safely in obedience to his orders before the British realised the blockade was broken and despatched a squadron or a ship of the line to contain him. Perhaps this was his reasoning; but undoubtedly the decision to fight came from deeper sources than reason.

Many and varied have been the criticisms levelled at Lawrence for going out with an allegedly untrained crew and raw officers, and fighting before he had worked his men up into a team. It is true that his new First Lieutenant was ill in hospital, and the other Lieutenants had again been moved up one, so that the two junior places had to be filled by Midshipmen, and true that these were young and one had not drilled before the day of action with the men he commanded. But again Lawrence had to face the alternative; a ship of the line might appear any day or a companion for this single frigate – and what chance would he have then? Besides, he had faith in his Lieutenants; the First, Ludlow, had been nine years at sea, having entered as a Midshipman at twelve years old. He was exceptionally able and together with Budd, the Second, had been with the *Chesa-*

peake during her last cruise and obviously knew her well. The two juniors, Cox and Ballard, had both sailed with him in his previous commands and had been promoted from Midshipman on his recommendation; he had no reason to doubt their capabilities – quite the reverse. Age was no bar; Lawrence himself had been about Cox's age when he had his first taste of hand-to-hand fighting in the Mediterranean, and only a year older when *First* Lieutenant at Decatur's brilliant *Philadelphia* exploit. As for experience in action, that could only come in action, and no amount of working up could provide more of it than they had in the *Hornet*.

The other criticisms are perhaps even less valid. The men were not raw: of the 388 officers, men and Marines on the *Chesapeake*'s pay list on 1st June, 279, or nearly three-quarters, had served in the previous cruise under Captain Evans. There were no landsmen among them, the lowest rating (apart from 'boys' – 13 in all) was 'Ordinary Seaman'; they were exceptionally well trained at the great guns, as Lawrence had found during his drills in harbour, and although many were, it is true, dissatisfied about not having had the money due for six prizes captured during their recent cruise, it is impossible to believe that they were drunk as some writers have stated, neither were they formed of a great proportion of foreigners as others would have it. Lawrence had observed them for nearly a fortnight; he knew them to be first-rate American sailors and gunners, many of whom had learnt their trade in the British Service – a few of whom were in fact British deserters. There was also a small party of less than a dozen men from the dockyard, or possibly from the *Constitution*, which was still under repair; these came aboard at the last moment and their hammocks and gear lay in the boats and across the booms when the frigate sailed.

Lawrence knew his men; he had every reason for confidence. The only thing he did not know was the exceptional quality of the opposition. And how should he have guessed that this *Shannon* which had been flaunting herself before Boston and sending in verbal challenges for weeks was not simply another lamb for the slaughter? How was he to know that she marked instead the final flowering and high point of the ancient art of broadside fire from carriage-mounted cannon and that a more destructive vessel of her force had probably never existed in the history of Naval warfare?

Lawrence had no idea. He had weighed what he did know in scales heavily weighted by his temperament, and had come to the inevitable conclusion. As he saw the *Shannon* teasing him on this bright morning with the light breeze fair in the west, he saw only his brilliant opportunity. He ordered the anchor hove short, and the ship prepared for sea.

Expecting that the pilot boat's report would be favourable, he had the quarter boats lowered and the women from the berth deck sent over the side with their scanty baggage; they expected to be back aboard that evening and cried no farewells – only screams of encouragement. As they landed by the fort they waved and cheered the British frigate and yelled taunts, looking forward to a closer view when their brave and boastful menfolk brought her in.

The citizens of Boston were equally sanguine. The day's work was forgotten as they rushed to the waterfront or the roofs of nearby buildings to view this latest British ship offering herself as a prize to their Naval heroes. Fishermen filled their boats with sightseers to follow the *Chesapeake* into action; the coffee houses were abuzz with organisations for a great celebration supper to which it was proposed to invite the surviving officers of the *Shannon* together with Lawrence and the rest of her conquerors. And at the Navy yard they cleared a wharf to accommodate her riven remains when she was brought in. Never was optimism about the result of apparently equal combat exaggerated to such heights of confidence.

Even if he had wished, *could* Lawrence have refused to go out?

The *Shannon*, meanwhile, tacked and beat to quarters, and the people went through the ritual of the great-gun drill without firing. Broke, who had told his clerk to write out the letter of challenge fairly from his draft, sealed it, then wrote a postcript on the outside, "We have thirteen American persons on board which I shall give you for as many British sailors if you will send them out; otherwise, being privateersmen, they must be detained." He had the hot-tempered Captain Eben Slocum freed and brought up, and told him that he was a free man if he would agree to deliver the letter. Slocum was quieter after his night in irons and he was shortly put in to a fishing schooner that the *Shannon*'s jollyboat ran aboard.

As the schooner left her side and pointed inshore for Marblehead Broke climbed the main shrouds with his long glass and settled himself in the top. He didn't expect to have to wait for Slocum to reach the shore. Under the circumstances this morning the letter should scarcely be necessary. He knew his man. The wind and weather were fair for sailing; the chance of breaking the blockade in single action in full view of the people of Boston would be too much for the spirited Captain of the *Chesapeake*. In any case it was obvious from the papers that the Americans were becoming quite too saucy, and they would not expect Lawrence to refuse the challenge presented by the *Shannon* alone.

He trained his glass over the masts and yards of the frigate standing up so boldly over the island, searching for another sign of movement. Below him the great cannon went rumbling and thudding against their port sills, then back again – and out. The only other sounds were made by the water plashing gently against the bow and the occasional hoarse orders from the officers of the quarters. The sun was warm against his neck and the breeze full in his face.

But after that first response from the Americans nothing further seemed to happen. She just lay there with the topsails slatting unsheeted. In the other direction Slocum's fisherman was having a long beat against the offshore breeze; he could not reach Marblehead or Salem for some time yet – but surely, surely Lawrence would never need a *paper* challenge . . .

At 11.30 Broke shut his telescope and climbed down to the officer of the watch on the quarterdeck. "Beat the retreat, if you please," he said with the disappointment obvious in his voice. "But, Wallis, I don't mean this for a general quarters. She will surely be out today or tomorrow."

Shannon beat back and forth across the entrance to the harbour under easy sail to the light and variable breeze, making little way, towing the jollyboat astern from a short painter. She had been left down after capturing the fishing schooner in order that the stern-chase guns would not be masked. She yawed across the smooth green shadows in the frigate's wake.

At midday Wallis ordered meridian. The Marine sentinel on the quarterdeck upturned his half-hour sandglass, and from the belfry forward came the four double peals followed immediately by the pipes shrilling to dinner. The men, animated by the pleasant weather and their close view right into the heart of enemy territory, excited by the prospect of a wild break in routine when the American frigate came out, clattered down to their mess tables.

On the quarterdeck Lieutenant Falkiner relieved Wallis for the afternoon watch. They both stood gazing over towards the *Chesapeake*'s spars and hanging topsail over the bright land. The glass was high and rising. The wind had blown the clouds off and the sky was a clear blue bowl of summer. Wallis had a recollection of his first action as a youth – a losing action – the roar of the guns like spasmodic thunder, smoke in his eyes and nostrils as the frigate jerked like a live thing, curses, cries from the sweating, blackened men at the tackles, groans, blood over the decks, and final horror, the rush of the enemy boarders over their bulwarks, fierce with strange French oaths, running, yelling, cutting as they came . . .

"She has not moved yet?" Falkiner said.

"The Captain is sure she will come out."

Presently the Marine at the sandglass called out the half-hour and the bell was struck once. The pipes shrilled for grog and the rough pitch of the men's voices from below swelled and grew more frenzied as the heady tots mixed with three parts water loosened their minds. The noise struck up through the gratings over the hatchway – roaring laughter, snatches of song, skylark, stage Irish obscenities to rile the new Paddys who were too stupid to understand anyway, all mixed with coarse boasts of what they were going to do to the Yankees when they dared come out. They knew they could. If anyone could turn the trick it was their flaming redhead Captain. A tartar at the great guns, but they knew they could handle them now and shoot straight across the surface whatever the roll on her – none of your dismasting games – into the hull and give it to the men and never mind about the rigging, the Captain said. They knew that if he could get her alongside yardarm to yardarm they could flush the boasting Yankees from their pride. If anyone could do it, the Shannons could.

The babble of sound floated up to Broke, who had taken his position with a telescope in the maintop again. But why wouldn't she move? Every minute gone was a minute of this fine day wasted – and would it eventually be just another day to add to his six and a half undistinguished years?

He could see that Slocum's boat had still not reached the shore.

As he looked back towards the *Chesapeake* his blood stopped momentarily, and then pumped hard. There was a cry simultaneously from the lookout, "She comes! Sir, the frigate has made sail!"

What a picture she made! She had sheeted home all together and was walking out over her short cable helped by the ebbing tide. He watched her through his glass for a moment to make sure there could be no mistake, then hurried down on deck.

The voices from below had ceased as the word spread like a thunderclap among the men. They were all on deck lining the bulwarks and hammock nettings and even in the lower shrouds, straining to get a better sight. And they were quiet. Now that the moment was upon them their high spirits gave way to a sort of awe. The Yankee frigate was coming for them.

Broke felt their eyes on him, and knew that Watt close by was waiting for a word. He stepped back to the main shrouds and levelled his telescope again. There could be no doubt. She was walking down steadily towards the lighthouse with the tide and the wind right behind her – she was surrounded by a clutch of small craft like ducklings in her wake, and among them some fair-sized cutters and a large schooner, probably armed, and all of them crowded with Americans coming out to see the sport. What a spectacle they made with their gay sails and myriad colours against the land! He could imagine his opponent, Lawrence, on the frigate's quarterdeck, a large, handsome, wilful fellow by all accounts – and confident too. He would expect to give these people of his a show.

He fought down his mounting excitement and turned to Watt. "I hope to have the pleasure of shaking hands with Captain Lawrence today." Watt smiled.

They wasted little time discussing the immediate situation because it was obvious to both that *Shannon* was far too close to Boston and that if by mischance they were dismasted or otherwise crippled they would be in danger from boarding parties from the shore. The helm was put up to wear ship, the jib set and when they were round on a south-easterly course the t'gallants and fore course were dropped and sheeted home. The *Chesapeake* meanwhile set all her studding sails alow and aloft and walked out after them, a splendid, tapering mass of white sunlit and shadowed canvas against the green land.

All the officers were up on the quarterdeck now, and those Marines and waisters on deck were talking with hushed excitement. Broke called them to silence. Then he went below to his great cabin for the last time before it was dismantled for action. He fell to his knees and committed his beloved Louisa to God's care, and his dear children, and the *Shannon* and all her people, and he prayed earnestly that he might not fail any of them when the moment of trial came. And if it were God's will – let it be *Shannon* to raise the proud old Union flag again.

Shortly afterwards his servant was stowing his gear ready for carrying below, and the carpenters were banging away at the timber partitions which formed his suite of rooms. They soon had them apart and carried them down to the hold with his few pieces of furniture and his books; now the gun deck presented an unbroken sweep down each side inboard of the cannon, a sweet sheer of planking from the manger right forward where the kids were tethered, down past the main hatch coaming, surrounded by the 18-pounder balls like strings of black beads in their shot racks, past the stump of the mainmast with its cluster of stanchions, up again to the great windows at the stern through which the sun was striking in diagonals. Dappled reflections off the water rippled along the beams overhead.

The chase to seawards continued slowly down the fitful breeze of afternoon. Broke had the carpenters erect a table on the quarterdeck and a canvas screen just forward to shield it from the men's gaze, and invited his commissioned officers to dine with him. They gathered around the white cloth agleam with his silver service and glassware, claret in decanters making a splash of colour between their shadows – Watt and Wallis, Falkiner and the two Marine officers, Johns and Law, each backed by his own servant, each a little constrained by the occasion and by an effort at unconcern. And whenever they stood to glance over the starboard-quarter hammocks, there, like fate itself, was the towering spread of the *Chesapeake*'s canvas, always just a fraction closer, the sun moulding white highlights on the starboard side of her studding sails, and the ripple at her bow. A picture for an artist against the clear blue of the sky! The small craft accompanying were straggling now; only the schooner seemed able to stay the pace in the light breeze.

When they had finished eating and the servants had cleared the plates, but while the port remained, Broke rose to his feet and looked at his officers in turn. "Well gentlemen, no doubt we shall shortly be in action," he started, as if announcing nothing more serious than a gun drill. "It will be a satisfaction to me if we all take wine with each other – and shake hands all round before we go to our quarters." This was an old custom which had fallen into disuse; he revived it mainly to reconcile two of those present who had quarrelled. The chairs scraped back; the officers stood with him and raised their glasses across the table, they bowed, straightened up and drank deeply to their friendship in silence.

Below decks all was ready for the action. In the steamy, dark cockpit below the steerage the surgeon and his mate had laid out their armament of saws, knives, probes, drills, forceps, which glistened dully in the candlelight from the heavy lanterns round about. The deck below was spread with old, scrubbed canvas; half-tubs gleaming with water stood ready to receive amputated limbs, others were placed by the sponges and bandages and tourniquets, still another half-tub filled with warm water was placed to take the coldness from the knives and saws before they entered flesh.

Forward the old gunner, having seen to the damp furze screens all around the hatchways up which his cartridges would be passed, and more damp screens before the entrances to the magazines themselves, was busy filling flannel cartridges with powder, helped by a little band of his mates, stacking them carefully inside the copper-lined door.

Above on the maindeck alternate cannon had been loaded with one ball additional to the one they always had in them at sea; the others had one round shot, one grape. By the side between each gunport was a half-tub of salt water in case of fire, and by each breech, but placed out of range of possible leaping, another half-tub of water with lighted slow matches stuck in the rim in case the lock failed. A third bucket contained fresh water for refreshing the crew. Nettings of wads were placed handy between the guns, and the rammers, sponges and worms laid in parallel on the deck, handles inboard as if at drill; the ends of all the tackles were neatly flaked, the flints carefully placed and adjusted in the locks, the tompions removed from the mouths which poked outboard; all that was needed before firing was the correct adjustment to the quoins for horizontal aim. The deck had been wet and sprinkled with sand, hoses were uncoiled like snakes over the hatch gratings; the pumps were rigged.

Similar preparations were visible on the fo'c'sle and quarterdeck for the carronade batteries, and the small arms had been laid inboard of them for the boarders. Above, the yards had been slung with chains and further secured against falling by stoppers to their halyards so that if cut lower down by shot they would still hold. Buckets of water had been prepared on hoists so that the sails could be wet down just before the action.

Meanwhile Lawrence, fearing once more that he might be following the *Shannon* into a trap, rounded to and lay pointing northwesterly towards Salem, and fired a gun. Broke had the *Shannon* brought to in the same direction and hove all aback, and fired a gun in reply. He discussed with the officers whether they were far enough from the harbour, but decided that as there was still plenty of daylight left it would be advisable to try and draw the *Chesapeake* still farther out. So when Lawrence, apparently satisfied with Broke's action, put his helm up and filled again, standing towards him, Broke did the same and continued running seawards.

By this time, about 4 o'clock, *Shannon* had run some fifteen miles from Boston, which was quite out of sight astern. Broke, his table and canvas screen cleared from the quarterdeck, shortly decided that the time was suitable for allowing the *Chesapeake* to close, and he ordered the t'gallants to be taken in and the staysails lowered. The hands were piped to grog and afterwards, while the strong spirit seered down their throats, the kids were brought up from the manger and thrown overboard. He watched the poor things struggling as they drifted astern.

The *Chesapeake* was barely four miles away, and closing the gap of

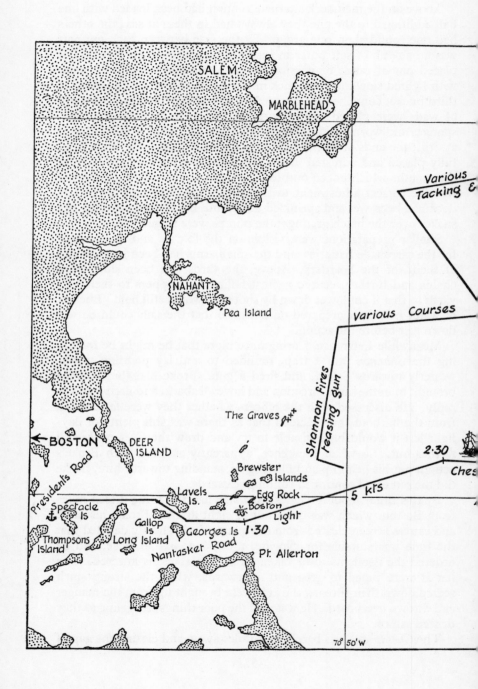

SALEM

MARBLEHEAD

Various
Tacking &

NAHANT

Pea Island

Various Courses

The Graves

Shannon Fires
teasing gun

BOSTON   DEER
               ISLAND

2·30

Ches

President's Road

Spectacle
Is.

Lavels
Is.

Brewster
Islands

Egg Rock
Boston
Light

5 kts

Thompsons
Island

Gallop
Is

Long Island

Georges Is

1·30

Nantasket Road

Pt. Allerton

70° 50′W

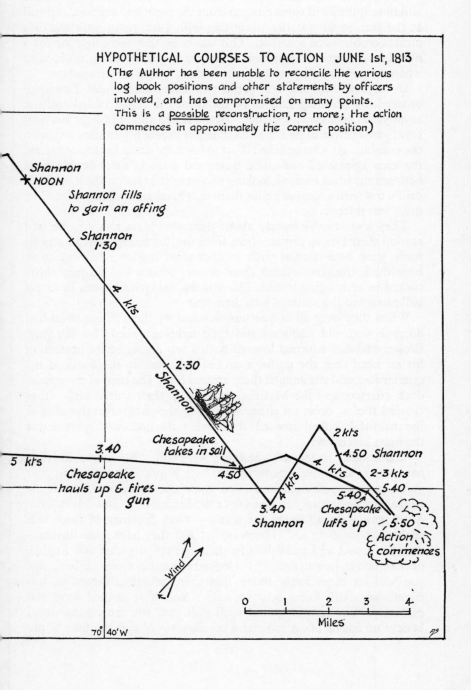

HYPOTHETICAL COURSES TO ACTION JUNE 1st, 1813
(The Author has been unable to reconcile the various
log book positions and other statements by officers
involved, and has compromised on many points.
This is a _possible_ reconstruction, no more; the action
commences in approximately the correct position)

Shannon
× NOON

Shannon fills
to gain an offing

Shannon
× 1·30

4 kts

× 2·30

Shannon

Chesapeake
takes in sail

2 kts

5 kts   3.40   ·4.50 Shannon

Chesapeake   4.50   4 kts   2-3 kts
hauls up & fires   5.40
gun   4 kts

3.40   5.40   Chesapeake
Shannon   luffs up   5·50

Action
commences

Wind

0   1   2   3   4
Miles

70° 40' W

blue water steadily. Her cloud of canvas was broken gaily by the red and blue splashes of three ensigns from the main and mizzen, and still at the fore royal was the white flag with FREE TRADE AND SAILOR'S RIGHTS emblazoned across it. This was what they were fighting for – not the economists' definition – simply the freedom to trade with whatever country they wished without the fear of impressment.

By 4.50 *Chesapeake* was some two miles astern and Lawrence ordered his studding sails to be taken in, the royals furled and the royal yards sent down on deck. Broke noted this, but kept his own royal yards across as he expected the light breeze might die away with the evening. At 5.10 he asked Watt to have the drum beat to quarters; the men assembled and stood quiet and grim in their double rows between the black cannon, looking almost as they had at the morning's drill – but with a tension about them that had been lacking then. The quiet was intense.

They had scarves loosely about their shoulders ready to be tied around their ears to protect them from the shattering blast in action; some were bare-chested with another scarf holding their white or blue duck trousers around their waists, others had striped shirts tucked in or hanging outside like smocks, everything clean in case a ball ploughed the material into their flesh.

When they were all at quarters watched by their officers who had donned worn old uniforms and their fighting swords for the fray, Broke, who had adorned himself with a top hat as better protection for his head than the uniform cocked hat, went to the break of the quarterdeck and summoned them around him. The men of the upper-deck quarters and the Marines, brilliant in their scarlet and white-crossed tunics, drew up either side along the gangways, the men of the maindeck looked upwards from below the boats and spars across the open hatchway.

"Shannons," he started when they were still. "Shannons, the time has come to show the superiority you have acquired in managing your guns, and in marksmanship. You know the Americans have lately triumphed on several occasions over the British flag. But this will not daunt you – we all know the truth – 'twas disparity of force that enabled them to do so." He paused. "But they have gone further – they have said and published in their newspapers that the English have forgotten how to fight." He looked around at them. "Shannons, you will let them know today that there are Englishmen in this frigate who still know how to fight. You have drilled long and earnestly. You have acquired such skill with the great guns that I believe no frigate afloat can stand beside you. *Now* is the time to put that drill to the test of action. Throw no shot away. Aim every one. Keep cool. Work steadily. Fire into her quarters – maindeck to maindeck, quarterdeck to quarterdeck. Don't try to dismast her. Kill the men and the ship is yours."

The sailors growled their appreciation. Broke held up a hand.

"And if it comes to close quarters, don't hit them about the head for they have steel caps on. Give it them through the body."

The low growl broke out again. Broke raised his voice, "You know the day – 'tis the glorious first of June. And I have great hopes of adding another shining laurel to it for I have no doubts that we will triumph. Remember your comrades – from the *Guerriere*, from the *Macedonian* and from the *Java* – you have the blood of *hundreds* to avenge today. The eyes of all Europe are upon you."

There was complete silence as Broke mentioned the three British frigates that had been lost, and now several of these sturdy sailormen around him wept openly with emotion.

One of them named Jacob West, who had been in the *Guerriere* when she was taken and subsequently repatriated and drafted to the *Shannon*, raised his voice, "Sir, I hope you will give us revenge for the *Guerriere* today."

"You shall have it, my man," Broke replied. "Now go quietly to your quarters. And don't cheer!"

The men dispersed back to their guns, the waisters and idlers to their stations for manning the braces, and the Marines drew up along either gangway, musquets held loosely. Broke stationed two of the *Shannon*'s Quartermasters at the weather spokes of the wheel, and a man named James Reader, alias Adam Read (a recaptured British sailor), at the lee wheel, making certain that a chance shot would not leave the steering unattended. Then he walked forward to his 9-pounder swivel crews and instructed them to concentrate on the American wheel. "She must not get away!"

The *Chesapeake* was well within range now but Lawrence was careful to keep just clear of the *Shannon*'s wake so that no guns would bear on her. She had shortened to fighting canvas and was coming on at between 3 and 4 knots under full topsails, foretopmast staysail and jib alone. Lawrence's men were waiting quietly at their quarters. Earlier there had been grumbling about the prize money owing, but Lawrence had sent them down to the purser by twos and threes to collect cheques, and calling them together had addressed them from the quarterdeck as Broke had addressed his people. After stirring their imagination and confidence by reciting the unbroken list of American frigate successes he had ended with a telling reference to his own latest victory. "*Peacock* her, my lads," he had finished, "*Peacock* her!" The Americans stood to their guns, certain that they would do just that. And it was very plain to them that 'Captain Jim' intended going in to close quarters straightaway, for he had instructed his Lieutenants to add canister and bar shot to the one round, one grape already in the guns.

Broke now shortened to single-reefed topsails and jib and lay the *Shannon* to with the wind just forward of the starboard beam. The jib was allowed to shiver, and the mainyard being braced square the maintopsail was shivering so that she barely had steerage way under the fore and mizzen-topsails alone. The spanker was held simply by the throat brail, ready to drop in an instant should they need leverage at the stern to turn her up into the wind quickly, and the cro'jack braces were manned. She lay like a wary fighter waiting to respond to whatever her opponent attempted.

The quiet minutes drew out agonisingly. The *Chesapeake*'s masts stood taller as she walked down towards the *Shannon*'s taffrail at a fine angle from the starboard quarter. Every detail was bright and clear. Her three ensigns and the motto flew gaily to leeward. The sun picked out the barrels of the Marines' rifles along the spar deck, and more rifles in the tops which were crowded with faces peering towards *Shannon*. The rigging was taut and through its tresses and furled canvas there was a clear view to the quarterdeck and the wheel and Captain Lawrence, standing high on a gun slide, tall and unmistakable in cocked hat, heavy gold epaulettes, snowy shirt above his best blue coat laced with gold and buttoned across his chest; he had dressed himself carefully for the occasion, his hair was braided in a queue and tied with black ribbon. His First Lieutenant, Augustus Ludlow, Sailing Master, White, and the Midshipmen aides stood near by.

Broke in his tall hat, with Watt close beside him, stood right aft at the *Shannon*'s taffrail watching the American vessel closely and trying to fathom which side she would attack. There were three courses open to her: first and most unlikely she could luff up suddenly and bring her port broadside to bear before the *Shannon* could answer with her full broadside – but she was coming too slowly to do this without risk of hanging in irons, especially if a chance shot carried away some vital rigging. Her most likely course would be to put her wheel up and come under the *Shannon*'s stern to rake. Alternatively she could come fairly alongside with her port bow ranging up the *Shannon*'s starboard quarter.

Broke's best plan according to accepted doctrine was to wear while she made her approach and try and half rake with the port broadside as she conformed – fractionally later – to his movement. Dacres had done this as the *Constitution* bore down upon him. Broke dismissed it; he knew the value of keeping his ship steady for his gunners to take good aim, and he had little faith in raking fire from a ship under way and swinging. Besides, this would throw the ships into action at comparatively long range, and the last thing he wanted was a man-oeuvring match which might leave him dismasted so close to his enemy's base and at this late hour. He wanted to draw Lawrence fairly alongside yardarm to yardarm where the ferocity of the close action would tell in favour of the ship with superior drill and discip-line; he expected this must be *Shannon*.

"Close quarters was always Captain Broke's teaching – his wish – his hope and his principle. It is then that every element in a sea fight even to the noise, the smoke and confusion has its greatest effect to weaken the energies and overpower the martial faculties of the enemy . . ." (Captain, former Midshipman, R. H. King.)

So he left his wheel steady and his jib and mainsail shivering, offering his barely moving frigate to Lawrence from whichever side he chose to take her, challenging him similarly to dispense with opening manoeuvres – but watching closely nevertheless, ready to meet whatever movement he chose.

Louisa and the children would be fast asleep in Suffolk now, oblivious of this strange exultation of his . . .

"Sir, may'nt we have three ensigns" – it was one of the carronade hands near by, his voice heavy with restrained excitement – "like she has, sir?"

Broke turned and glanced briefly up at the *Shannon*'s single, faded blue ensign fluttering from the gaff.

"No. One is sufficient." He added, "We have ever been an un-pretending ship." But he called out to the Scot who was captain of the mizzentop, "Make fast a stop at each side of the flag!"

When he turned to observe the American frigate again it appeared that she had put her helm up. Watt said, "She's bearing up to rake!" Broke called out for the jib to be sheeted in and the wheel starboarded, and walking forward with his speaking trumpet, called down to the gun deck through the open skylight which normally served his cabin, telling the men to lie down on deck. "Stand by for raking fire from aft!"

Whether Lawrence intended to rake, but thought better of it when he saw the *Shannon* coming round to answer him, or whether it was just a temporary adjustment in his line of approach, he almost immediately resumed his former course. Broke, watching carefully, did likewise. Now he knew he had his man; he had accepted the challenge. He was going to run alongside! To make their speeds more nearly equal therefore he ordered the maintopsail braced sharp up so that it would fill like the fore and mizzen, and then walking to his skylight again, called out to his maindeck gunners to fire when they bore on the *Chesapeake*'s second maindeck port from forward. Wallis at the after quarters and Falkiner forward had the quoins of the starboard battery set to give horizontal fire to windward under the present easy press of the topsails.

Broke, meanwhile, walked forward towards the starboard gangway and stood in the open entrance port where he had a clear view around his vessel over the waist hammocks, and would be able to see his first guns taking effect. His every action had been under the keenest surveillance from the silent, waiting men of the upper-deck quarters. Now one of them named Rowlands, who had been in the *Guerriere* when taken and was craning over the canvas screen around the maintop to get a better view, was so delighted with Broke's calm and self possession and the precision of his orders that he ejaculated, "Ah, that's the man for me. She's ours!" And picking up his musket from where he had laid it, he concentrated on the American frigate, now nearly upon them.

Lawrence was bringing her up in fine style. Aware of all eyes from the small spectator craft which had caught up to within a mile or two while the frigates shortened sail – conscious like a sportsman on a home pitch of their admiration and support, he carried his ship up and almost aboard the *Shannon*'s quarter with their plaudits ringing in imagination. This was how the *Hornet* had made her approach to the kill – "*Peacock* her, my lads!" – but he was coming in closer even than that, buoyed up by thoughts of another quick and shattering victory. His Marines were waiting in orderly ranks. He aimed to give them every opportunity with their rifles.

Stephen Decatur: "Lawrence had no talk, but he inspired all about him with ardor; he always saw the best thing to be done, and he knew the best way to execute it, and he had no more dodge in him than the mainmast."

Lawrence held on as close as good seamanship allowed without danger of an accidental collision; his bowsprit reached out almost to the *Shannon*'s taffrail. He noted the worn and pealing paint below her gunports, the streaks of rust down from the sills and channels, the patched sails, the faded Union flag at the fore royal, the old blue ensign at the gaff, the jollyboat swaying slowly in the smooth of her wake – another tired craft, too long on the station?

He called out, "Luff her!"

The Quartermaster lent his weight to the spokes. The *Chesapeake*'s bow swung up into the wind paralleling *Shannon*'s course with only 40 yards separating them laterally. The American company roared out three cheers which struck fiercely across the small gap of water to the British as if they were already aboard.

The Shannons gave no reply; it was one of Broke's peculiarities to insist on silence in action as well as drill so that orders might not be misheard. So they waited quietly, screwing their courage in the awful stillness before the holocaust broke, holding tight lips, tight nerves, expecting a fierce contest but determined not to submit – tight scarves drawn about their ears, they watched the gun captains bending over the sights all down the starboard battery, all the guns laid precisely horizontal for the slight list – "Throw no shot away. Aim every one. Keep cool. Work steadily. Fire into her quarters – maindeck to maindeck, quarterdeck to quarterdeck. Don't try to dismast her. Kill the men and the ship is yours. The eyes of all Europe are upon you . . ."

The ripple of water from the bow of the American could be heard distinctly through the ports as they waited. Billy Mindham, captain of the aftermost maindeck gun, suddenly saw her martingale stays down to the dolphin striker showing very close against the bright afternoon, passing slowly forward across his sights, then the dark stem with leaves picked out in gold chasing up to the proud black scroll of the fiddlehead, the broad yellow band leading down from it around the curve of the bow, down to the level of the gunport sills as she came on – he could see each plank and fastening clearly, each scratch in the fresh paint carved in his retina. As the first bridle port moved across the barrel of his piece, the dispart stood fairly in its centre. He felt a tight ball of excitement in his throat; they had her! *Shannon* was quite steady under the easy canvas, the guns were exactly lined for height – this was ten times easier than practice at a mark . . .

He could see the second port with the muzzle of its gun poking through – now! He jerked the lanyard, the lock snapped, splutter of powder, sparks upwards and the great breech came leaping towards him like thunder, smoke clouding back through the port and blinding all view. As the trucks thumped to the deck and the tackle men hauled frantically taut he heard the aftermost carronade go off just above his head, and then a fraction later there was a roar from his left hand as the thirteenth maindeck gun came on target. There was a choking smell in his nostrils, fighting blood rushing to his head.

Broke, standing above in the open gangway port in his tall hat, watching the shadow of the *Chesapeake* making long, clear patterns of masts and rigging and deep sails across the smooth water just astern of him and up his beloved *Shannon*'s weathered quarter to the canvas over the hammock nettings, saw his first two maindeck shots splintering home right on target. He was aware of the crackling of small arms from the American Marines and the scream of a ball through the air, then his own twelfth maindeck gun went off and almost simultaneously the second carronade from the stern. He left the entrance port and walked back up the quarterdeck, satisfied that his broadside was horizontal and all guns would be effective; as he went he noticed the *Chesapeake*'s jib suddenly lose its wind and shiver slack – the sheet had been cut already.

Forward in the American frigate the execution was dreadful. Most of the gun's crew, standing by the right of the foremost gun which was the *Shannon*'s point of aim, were dead or injured. Some had been laid flat against the timbers of the manger, pieces of others were blown straight across to the opposite port. The Lieutenant of the first division, Budd, together with other survivors, pulled the bodies clear so that the gun could be fired, despatched the wounded down to the cockpit, the dead into the sea.

As the *Chesapeake* ranged up with almost a knot superior speed, so the destruction spread aft. The two balls or ball and grape crashing from each methodically aimed British gun in turn, travelling comparatively slowly before their charges of old and often damp and clogging powder, smashed through the side timbers spreading jagged, flying splinters and mowing the guns' crews down. Above them the British carronades, loaded with one round and one grape each, were spreading equal destruction along the upper deck and gangway, and the 9-pounders detailed by Broke for dismantling the wheel had already despatched the original Quartermaster. Another had taken his place. Captain Lawrence himself had a musquet ball in his leg from one of the topmen; his snowy white breeches were spreading with red.

He realised that he had too much speed, a situation aggravated by the fact that his canvas was now blanketing the *Shannon*'s and further increasing the difference in their rates of sailing, and he ordered the wheel put down for a pilot's luff, a temporary yaw into the wind to shiver the sails and take the way off. This manoeuvre was helped by the loss of wind from his jib, and the *Chesapeake* turned away, veering her stern half towards the *Shannon*. All her guns were in bearing by now, and the comparatively unhurt midships and after crews had begun firing with an accuracy in training to equal the *Shannon*'s own – but being lee guns and without the meticulous arrangements for horizontal fire that obtained in the British ship, too many went below the maindeck and banged against the copper exposed above the waterline. A number took effect among the guns' crews though, bringing death and splinters, the sudden shock of wounds, smashed bone and muscle, limbs flying and blood pulsing through clean cloth, spreading, tacky under boots and bare feet.

The immaculate silence which had been observed as at drill disintegrated into a grunting, oathing, even cheering confusion of sound as the crews reloaded feverishly and the tackle men hauled the great pieces out with a run.

"Now such a leaping, tugging, clattering of ropes and grumbling of blocks as if all the tenants of the lower regions, black from the smoke, had broken loose and gone mad. More smoke bursting forth from the many black iron mouths and whirling rapidly in thick rings, til it swells outside into hills and mountains, through which the sharp red tongue of death darts, flash after flash, and mingling fire and smoke slowly rolls upwards like a curtain in awful beauty, and exhibits the glistening water and the hulls of the combatants beneath, while the lofty mastheads and points of yard-arms seem as if cut away from the bodies to which they belong, and sustained or resting on the ridges of the dense and massy vapours alone. And amid the breaks in the cannon's peal the shrieks and cries of the wounded mingling with the deep roar of the outpoured and constantly reiterrated hurra, hurra, hurra, sweep over the sea. Sulphur and fire, agony, death and horror are riding and revelling on its bosom; yet how gently playful is its face . . ."

In brief intervals when the piled up smoke blew clear, the marksmen in the *Shannon*'s tops had vivid glimpses down on the American's upper deck; the planking was scarcely visible – "the hammocks, splinters and wreck of all kinds driven across the deck formed a complete cloud". The American Marine Officer, Lieutenant James Broom, and the Sailing Master, William White, were taken off as also were two Midshipmen and a number of Marines, and Lawrence, having limped down from his gun slide, leant on the binnacle for support. Two of his helmsmen had been killed and a third was at the wheel.

The easy peacock had turned into a hawk with red claws.

Down below on his gun deck the Fourth Lieutenant fell mortally

167

wounded, and forward in the first division, whose guns were now out of bearing, Lieutenant Budd realised with a shock of horror that out of some one hundred and fifty men who had started the action on the gun deck only about fifty remained on their feet working their pieces.

As the *Chesapeake* continued to turn up into the wind most of her shot struck forward in the *Shannon*. Thomas Selby, Able Seaman on the fo'c'sle, had his head smashed from his body, Neil Gilchrist was cut in two by a 32-pounder ball, Thomas Barry, a young lad, was taken off by a star shot across his middle. A 32-pounder carronade ball struck a case of shot for the *Shannon*'s 12-pounder which was stowed in the main chains, driving it through the timbers to scatter like lead hail across the gun deck. The Shannons moved their wounded from the danger space by the leaping cannon and into the arms of the sick-bay party, pitched the lifeless through the ports and found themselves caught up in a primaeval lust for killing which swept the quarters like a red cloud, turning them berserk; they cheered and yelled obscenities, dripping sweat as they worked mindlessly with superhuman frenzy, at the tackles and sponges and rammers whose feel and motion they knew as well as their own leathery palms.

"It is a delirium of joy, a very fury of delight! And that loud, exulting shout again announces more destruction, more human slaughter . . . the bustle, halooing, hurraing, crashing, thundering, whizzing and whistling made me drunk and delirious like a fellow in a tavern who smashes tables and chairs, dishes and glasses, dashes his fists through the doorpanels and the windows all senseless of the scarifying and bruises he inflicts upon himself . . ."

The *Shannon* reeled and shook to the discharge of her own guns and the occasional staggering shock of the enemy's blows as the *Chesapeake*'s well-drilled crews, decimated as some were, still poured in a ragged volley from the midships and after guns.

On the American quarterdeck the third helmsman fell, and the wheel itself was smashed and the tiller ropes cut by Broke's dismantling guns. The *Chesapeake*, out of control and with the helm still slightly alee, continued to luff into the wind, helped round by her spanker, whose brails had been shot away so that the canvas blew out and flattened against the mizzen-rigging. The foretopsail halyard had also been cut by a shot, and the yard having no chain slings or preventer ties – a sign of careless overconfidence perhaps – had fallen on the lifts and shivered the canvas; her head turned away farther from the *Shannon*.

Broke, seeing this, and thinking amidst the smoke and deafening confusion that she was trying to disengage, ordered the wheel down to chase her, then walked forward to direct the 9-pounders to aim for the *Chesapeake*'s head yards, not realising that these had already been disabled. As he passed by the main shrouds, lifting his leg high over an obstacle on deck, a 32-pounder ball from the *Chesapeake* knocked a monkeytail from the 9-pounder swivel and flew on, according to witnesses, between his legs. The captain of the gun, Driscoll, fell to the deck with both kneecaps fractured and driven upwards by the flying metal. He was carried to the mainmast where he sat weeping with mortification at being thrown out of the fight. The loader of the same gun received a grape shot just below his stomach which caused him dreadful agony. He loaded the gun nevertheless, then fell to the deck in torment, beseeching anyone near by to put a hand into the wound and remove the shot. "I shall do well enough if you will only do that." He died later.

By now all the *Shannon*'s aftermost guns were out of bearing as the *Chesapeake*, despite her luff, had surged on past them. The carronade crews from the quarterdeck had consequently left their pieces at a word from Broke, picked up muskets and swarmed forward on to the booms and the boats, from where they started firing over the heads of their own Marines drawn up along the gangway into the blue mass of the opposing Marines.

Their fire winged diagonally across the American decks as the *Chesapeake*'s totally unbalanced canvas accelerated her turn into the wind. Her yards were caught aback. The canvas slapped loosely against the masts and she lost way, then started drifting astern, back towards her eager adversary. Broke's Second Lieutenant of Marines, John Law, saw her approaching through the smoke clouding up from the forward guns and, hoping to get some orders for his division, which was still drawn up out of the fight on the disengaged gangway, observed to Broke that she was preparing to board.

"No, sir," Broke replied. "She is crippled and cannot help herself." Nevertheless he ordered Law to move his men on to the fo'c'sle. Then, directing his forward carronades to fire among the massed American Marines, he ordered the helm up and the mizzen-topsail to be shivered in an attempt to throw the *Shannon* away from the approaching stern of the other. She was helpless in irons and he wanted to pour in more shot before there was any question of boarding. Unfortunately the *Shannon*'s jib stay was parted by a shot at this moment, and she fell off very slowly.

On the wreck-strewn quarterdeck of the *Chesapeake* Lawrence realised that his ship was falling foul of the Britisher and ordered the boarders up. Lieutenant Ludlow yelled down through the hatchway; Midshipman William E. McKinney, a bare fourteen years old, scampered down the main ladder and went forward to tell Lieutenant Budd at the first division, then worked his way aft, piping out his instructions to Lieutenant Cox of the second division, and calling out to the third division, whose aftermost guns were still in bearing and firing. Meanwhile another of Lawrence's aides, Curtis, was trying to find the Negro bugler, William Brown. This man, who had no duty in action save to stand with his bugle at the break of the quarterdeck, a passive spectator of the wreck and carnage, had not unnaturally tried to find shelter from the musquetry sweeping the deck, and was crouching under the disengaged side of the long boat which was stowed in its chocks just three feet forward of his duty position. When Curtis at last found him after searching right forward along the gangways he yelled at him to blow – blow for the boarders – but the wretched man was so terrified or stupefied by the noise and frantic confusion that he just crouched there, trembling. Curtis left and ran down the main hatchway to call the boarders by word of mouth.

The confusion was, if anything, worse below. The *Shannon*'s maindeck fire was half raking from the port quarter as the *Chesapeake* hung in the wind, drifting down towards the muzzles. Lawrence's stern windows had been beaten in and the fir beams and timbers had been shivered into clouds of splinters bringing death and terror to the men of the after quarters, who had been virtually untouched at the commencement of the action. The men of the first division, up forward, who had taken the first brutal assault of the *Shannon*'s guns one after the other in methodical progression up her side, and whose own guns had been out of bearing for some minutes, had no work to take their minds off the crashes and screams from aft, and were either lying on deck to try to escape the fire or crowding over to the disengaged starboard side, where they took refuge by the galley. A few men from the comparatively unhurt second division in the waist had followed their Lieutenant, Cox, as he rushed for the main hatchway with drawn sword crying "Boarders away!" but most were retiring to starboard and mingling with the beaten men of the first division.

There was also a steady stream of wounded being taken below to the cockpit. Lieutenant Ludlow, hit by a musquet ball, was among them, leaving Lawrence, the only officer on the upper deck – apart from some Midshipmen forward. Already Lieutenant Ballard of the third division, which was now taking the hardest pounding, had been carried below by his Midshipmen, Horatio Baty.

Lieutenant Cox, meanwhile, gained the quarterdeck only to find that his Captain had been hit with a second musket ball, this time a desperate wound just above the groin, and was clinging painfully to the binnacle to keep himself upright. Cox, who had been with Lawrence all his sea life and who had the same affection and respect for him as Broke's sea children for their Captain, sheathed his sword and ordering the men behind him to "Rush on!" hurried to hold up his Captain. Lawrence asked him to show him the way to the cockpit, and Cox, helped by two sailors, took him painfully to the ladder and down. As they reached the gun deck Lawrence recognised his young aide, McKinney, and called out to him to hurry up the boarders.

On the *Chesapeake*'s fo'c'sle the Boatswain, Adams, had been mortally wounded; Midshipman John D. Fisher had rushed aft on first hearing the call for boarders, but seeing no signs of an organised body of men there, simply a few leaderless individuals held in an enfilading fire from the whole length of the *Shannon*, and a few carronade men valiantly working their pieces through the roar and the smoke, which had practically obliterated their opponent, he thought a mistake must have been made, and returned forward again. Here he found that an order had been passed to board the fore tack and hall aft the head sheets to shoot the ship clear. The wounded Adams growled, "They are shot away!"

But it was too late anyway. The *Chesapeake* had been increasing her pace astern, and now her wrecked port quarter gallery crunched against the *Shannon*'s timbers in the way of the fifth maindeck gun from forward, and the fluke of the *Shannon*'s working anchor, which had been stowed on the gangway to be out of the way, tore in and held. At the same time the American's spanker boom swung over the *Shannon*'s Marines, lined up two or three deep and still firing as fast as they could load. Broke's Boatswain Stevens, hurried to lash the boom inboard to keep the ships together.

Broke, meanwhile, had been leading a charmed life. Having narrowly missed the ball and monkeytail that put Driscoll out of the fight, missed all the American Marines' rifle balls aimed at his tall hat, he had been standing beside his clerk, John Dunn, and his purser, George Aldham, and the Marine Sergeant, Molyneux, when shot from one of the American's after carronades had struck the bow of the launch just forward of him and knocked a cloud of splinters away to leeward, temporarily halting the Marines of the second division, who were still moving along the port gangway in orderly fashion to take up station on the fo'c'sle. Almost immediately afterwards another of the American carronades erupted only feet away, knocking in the hammocks just by him and swathing both Dunn and Aldham to the deck with pockets of grape across their lower stomachs and hips. They lived scarcely an hour afterwards.

Broke was not conscious of his near escapes as, standing on a fo'c'sle carronade slide, he peered over to try and ascertain the situation on the *Chesapeake*'s decks. He had no intention of boarding her himself, but he suddenly realised that there was no one opposed to him. The American Marines had long been in an intolerable position massed on the gangways under the concentrated, half-raking fire of grape from the *Shannon*'s forward carronades as well as the *Shannon*'s first division of Marines and the guns' crews of the after quarters in the boats above them, besides the expert and chosen marksmen from the tops; now those that remained, officerless, were falling back on the fo'c'sle. The guns' crews of the *Chesapeake*'s after carronades were also dispersing forward in smoke caused by a grenade which had exploded the arms chest by the American's mizzen and spread flame briefly up the luff of the spanker.

Now the quarterdeck lay just four feet from him – practically deserted!

As he saw all this through the thinning smoke a sailor just forward came to the same conclusion and leaped up on to the fo'c'sle hammock cloth shouting, "Captain Broke, now is a fine time to board her, for damn the man that's alive on her quarterdeck." He crossed over to the *Chesapeake*'s bulwarks, but a shot from a stalwart American Marine dropped him.

Broke saw the opportunity to board was fleeting: the ships were touching at a small point only, and the *Chesapeake*'s head was being blown round before the wind. Her yards were still braced sharp up and directly her sails filled she would tear herself away from the lashings Stevens was putting on the spanker boom. There wasn't a moment to be lost; he must throw as many men over as possible in the brief time they had. He was the nearest.

Dropping his speaking trumpet, he drew his sword and crying, "Follow me who can!" climbed to the working anchor, thence over the hammocks just abaft the fo'c'sle bulwarks and down on to the protruding muzzle of the *Chesapeake*'s deserted aftermost carronade, using it as a step up to the hammocks atop her bulwarks. Then he dropped down on to the enemy quarterdeck.

Sergeant Molyneux followed close behind, and William Stack, his coxswain, and Bill Mindham, captain of the aftermost maindeck gun long since out of bearing; several others were swarming over the bulwarks with cutlasses, and more creeping and running along the

172

spanker boom from out of the boats where they had been firing musquets. An Irish sailor named James Bulger leaped over without any weapons at all, realising through the red haze over his brain that there would be arms aplenty on the enemy's deck; the first thing he saw was a boarding pike, and seizing it, he went roaring after the others who were following the shiny black hat of their Captain. Lieutenant Charles Falkiner, who had come up from the gun deck as the ships fell together, saw his opportunity and jumped across, so did Lieutenant Watt, after seizing the white ensign which he always laid ready to hand across the capstan before going into action.

Broke, running forward on the deserted, blood- and wreck-strewn quarterdeck, saw a lone figure by the mizzen standing his ground and pointing a pistol at him. He brought his sword up in a swinging back-hand cut and laid the man's pistol arm open against the mast, then ran on towards the port gangway, towards the inert forms of Marines, and others who were lying wounded and had thrown their arms from them.

Some way ahead of him a small American party rallied on the fo'c'sle and prepared to face the attack.

Down below in the stench, blood and dim, wavering light, groans and involuntary sharp cries of the mutilated lined sitting and lying before the entrance to the cockpit, the surgeon, John Dix, hurried to Captain Lawrence as he was supported in great pain down to the stanchions at the foot of the ladder. Lawrence called for his aides. "Tell the men to fire faster! Don't give up the ship!" They carried him straight to the operating table. "Doctor," he said, "go on deck and tell the commanding officer to fight the ship till she sinks." He countermanded the order immediately and told the surgeon's assistant to send the loblolly boy instead.

Lieutenant Cox, having left him at the ladder, returned to the maindeck fired by his spirit, and seeing that the after guns still bore against the *Shannon*'s side, helped Midshipman Russell, alone at the thirteenth gun, to depress and fire it. Then they both went to the fourteenth gun and fired that. There was no one else; the men had either been driven from their quarters by the terrible pounding and splinters or had gone up at the cry of boarders.

Lieutenant Ludlow, although wounded and receiving attention in the cockpit as the ships fell together, led a number of them in a rally up the main hatchway and succeeded in pushing a party of Shannons, following in the rear of Broke, back as far as the binnacle before another wave of oathing, yelling Englishmen came storming over the hammocks with pikes and cutlasses and forced them to retreat again.

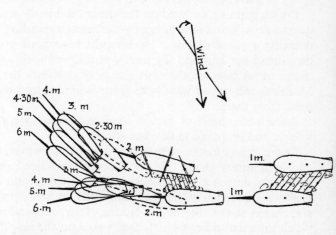

AUTHOR'S RECONSTRUCTION (FROM EXCEPTIONALLY CON
EVIDENCE) OF COURSE OF THE ACTION. JUNE 1st

Wind

4.30m
4.m
5m
6m
3. m
2·30 m
2 m
1m.
3 m
4. m
5.m
6·m
2.m
1m

Shannon   3 kts at start
Chesapeake   4 kts at start

5·50 p.m. 0m   Shannon's 14th main deck gun fires

5· 51   1m   Firing general.

5·52   2m   Chesapeake starts pilots' luff - squares mainyard
                Shannon's speed has been reduced by her sails being
                blanketed by Chesapeake.

5·52½   2m 30secs (pecked outlines) Shannon, believing Chesapeake
                to be disengaging, follows her into wind. Speed
                further reduced by blanketing from Chesapeake.

5·53   3m   Chesapeake continues luff into wind out of control.
                Much reduced headway by squared main yard

CHESAPEAKE
4 kts.

SHANNON
3 kts

0 m

0 m

5.54 p.m   4 m   Chesapeake stops in wind and starts drifting astern
                   and crabwise. Shannon shivers mizzen topsail and
                   attempts to keep away, but by now she is making little
                   headway, and with the loss of her jib stay she only falls
                   off slowly

5.56   5m)   Chesapeake continues crabwise drift down onto Shannon,
            6m)   who is unable due to loss of headway and blanketting
                   of sails to escape. Chesapeake's quarter strikes 50
                   feet aft from Shannon's bow. Thereafter the
                   Chesapeake is blown round across Shannon's bow.

        0   200   400   600
        |_____|_____|_____| feet

Foremost in the charge was John Collier. He saw an American Marine pointing a rifle as he rushed him, heard the explosion and felt the blast as the ball flew by his ear – there was a cry behind as the next man took the shot in the throat and fell. Collier came on. The Marine threw down his useless rifle and turned and ran. Collier followed him down the starboard gangway towards the fo'c'sle where Broke's small party of boarders, having pressed through a disorderly volley of small-arms fire, was meeting spirited cutlass and bayonet resistance from the Marines and a number of former British sailors who had deserted to the American service; these knew they would tread air at the yardarm if they were captured. Lieutenant Budd had rallied another small party from the gun deck up the fore hatchway, and the fighting was warm.

Then the second wave of English led by Collier rushed into them. The Marine who was being chased jumped through one of the bow ports and climbed down to enter his ship again by the maindeck bridle port; others followed him. Lieutenant Budd received a sabre cut across the arm and fell back down the hatchway he had emerged from.

Aft of them Lieutenant Ludlow had also received a severe cutlass wound, although his was across the head, and he fell; the remnants of his party were fleeing before the blood-maddened Englishmen and the Irish, wild with excitement. James Bulger's American boarding pike was red at the tip; he charged into the fo'c'sle fray mouthing Gaelic execrations – "And then did I not spit them, beJasus!"

Lacking officers, lacking support from below and driven back by the irresistible fury of the boarders, the American resistance fell apart, some bolted out of the carronade ports down over the side like the Marine, others leaped for the fore hatchway and tumbled down.

On the gun deck below, Lieutenant Cox became aware of the commotion from forward as they clattered and fell off the ladder, while others from the gun deck, having removed the gratings from the hatchway down to the berth deck below, jostled each other to get down. The panic was contagious. He ran towards them, drawing his sword.

"You damned cowardly sons of bitches! What are you jumping below for?"

A Midshipman, Higginbotham, who was near by, asked Cox if he should try to stop them by cutting a few down.

Cox looked at the stampede; they were too tightly crowded and too terrorised. "No, sir," he said sadly, "it is of no use."

By this time the American frigate's topsails had filled and torn her away from the lashings which Stevens had been putting on the boom until struck in the arm by grape from the American mizzen-top swivel. Now, leaving some of her port quarter gallery on the fluke of *Shannon*'s work anchor, the *Chesapeake* walked away forward. As her port side crunched against the British fo'c'sle the after end of her foreyard, which was still braced sharp up, came in contact with the forward end of the *Shannon*'s foreyard, which was also braced up sharp, and the Midshipman from the *Shannon*'s foretop, John Smith, seeing the split-second opportunity presented, ran out along the yard and over on to the *Chesapeake*'s. By this time most of the American foretopmen, seeing their fo'c'sle virtually overrun, were fleeing down the shrouds; the sight of Smith storming towards them along their own yard with a French cavalry sabre he had acquired from a captured privateer was enough to persuade the rest to go, and they scampered over the weather side. The last to escape was a large Midshipman wearing enormous fisherman's boots; he jumped for a backstay which had been cut by shot and was dangling over the fo'c'sle, and slid down it. Smith jumped on to the same stay after him and followed him down so closely that they fell on deck together with the American lad underneath. Broke was near by and he put out an arm to restrain Smith as the terrified American tumbled away.

Meanwhile Midshipman Cosnahan, stationed in *Shannon*'s main-top, had found his aim from over the top cloth much impaired by the lower corner of the topsail, and had scrambled down and seated himself astride the mainyard by the slings. From here he had a splendid view of the American mizzen-top, whose seven occupants were keeping up a spirited fire on the British boarders below them. Cosnahan started picking them off one by one, passing his empty musquet up through the lubber's hole into the top after each shot, and receiving another loaded one down. He despatched three Americans in this way, three others fled, but one man, hidden from him by the timber of the lower mast and topmast together, remained firing down on the English boarders. He could not be removed until one of these came running up the shrouds and grappled him with bare hands. After a short struggle the Britisher, who was a large, muscular fellow, shouted, "Stand from under!" and the American sailed from the top and crashed into the starboard quarter boat.

Now, as the *Chesapeake* forged across the *Shannon*'s bow, carrying away the British jib stay, jib, flying jib-boom, spritsail yard and rigging, she ceased to touch the side at any point, and the Marines and others preparing to follow the first boarders found a widening gap of sea preventing them. In all perhaps sixty men, perhaps less, had gained the enemy's deck in the minute or so available. But in the conditions they were enough. The American organisation had been completely shattered by the grape and musquetry sweeping the deck prior to the boarding, and the guns' crews of the maindeck had been demoralised by the raking fire to which most of them had been unable to reply; they had consequently lacked the cool discipline necessary to resist such a ferocious charge as the British made, and since losing both the surviving officers who had attempted a rally, all cohesion was lost. They were simply individuals trying to escape the vengeance which the demonic masks of the boarders promised. As the American frigate sailed herself away from the *Shannon* her upper deck was virtually a British possession.

Broke saw the victory clear cut. He tried to tear his frenzied men from slaughtering the few outnumbered Americans and British deserters who still fought for their lives on the fo'c'sle but as he was concentrated on this, three others, probably those chased down from the foretop by Smith, rushed on him from behind with weapons picked up from the deck. Collier fortunately near by, yelled a warning, and Broke turned in time to knock aside the first thrust from a boarding pike and put his sword through the man. Before he could recover, the second assailant swung a clubbed musquet which knocked off his hat and crashed down on his shoulder, and the third with a sabre dealt him a ferocious cut from half behind on his left, parting his skull down to the brain cavity. Broke, stunned, fell to the deck with blood welling from the wound and down the side of his face and neck. The American was about to finish him off on the deck when a British Marine, John Hill, ran the man through with a bayonet. The other two Americans were making off as the British rallied to their Captain's aid. Collier yelled, "One of them fellows has cut the Captain's head —" and William Stack, Broke's Coxswain, chased the nearest over the booms and despatched him from behind with his cutlass as he was going below. The other was hacked to death by Collier and the other enraged Shannons.

Broke, faint and weak, the whole side of his face, muffler, shirt and uniform red with his own blood all mixed up with the contents of a burst cask of quicklime which lay scattered over the deck, tried to lever himself into a sitting position. Midshipman Smith hurried to help him, as did Bill Mindham, Captain of the fourteenth maindeck gun.

Meanwhile another tragedy had overtaken the British on the quarterdeck. Watt, who had boarded with his white ensign, had been temporarily halted by a shot through the foot as he dropped on to the

American deck. By the time he had recovered himself and gone to the mizzen-halyards to haul down the American flag and raise his ensign over it he found that some other Shannon had beaten him to it, and a small blue ensign was already waving above the 'Stars and Stripes'. Determined on his larger flag, however, he ordered both to be hauled down and was about to bend on the white ensign when a charge of grape from the *Shannon*'s seventh maindeck gun carried off the top of his head and killed and wounded five others among his party. This gun had been engaging the *Chesapeake* through Lawrence's stern windows while the ships had been locked together, and it seems likely that it was elevated and fired into Watt's group as the ships separated because the gunners saw the blue ensign coming down and naturally thought the party must be American. It may simply have been a case of excitement, the lock tripped before the quoin was properly home.

The British recovered quickly from the shock and hauled up the blue ensign again over the 'Stars and Stripes'. Lieutenant Wallis in *Shannon*'s maindeck ordered the cease fire, and went up to the quarterdeck to try to ascertain the position. And forward in the *Chesapeake* Bill Mindham, binding Broke's head with the neckerchief he had been wearing about his own head, drew his Captain's attention to the symbols of victory.

"Look there, sir. There goes the old ensign up over the Yankee colours!"

Then with Smith's help he lifted Broke to his feet and supported him slowly along the gangway to the quarterdeck and sat him down on a carronade slide with his back against the bulwarks.

Meanwhile the boarders had rushed down the main hatchway, chasing a few Americans before them. These had fled on down the steerage ladders while the British made hot forward to where the last of the fo'c'sle party were squeezing down the fore hatchway to the berth deck. Some of these faced them and there was a ragged volley of rifle fire, but the British had their blood up and the scent of victory in their nostrils, and once again the fury of their onslaught drove the unorganised, leaderless Americans back. Both Lieutenants Budd and Ludlow had been taken to the cockpit; after the first few shots there was little resistance.

Captain Lawrence, lying below, heard the rush down the ladders and asked what was happening. On being told that this was the enemy boarding, he cried in an agony of the spirit, "Then blow her up! Blow the ship up!"

Two decks above Broke sat dizzily on the carronade slide suddenly cold in the shade of the bulwarks and faint from loss of blood, but aware through the confusion of shouting and pounding feet, the press of movement, light and colour and the deep, throbbing pain splitting his skull that they had won – *won*. The old blue ensign flew proudly over the Yankee flag – he was sitting on the Yankee quarterdeck – British. He remembered coming aboard – over the hammocks, dropping down on the planks – deserted – only that one strange fellow aiming his pistol at him – it seemed but a moment ago . . .

Midshipman Smith had left him. After cutting the halliards to the main peak so that the last American flag fluttered down from aloft, he had gone below in the wake of the tumultuous boarders. The maindeck that greeted his eye was a terrible scene of ravage. The rays of the low evening sun were striking in diagonally from the port quarter, through the great, shattered windows which had received most of the fire, glinting along the muzzles of the deserted guns, all awry on their split carriages and missing trucks, ropes and side tackles astraggle – sunlight lighting jagged holes in the side timbers where solid shot had entered, brightening the splinters of raw wood. Below, the scuppers were dark with blood; patches and spurts of blood stained the deck and even the beams overhead, and fragments of flesh, scalp skin with pigtails, unrecognisable pieces of gore, slivers of moments-ago living tissue were plastered loosely about the timbers. On the starboard side forward the fingers of a dismembered hand were sticking above a port as if their owner had pushed them through from outboard. Pieces of limbs still covered with clothing, stained deep red through and through were scattered among the wreck and loose ropes on deck as if kicked out of the way, and among them the still forms of those who had been killed in the rush of boarders, and others lying, moving faintly.

Amidst this ghastly scene, which was pointed up by the highlights of bright sun and contrasting shadow, the Shannons moved like tigers, indifferent to or unaware of the carnage, exulting in their success like the victors of a needle match at football. There wasn't a Chesapeake to be seen on his feet. All the Americans had fled or been driven below; the British were securing the gratings over them. Smith, glad of the opportunity to get back into the fresh air, was about to mount the ladder and convey the stirring news to Broke while he still lived when one of the *Shannon's* maindeck guns went off – as it turned out later, by accident – and the ball mowed straight across the deck and through the port-side timbers, fortunately without wounding anyone. He ran to a gunport and cupped his hands over his mouth. "Cease fire! This ship is secured!"

As if to disprove it there was a rifle shot from the berth deck below, and a British Marine, William Young, who was standing guard over the main hatchway, fell mortally wounded. Blood surged up to the dizzy brains of the Shannons, and they pointed their muskets among the penned Americans below them and fired as fast as they could load or find discarded weapons on the deck.

This fresh outbreak of shots and screams shattered the calm of the upper deck, and Broke, now barely conscious from loss of blood, and wavering, ashen-faced, on his carronade slide, asked what was happening. On being told, he directed that the Americans be driven into the hold. It was his last order in the contest; he passed out.

Meanwhile Lieutenant Falkiner, who had been resting on the booms between the gangways to recover his breath after the heady rush and excitement of the fighting, had jumped to his feet at the noise and rushed below. Seeing his men out of control and firing down at the helpless prisoners, he lined his pistol at the head of the nearest and shouted that he would blow out the brains of the next man to fire a shot. In the quiet that followed this announcement he called to the Americans to send up the man who had killed William Young.

"The *Chesapeake* is taken," he added. "We have three hundred men aboard. If there is another act of hostility you will be called up on deck one by one – and shot."

The contest was over. From the time of the first *Shannon* gun until the last mistaken shot through the maindeck it had lasted eleven minutes by Lieutenant Wallis's watch. Wallis had handed it to the gunner, Richard Meehan, as they went to quarters, and the gunner had timed the shots in the security of his magazine below decks.

Both ships had swung round before the wind now and were heading easterly within easy hail of each other, the *Chesapeake* drifting out of control, the *Shannon*, under the command of Lieutenant Wallis, coming up under her lee. The *Shannon*'s jollyboat was hove alongside, a party of Marines and sailors under Lieutenant Johns, R.M., embarked and they pulled across the short space of water and scrambled up the side of the prize shouting greetings and congratulations. As they reached the deck they fell silent. Broke was lying propped half against the bulkhead with a quiet group around him. His face was white beneath its weathering, Mindham's neckerchief, dark with blood over the left side, obscured his forehead and beneath it his red hair was scattered and clotted. Patches of white lime looked like a crude powdering over it.

"He breathes yet," someone said.

They lifted him gently and, slinging ropes under, eased him down into the jollyboat, then pulled back to the *Shannon* and lifted him carefully aboard. His cot was rigged up in the space which had been his cabin, and a canvas screen hurriedly erected around it as a temporary shelter before the partitions were restored. Doctor Jack left his wounded in charge of the assistant surgeon and came up to attend him. Wallis hovered anxiously near by. They removed his stained coat and muffler, his formerly white shirt and Mindham's stiff neckerchief. Jack washed the blood off his face and neck, and parting the tangle of matted hair, gradually revealed a deep cleavage extending for some 4 inches over his left ear towards the corner of his mouth. Between the depressed sides of the wound at the top of his head they could see the outer membrane of his brain pulsing gently.

Wallis was appalled at the severity of the gash; it seemed impossible that Broke could survive. And the doctor gave him no hope. Strong as he was, the Captain's chances were slim indeed.

While undressing him they had found a delicate chain with a blue satin satchel, now tacky with blood, hanging around his neck. Inside was a lock of blonde hair. When they had put clean bandages around his head and settled him back in his cot Wallis took the keepsake down to his cabin and stowed it carefully. He would deliver it to Louisa after Broke died.

CHAPTER EIGHT

THE schooner and small spectator craft which had lain hove to well out of gunshot to windward of the combatants were starting the long beat homeward, their passengers silent, sad and disappointed. They had been unable to comprehend it when the *Chesapeake*'s colours first came down – an American defeat was inconceivable – it was a mistake – it would soon be put to rights. When the British ensign went up a second time and stayed flying over their own as the guns ceased and the smoke drifted away and thinned, the bitter truth could no longer be denied. The *Chesapeake* was beaten – and in scarcely any time at all.

In Boston, whose citizens, lining the roofs in excited anticipation, had been spared this painful sight just over their horizon, the news spread and was received like a bad dream, something insubstantial to be dispersed in the light of the next day. When the dream was confirmed "the whole town became one scene of silence and mourning". The grand celebration supper was cancelled, the silent tables cleared.

The first stories about 'infernal machines' thrown from the British ship, and the rawness of the *Chesapeake*'s crew in contrast to the long-service Shannons, the stories and excuses blossomed out of wounded pride to account for the unprecedented speed of the British victory – indeed the sheer unexpectedness of the victory itself.

Far out in the Bay, as the sun sank and tinged the waters with pale fire, those Shannons fortunate enough to have been spared from shot, splinters, sabre or pike swarmed over the lower rigging of both the scarred ships lying still after the convulsion of battle, and knotted the severed sheets and brails, or rove fresh ones and extemporised shrouds to hold the wounded lower masts. Others sluiced down the slippery red decks below, and tossed the more obvious pieces of flesh and bone over the side. The remaining dead from both vessels were sown up in hammocks with round shot at their feet and committed to the deep. Some of those most seriously wounded, feeling the warmed steel of the surgeons, still perspiring from their butcher's work in the stifling agonies of the cockpits, suffered feverishly envious thoughts of their shipmates who had been carried off quickly. Above them the two rival Captains lay heavily asleep with wounds that had been diagnosed as mortal. Lawrence, his own quarters shattered, lay in the *Chesapeake*'s wardroom; his First Lieutenant, Augustus Ludlow, scarred with a cutlass across his scalp, had been carried across to the *Shannon* and lay one deck below Broke in Watt's old cabin.

The American prisoners penned below the gratings were growling with resentment and defiance, and Lieutenant Falkiner, who had been placed in charge of the prize while Wallis, as senior surviving officer, commanded the *Shannon*, had a number of them brought up one by one under the musquets of the Marines, and manacled, ironically, with handcuffs which Lawrence had shipped in quantity from Boston for use on the British. The men were then transferred to the *Shannon*. When the remainder still showed fight and threatened to break out and blow up or retake the ship, Falkiner had the carpenters cut scuttles in the deck either side of the hatchway and pointed two of their own 18-pounders, loaded with grape, down through the apertures at the mass of malcontents.

The British Marines guarding them amused themselves with jests about the names the Americans gave to their guns. These were engraved in copper on each piece; they read like a roll call of patriotism – now so pathetically thwarted – Brother Jonathan, True Blue, Yankee Protection, Putnam, Raging Eagle, Viper, General Warren, Mad Anthony, America, Washington, Liberty for Ever, Dreadnought, Defiance, Liberty or Death . . .

When the essential work on the shrouds and running rigging had been completed, the two ships set sail and drifted eastwards before a light breeze to make a better offing. The British able-bodied sailors, divided into two parties to man both ships, continued their repairs aloft. The carpenter's gangs manned the pumps and stopped and caulked those low shot holes which were leaking quantites of water into *Shannon*'s bilges. Lieutenant Wallis wrote a brief account of the action in the Log Book; as the Captain's clerk had been killed most details of time ceased at 5.50.

". . . grappled the enemy and boarded him, and after an action of ten minutes succeeded in hauling down his flag, pendant and ensigns. Cleared the enemy and sent the jollyboat to exchange prisoners. In boarding lost the life of Mr. Watt, First Lt., and several men.

"Captain most severely wounded by one of the enemy whilst endeavouring to rescue him from his own men. Could not ascertain our own loss or that of the enemy from the lateness of the evening, and the greater part of the ship's company having boarded the *Chesapeake*. Out yawl (having repaired her) and sent her to exchange prisoners. Found our masts considerably wounded and the rigging and hull of the ship much cut up."

The weary sailors worked throughout the dark hours, "the fact being that our lower rigging was all cut through, and the masts consequently unsupported, so that had any sea been on they would have gone over the side". The *Chesapeake*'s masts had been similarly weakened, most of the lee shrouds having been cut, and even on the disengaged, weather side 8 out of 9 foremast shrouds were gone, 7 out of 10 mainmast and 2 out of the 6 at the mizzen. It was fortunate that the sea remained as calm as it had been throughout the day.

By 4.0 a.m. on the morning of 2nd June as the first light streaked the sky they had made some twenty miles of easting and Wallis, judging this sufficient to be out of immediate danger from any small-boat reprisal parties, hove to and divided the increasingly fractious prisoners more equally between the two vessels.

The *Shannon*'s muster list had been checked off by this time, and it was found that 23 men had been killed and 57 wounded besides the Captain, several of whom, among them the veteran Boatswain, Stevens, had little chance of survival. The Americans had 99 wounded, of whom 46 were classified as severely or dangerously; their loss in dead was at least 48. The total butcher's bill for the action was therefore at the least estimate 228, in itself high for a single-frigate action, but the fact that it had occurred in the space of only 11 minutes raised the encounter to a unique position in Naval warfare: never before had such slaughter been accomplished so quickly. The casualty rate had been over 20 per minute. That most sanguinary encounter between the *Amelia* frigate and *L'Arethuse* which had so pained *The Times* had averaged less than 2 per minute over the period of close action, the *United States/Macedonian* about 2 per minute and the *Constitution/Java* less than 2 per minute during the close action. Thus the *Shannon/Chesapeake* contest was ten times more fearful than any of these. Lawrence's ship had inflicted such casualties as she had in the short space of time allowed her gunners before they were knocked out of the fight by the *Chesapeake*'s superior sailing speed and then her luff; this is conclusive evidence that she had been a most worthy opponent for Broke and the Shannons.

For nine, wearisome, sea-going years Broke had been waiting, hoping, dreaming, praying, continually seeking for a chance of glory; when at last he forced the chance he had a spirited opponent in Lawrence. And together they produced the most shattering frigate action in history.

.   .   .

A light breeze from the south-west sprang up during the afternoon of 2nd June and the two ships filled to it and set course northwards for Halifax. During the next few days Lawrence, stricken in mind by remembrance of his ship being boarded and taken, and suffering acute pain from peritonitis arising out of the musket ball embedded in his lower body, sank into a delirious coma. Feverish images of the rush of men down the *Chesapeake*'s companionways tumbled about in his brain – the dim battle lanterns of his imagination shook and weaved to the crash of shot entering his timbers; he tossed and waved his arms to his aides to hurry up the boarders, crying out again and again, "Don't give up the ship!"

He died on 4th June off the Sambro Light at the entrance to Halifax.

His First Lieutenant Ludlow was meanwhile making a good recovery. Wallis visited him in Watt's old cabin every morning after the surgeon had dressed his wounds, and they frequently discussed the course of the fight, and the 'ifs' and 'buts' whose echoes are heard down to this day.

"Well, I must say, it was a gloriously stand-up affair," Ludlow remarked after one such discussion. "I fully expected a different result, but the day was nobly won by yourselves." He smiled painfully. "Nevertheless, I hope to live, and should like to try it again."

Ludlow was scornful of one of his brother officers who complained that the action had been won by unfair means. "Let me hear no more of it," he retorted. "We were fairly beaten."

Broke was still fighting. He lay motionless in his cot, hardly speaking, his face ashen, the top of his head swathed in bandages. When the doctor or Wallis, in the few moments he could spare from his sleepless duty in charge of the two vessels, came to see him his replies were in lifeless monosyllable. Some of the Midshipmen, particularly his aide, Tommy Fenn, who was a noted humorist and general favourite in the ship, visited him and tried to rouse his spirits with highly coloured accounts of different phases of the action, but while he listened politely enough there were few flickers of the old, cheerful Broke. The nearest he came to showing animation was when he asked for the fifer to play him 'Yankee doodle dandy' one day.

"I think nothing will cheer me up so much as that tune."

The fifer took up a position just outside his door and performed the duty with such spirit that the Americans in the hold became suddenly alive with expectations of recapture, and the Shannons on their watch below tumbled up on deck in alarm.

For the rest, the *Shannon* was a quiet ship on her journey northwards. The doctor had advised Wallis that all noise should be kept to a minimum for fear of hurting the Captain's head, and the men had been instructed accordingly. They padded about the decks, and the Petty Officers cut out all unnecessary orders and delivered the vital ones as softly as their coarsened throats and the hearing of their sailors would permit.

The weather was kind too, wafting the ships north with light airs so that they were enabled to set the royals and studding sails and walk away steadily. Broke lay still, suffering terrible headaches, feeling the easy swing in his cot and hearing the familiar groan and creak of the tiller ropes as if in a dream. Ever at the back of his consciousness, like a warm glow between the stabbing pains through his head, was the knowledge that the *Shannon* had restored the splendid old flag to its former proud position – and now he could go home. No longer any need to wear out his youth and poor Louisa's to prove himself. It had been a victory in fair and equal combat as complete in its way as anyone could possibly have wished for.

But overlaying this comfortable pillow of his mind was the shadow of death. He knew from odd, unguarded looks glimpsed on his surgeon's face that his wound was dangerous. And he could feel himself weak as a straw and useless from loss of blood.

Death was all part of the lottery, but not *now* – please God, not now that he had everything to live for. Not at the very moment of his release from service, when he could expect to retire honourably to Louisa and the family and the peaceful, domestic affairs he had been denied these nine years. His thoughts dwelled more and more on Suffolk and the children. He prayed for Louisa as the days merged and blurred together, and willed himself to live – *live*. June was a pleasant time in England.

. . .

The ships were delayed by fog when they reached the Sambro, and there was a temporary scare when three men-of-war bore up out of the murk and chased them. Wallis had a feeling that they might be Rodgers' squadron come to recapture their *Chesapeake*, but they proved fortunately to be nothing more alarming than British 74s and a frigate *en route* to join Sir John Warren's flag. They were signalled the glad tidings.

The whole of the following day was obscured by fog, and the ships hung under topsails south of the Sambro firing signal guns which sent splintering echoes through Broke's semi-conscious moments. On the next day, Sunday, 6th June, the mist dispersed sufficiently for a glimpse into the harbour mouth; all sail was set to the light airs and the two ships headed for the breakwaters, the *Shannon* leading, soon joined by her prize under Falkiner, who brought her close astern. At 1 p.m. Wallis made the ship's numbers to the shore.

By the time the light breeze had brought them up to the entrance later in the afternoon the whole town had been alerted to the brilliant news, and were turning out of houses and churches and running to the waterfront to witness the sight.

A young Englishman, later Mr. Justice Haliburton, M.P., was among them.

"I was attending divine service in St. Paul's Church at that time, when a person was seen to enter hurriedly, whisper something to a friend in the garrison pew, and as hastily withdraw. The effect was electrical, for whatever the news was, it flew from pew to pew, and one by one the congregation left the Church. My own impression was that there was a fire in the immediate vicinity of St. Paul's; and the movement soon became so general that I, too, left the building to enquire into the cause of the commotion. I was informed by a person in the crowd that an English man of war was coming up the harbour with an American frigate as her prize. By that time the ships were in full view near St. George's Island and slowly moving through the water. Every housetop and every wharf was crowded with groups of excited people, and as the ships successively passed, they were greeted with vociferous cheers. Halifax was never in such a state of excitement before or since . . .

"It soon became known that the ships now approaching were the *Shannon* and the *Chesapeake*, and that the former was in charge of Lieutenant Provo Wallis, a native of Halifax, who was in temporary command in consequence of the severe and dangerous wounds of her gallant Captain. This circumstance naturally added to the enthusiasm of the citizens, for they felt that, through him, they had some share in the honour of the achievement . . ."

For young Wallis it was a homecoming past the bounds of imagination. All the British warships in harbour were manning their yards in honour, and those with bands were sending thrilling martial tunes across the water to greet the conquering heroes. As *Shannon* passed each ship in turn she was greeted with a storm of cheering. She had done far more than simply take a hostile frigate, she had restored to the British sailors their badly shaken self-respect.

Directly they came to anchor, as Wallis was arranging for the wounded to be sent ashore to the hospital, swarms of small boats were crowding around them, filled with noisy, excited people, all anxious to have a closer glimpse of the embattled ships. Wallis turned them away from the *Shannon* so that Broke would be as little disturbed as possible, and they pulled across to the *Chesapeake* instead. Young Haliburton was in one of them.

". . . internally the scene was one never to be forgotten by a landsman. The deck had not been cleaned, and the coils and folds of rope were steeped in gore as if in a slaughterhouse. She was a fir-built ship and her splinters had wounded nearly as many men as the *Shannon*'s shot. Pieces of skin with pendant hair were adhering to the sides of the ship, and in one place I saw portions of fingers protruding . . . while several of the sailors, to whom liquor had evidently been handed through the portholes by visitors in boats, were lying asleep on the bloody floor as if they had fallen in action and had expired where they lay. Altogether it was a scene of devastation as difficult to forget as to describe. It is one of the most painful reminiscences of my youth."

But for John Pechell, one of the many Naval officers who visited the *Chesapeake*, the scene of ravage produced a different reaction. This evidence of what well-laid guns could accomplish in so short a time turned his thoughts to that branch of his profession, and he became from that day a gunnery enthusiast – with what results for the Service will become apparent.

One of the first visitors allowed aboard the *Shannon* herself was Broke's friend, Captain the Hon. Philip Wodehouse, Commissioner of the Dockyard, and he immediately went aft to the Captain's sleeping cabin. The sight of Broke lying motionless and white with scarcely a flicker of life except in his pained eyes shocked him deeply, and after some words of congratulation, which he kept brief so as not to exhaust the weak figure beneath the bandages, he returned on deck and leaning sorrowfully against the capstan, told Wallis that his old friend could never recover. "He is nearly gone, sir," he said with wet eyes. "He cannot last much longer."

"Leave it to me, sir," Wallis replied briskly. "Have his room ready in half an hour and I'll answer to him being there."

The continuous responsibility and long hours of duty since he had taken command of the *Shannon* had left Wallis tired to exhaustion, but his senses were keyed up to a pitch of awareness. The fact that Broke had resisted, quite unexpectedly, even as long as this gave him some cause for hope. While Wodehouse hurried over the side into his boat to prepare a bed in his home, Wallis returned below to his Captain.

"Now, sir, I want you freed from all this noise and disturbance. I have had everything prepared, and I want to take you on shore."

"Do with me as you will," Broke murmured.

Wallis had his men lift the Captain's cot bodily from its lashings, and slowly, carefully, up on deck to the gangway entrance, where he was lowered over the side into the launch, manned to receive him. Then he was pulled ashore and carried up the silent wharf to his friend's house in the dockyard.

The following day Doctor Rowlands, Surgeon of the Naval Hospital at Halifax, was called in. He found Broke in "a very weak state, with an extensive sabre wound on the side of his head, the brain exposed to view for three inches or more; he was unable to converse save in monosyllables . . . owing to his severe wounds, loss of blood, and the shock his whole frame must have experienced by the blow on his head".

On 8th June, as Broke still lay motionless between the Wodehouse sheets, the body of his gallant rival, Lawrence, was lowered over the side of the *Chesapeake* in a mahogany coffin draped with the colours he had defended with such spirit, his sword placed on top. A twelve-oared barge lay ready to receive him, and then pulled for the shore with slow strokes to a discharge of minute guns followed by a convoy of gigs and pinnaces containing Naval and garrison officers. Arrived at King's wharf, the party disembarked and reformed the solemn procession on shore behind a funeral firing party, each with a black band around his left arm. Following the coffin came the surviving American officers and Midshipmen from the *Chesapeake*, then British garrison officers, Post Captains of the Royal Navy, staff officers and finally the dignitaries and citizens of Halifax.

"Six of the oldest (Royal) Navy Captains carried the pall, which was one of the colours of the *Chesapeake*. This, they said, was considered a particular mark of respect by naval men, as it was a token that he had defended his colours bravely, and that at this time they should not be parted from him. The procession was very long, and everything was conducted in the most solemn manner; and the wounded officers of both nations who followed in the procession made the scene very affecting. I never attended a funeral in my life where my feelings were so much struck. There was not the least mark of exultation that I saw, even amongst the commonest people."

Meanwhile, Lawrence's First Lieutenant, whose head wound had seemed to be making good progress before they reached Halifax, suddenly grew worse in the hospital, and he shortly died; he was interred near Lawrence. Both coffins were later removed into an American ship which sailed in under a flag of truce. They were borne to Salem and reburied with great ceremonial only to be removed shortly afterwards to their final resting place in Trinity Churchyard, Broadway, New York, after another solemn procession from the battery, through Greenwich to Chambers Street, watched and followed by a crowd of some thirty thousand.

In 1816 a memorial was erected in the churchyard, on which was inscribed:

> The heroic commander of the *Chesapeake*,
> whose remains are here deposited,
> with his expiring breath
> expressed his devotion to his country;
> neither the fury of battle,
> the anguish of a mortal wound,
> nor the horrors of approaching death,
> could subdue his gallant spirit.
> His dying words were
> "DON'T GIVE UP THE SHIP"

Meanwhile, the senior Naval officer, Halifax, Captain the Hon. Bladen Capel, burning to convey the great news of the action to England in an official despatch, had asked Wallis to make one out. Wallis asked him if he could wait a few days to see whether Captain Broke might not be able to dictate a letter himself.

Wallis: "I had no wish to seize the opportunity of, as I foolishly thought, putting myself forward; besides, I loved Broke and was anxious he should tell his own story."

"Very well, sir!" Capel replied, and a few days later was able to extract some details of the action in dictation from Broke, who had begun to make a slow recovery under the attentions of the hospital surgeon and Wodehouse. It is an interesting coincidence that although the *Shannon*'s log book recorded the time of the action as 10 minutes, and Wallis's watch had recorded it as 11 minutes, exactly as Lawrence's clerk had recorded the time of his *Peacock* action, Broke, like Lawrence, thought 15 minutes quite short enough and made it so in his official despatch. As he confided to Midshipman King on 26th June, "I stated fifteen minutes that there might not be any disputes. I thought I could give them the difference."

Falkiner was sent with the despatch aboard the brig-of-war *Nova Scotia*, for England, and Broke meanwhile managed to write out a brief note for Louisa to reassure her by the same post.

> "Halifax, June 11th
> "My beloved Loo, I am happy to tell you that we have at last gained a glorious victory and, thank God! I am fast recovering of my wounds and trust shall be quite well in another week, and shall very soon return to my affectionate Loo's arms. I was wounded in head, which also deprived me of use of right hand; but I mend fast. The papers will tell you particulars. My kind friend Wodehouse is nursing me carefully, and has written to my dear mother. I will write again soon. Heaven bless you all. Kiss little dears for your affectionate
>
> "P. B. V. Broke
> "Samwell slightly hurt but almost well."

The reference to Midshipman Samwell, whose family were Suffolk neighbours, was typical of his concern for his young charges, most of whom had come out of the action miraculously unscathed.

In another week Broke was feeling strong enough to write a longer letter home.

"Halifax, June 19th

"I am, thank God! recovering fast, tho' it will yet be some days before my wound is sufficiently closed to allow me to live well and in good condition again. The constant headaches are now leaving me; I wish my beloved Loo's were as surely removed: they made me think of you, poor Gentle! I have been living on rice milk, but am now going to eat vegetables etc; in another week I shall live like other people. The Doctors ordered me not to talk or think, indeed I could not without painful exertion till lately. But now Wodehouse and my other friends come and chat with me, and I walk about upon the lawn. I wish it was in our shady old avenue at Nacton with my sweet Loo. I read idle books to kill time, but cannot study yet. The dictating of my public letter was a painful effort to me, but I am stronger now . . . I am regaining the use of my hand quickly; it was taken away by the blows on my head. Samwell had a musquet shot through the flesh of his thigh, but is doing extremely well. Poor stack (his cox'n) lost an arm; I mean to get him made cook of the *Chesapeake* . . . Poor Mrs. Aldham! we expect her here. I have no doubt Etough, Smith and Leake will be made lieutenants directly and some more soon. Samwell should have his time sent out, but I fear he is not of age yet. Tommy Fenn is well, and shot at the enemy bravely with a *little gun*. Barker and Grimley well. Driscoll getting on fast. I have recommended him strongly. Stokes and Mayne both well . . .

"Please God we shall soon meet; but live happy till we do my beloved Loo, and enjoy yourself with the dear children God has blessed us with, and with the amiable friends you have around you. Tell mama I will write her soon. Give my love to all around you and in Suffolk. Heaven bless you all for your affectionate P. B. V. Broke."

"The foolish Americans have been publishing a thousand absurd lies. Not liking to believe that their ship was bigger than *Shannon*, and got such a terrible beating by *fair play* as she did, the simpletons say we used *infernal machines*. They are sadly disappointed. They had *fetters* for *us all* upon deck ready, which came to their use.

"I open this again for a *cruel* task. I know how my beloved Loo will feel for a person who has been so kind and attentive to her and to the dear children, but poor Mrs. Samwell's son is gone. Only the night before the doctors considered him safe, and I thought of nothing but his promotion, but his wound took a sudden turn . . ."

Meanwhile, Louisa, staying with friends in Budleigh Salterton and unaware of the action or of her husband's wound, only wondering how much longer the Admiralty would keep him from her, had asked her brother to try and find out from one of the Lords whom he knew personally when they were likely to allow her Philip's return.

"Budleigh Salterton   June 24th
". . . I yesterday got his answer which although most gratifying in one sense is far from being satisfactory to me in the other, but I am still willing to flatter myself that Admiral Hope knows more than Sir Geo Warrender whom my brother asked. I will copy you what he says: 'No one can stand higher in the opinion of the Admiralty than Captain Broke, they consider him one of the finest officers in the service and as such think they will not order him home as long as it is possible for him to remain there.' He spoke of your having given up the certainty of immense prize money to convoy the Jamaica fleet safe and my brother adds that nothing could be more gratifying than the manner in which he spoke of you and which he trusts will repay me fully for my disappointment at not seeing you so soon as I had expected – but my husband cannot stand higher in my opinion than he does, therefore *nothing* in this world can compensate me for the loss of his dear and valuable society – time never to be recalled . . .

"Our dear children wish kindest love to their dear papa and Willy says 'tell him to come home' . . . he neither wants to be told or reminded of what is so near to his heart. May God speedily place him in a situation to do so without reproach – may he bless and preserve you in all happiness for the sake of your affect[e] anxious Loo."

Before this letter was written rumours of the *Chesapeake* (Captain Evans) having been captured had been appearing in the papers. When the news was confirmed on 7th July by Lieutenant Falkiner's arrival with the official despatches the country went wild with delight. Mr. Croker, secretary to the Admiralty, who had to defend their Lordships against spirited charges brought by Lord Cochrane that British seamen were decayed and disheartened by maladministration, seized upon the fortunate timing of the news as manna suddenly dropped from heaven, and made a stirring speech in the Commons.

"The communication which I am about to make to the House has not been sought or prepared by me. It has presented itself to me, as if from a divinity to confute and confound the noble Lord's mis-representations and libels, to rescue the honour of the British Navy from all foul and malignant attacks, and raise the glory of the British flag still higher than ever . . ."

He did not wish to trouble the House at any length with the character of the Captain of the *Shannon*, and thought it sufficient to say that Captain Broke was an officer "no less distinguished for indefatigable activity and unwearied enterprise than for his skill and valour". Nevertheless, he went on to instance those many occasions when Broke had sacrificed the chance of prizes, and even sent those he took to the bottom rather than weaken his ship or squadron. Finally he came to the details that his listeners were burning to hear.

"The action which he fought with the *Chesapeake* is, in every respect, unexampled. It is not – and I know it is a bold assertion I make – to be equalled by any engagement which graces the naval annals of Great Britain. The enemy's ship was superior in size and weight of metal, superior in numbers —"

He was interrupted by loud cheers.

"All this superiority serves but to heighten the brilliancy of Captain Broke's achievement. And a peculiar circumstance occurred which gives the victory a new and richer colouring. Captain Broke was wounded. This, indeed, is not extraordinary, but the place on which he received his wounds inspires an interest which will be deeply felt but cannot be adequately described – he was wounded on the deck of the enemy's ship . . ."

The cheers renewed enthusiastically, and were kept up at intervals throughout the rest of the eulogy.

The *Naval Chronicle* echoed the applause in its editorial columns: "The capture of the *Chesapeake* is confessedly the most brilliant act of heroism ever performed, and perhaps can never be excelled . . ."

And poets and Naval officers of literary talent rushed into print with laudatory poems:

Three fatal fights Britannia saw with mixed surprise and woe,
For thrice she saw the Union Flag by hostile hands laid low.
Then casting round an anxious eye amongst her naval men,
Her choice she made, that choice was Broke to raise her flag again.

The glorious wound that decks thy brow, your foes affrighted view.
Thy blood that stained the well-earned prize proclaims their terrors true.

Hail Suffolk's pride! Such fame may I, a son of Suffolk share,
Or if I fall, like glorious Watt, to fall what hour so fair.
And prove tho' thrice superior force might transient trophies gain,
Britannia rules the wat'ry world, sole Empress of the Main.

Edward Stewart, R.N. Lt. *Royal Oak*

There were scores of others; here is *Impromptu*:

> *The bold* Chesapeake
> *Came out on a freak*
> *And swore she'd soon silence our cannon;*
> *While the Yankees in port*
> *Stood to laugh at the sport*
> *And see her tow in the brave* Shannon.
>
> *Quite sure of the game*
> *As from harbour they came*
> *A dinner and wine they bespoke;*
> *But for meat they got* balls
> *From our stout wooden walls*
> *And the dinner engagement was* BROKE.

The other officers were not forgotten. Lady Falkiner, in the Reading Room of the Marine Library at Brighton, was scanning a morning paper which had just arrived when she was seen to put it down suddenly in a state of great agitation, then burst into tears. Her husband asked anxiously what the matter was. Unable to reply through her sobs, she simply pointed to a paragraph, and handing him the sheet, fled the room. He looked at it in some alarm – changing quickly to elation. "Lord Melville thought so highly of the engagement that Lieutenants Wallis and Falkiner were to be promoted Commanders . . ."

References to the action and to Broke's alleged challenge to Captain Lawrence continued to occupy the newspapers for weeks. Louisa found herself congratulated by complete strangers, and receiving letters from friends and family well-wishers every day.

> "Budleigh Salterton July 11th
> "The newspapers we took in the carriage were filled with joy and exultation at your success and such praises bestowed in the House by Mr. Croker and others on your gallant and noble conduct as was almost too much for your Loo – it was indeed most gratifying to me to hear you so highly spoken of by the *whole country*. You will say it is enough to make me proud that I ever was and had good reason to be of you, but my beloved Philip is it true that *you* challenged the *Chesapeake* for the papers of today mention that as being the case? I know not whether to give credit to it or no . . . how *anxious* I am for later accounts of you to know that you are continuing to do well, your dear head healed and your strength regained and you ordered

home . . . but I must and will endeavour to be calm and patient, trusting in a merciful providence for his support and protection, ever grateful for his goodness in saving so valuable a life . . ."

And on 18th July.

"I have for the last week my beloved Philip received so many congratulations on your safety and success that I have been writing three or four letters every day . . . no further accounts from *you* (although daily reports in the papers) I cannot express to you how *very anxious* I am for your next accounts of you to be assured of your continued well doing, to know that your wounds are healed and that *you* have got orders from Sir John . . . to return home . . . God bless you my beloved husband. Our dear children unite in kindred love and kisses with your ever faithful and affectionate Loo."

Broke's brother, now a Lieutenant Colonel with Wellington's army, itself heady with the latest success at Vittoria, virtually liberating Spain, wrote exultantly,

"I cannot say how happy your success has made me, nor could I describe the joy and satisfaction which the gallantry of your achievement has created here; what the sensations were in England we hear of, that they were generally of the highest joy . . ."

And Lord Wellington, striding the Pyrenees, proposed, on the anniversary dinner of the Battle of Salamanca, a toast to "Captain Broke and the *Shannon!*"

This was being echoed in the London salons and after Naval dinners at Portsmouth and Plymouth: "Gentlemen, I give you – an Irish river and an English Broke!"

Most gratifying to Broke himself, after the letters from wife and family, were those from his professional friends on the station who knew him and the *Shannon* so well, and who could put their finger unerringly on the *cause* of his success.

The Captain of the Fleet, Sir Henry Hotham, for instance:

"*San Domingo*, Hampton Roads   June 27th '13
". . . Your action, my dear Broke, proves to the service and to yourself, the advantages which have resulted from the great pains you have taken to make your ship and your people perfect in the use of the guns; and which has been conspicuous to everybody, and was so strongly in my mind, that I have placed my faith in the

result of any action you might have since the commencement of this war, and I am delighted that I have placed a proper confidence in her, especially as I saw so many excellent arrangements on board the *Shannon* that I copied them in the *Defiance* and *Northumberland* with the best effects. I wish all our brother officers had given as much of their attention to the important part of the service of the management of the guns that you have, we should not then have made so poor a figure as we have done before you set us up again . . .

> "I remain, my dear Broke,
> "Most sincerely, your warm and affectionate friend,
> "H. Hotham."

And from Admiral Sir James Alexander Gordon, G.C.B.:

> "St. John,   June 13th 1813
> ". . . I have been suffering from a severe illness, but your success has done more for me than all the Doctors. To have taken her at all would have been most meritorious and gratifying to all of us; but the decided style of the thing was your own entirely, and only to be achieved by the discipline and experience of the *Shannon*'s crew . . ."

Their Lordships made a similar appreciation.

> "Admiralty Office, July 9th 1813
> "My Lords have before had occasion to observe with great approbation the zeal, judgment and activity which have characterised Captain Broke's proceedings since the commencement of the war; and they now receive with the highest satisfaction a proof of professional skill and gallantry in battle which has seldom been equalled and certainly never surpassed; and the decision, celerity and effect with which the force of H.M.S. was directed against the enemy, mark no less the personal bravery of the officers, seamen and marines, than the high discipline and practice in arms to which the ship's company must have been sedulously and successfully trained . . ."

Although Lord Melville, First Lord of the Admiralty, and Broke's Commander-in-Chief, Sir John Borlase Warren, expected to reward him with one of the new 74s, or, if he wished, one of the new large frigates being built to match the Americans', when he was fully recovered, those who knew him best interpreted his feelings far more accurately.

"*San Domingo*, Hampton Roads   July 13th

". . . How happily all things are come to pass in the way you most wished; you may now return to England crowned with laurels and honour, and you will naturally be received by your wife, and by all your friends in a manner infinitely more gratifying to you than ever; and your past, long and anxious services may be followed by as much ease and quiet as you choose to indulge in. You are truly to be envied . . .

"Ever very affectionately and faithfully yours,
"H. Hotham."

Meanwhile Broke was continuing the slow, uphill journey towards recovery. He was beginning to eat solid foods and regain erratic use of his right hand, while the persistent headaches with which he had been plagued since the action were losing some of their severity and becoming infrequent.

". . . I sit and read *idle books* or creep about on Wodehouse's lawn for the air, and the ladies have very kindly sent me flowers to decorate my room; so I dress and plant them on the tables round me, to gaze on them and think of my Loo . . . My garden is refreshed by fresh presents every morning. Wodehouse, Capel and Byron (all living here) come and chat quietly to me, with some other friends; and today some of my fair acquaintance came to congratulate me and prattle and smile on me to comfort me in my confinement. Oh, my poor Loo, what a delight it would have been to have been at home in all this painful nursing with my gentle, tender wife to watch and soothe me!"

"June 29th

". . . Any serious occupation or study is too fatiguing for me yet, but I get bodily strength fast, and (*the ladies tell me*) am recovering my beauty wonderfully. Mrs. Dixon made me a pretty light bonnet to go over all the turbans and dressings on my head to keep the sun off. 'Tis something like a beefeater's cap, only of grey velvet; so I must look pretty in my plaid mantle . . ."

His head continued to make good progress through the heat of July, and the doctors, proud of their performance, regarded him as their star patient. In the evenings Wodehouse used to take him out for quiet rides behind a 'grave, sober old coach horse', or on the water in his gig. They made frequent excursions to the *Chesapeake*, which was being repaired and fitted out for the British service, and Broke delighted in walking around her slowly, examining the *Shannon*'s handiwork in detail, and talking about the action with those many former Shannons who had been drafted into her. For the engagement, at least in retrospect, represented "one of the happiest moments" in his life, "as affording me the privilege of retiring with honor to my beloved Loo, and conscious of having earned my liberty".

His one regret, apart from the death of Lawrence and so many of the American officers and Midshipmen, was the sword stroke he had been forced to make against the lone figure by the mizzen-mast after he boarded. He had learned since that the man had been a Mr. Livermore, acting chaplain on board the *Chesapeake*; it worried his conscience that he should have struck thus at a man of God. But for the rest he was satisfied.

"Halifax, July 20th 1813

"Now my friend Admiral Hope is out there is no acquaintance of mine on the Bd. (of Admiralty) – but I now hope not to have any favors to ask these grandees for some years except to help my *young officers*. It is a great happiness to me to be able to leave them all in so prosperous a way – to see my *sea children* settled before I leave them – except poor Sll but we were altogether very fortunate in that rank – our enemy lost 8 or 9! All my old *élèves* will make good officers and do *Shannon credit*. Indeed I regard the bringing up such a family as an essential part of my eight years services and it is one that has cost me great care and anxiety – I have a right now to bring up *my own children* surely, and please God will – with my gentle Loo's aid."

.   .   .

Summer turned into autumn. The *Shannon*, with a relief Captain and with some of the Midshipmen who had started out as young lads with Broke – Etough, Smith, King – now promoted Lieutenants, made a cruise and returned with some merchant prizes; it was too much to expect of fortune that she would meet one of the lone American cruisers.

Broke's strength returned; skin grew over the terrible wound parting his scalp, and he found himself able to write less awkwardly, although not without great effort, and ride and take part in most of the activities he had previously enjoyed. His head was still swathed in a protective bandage like a turban and as his hair was shorn he had taken to wearing a gaily coloured silk handkerchief in its place, which flowed from beneath the felt hat which topped his bandages.

Every post he received contained fresh news of honours being prepared for his return, the Freedom of the City of London, a sword, value one hundred guineas, artists wishing to paint portraits of him

o

and *Shannon*, more laudatory poems and fresh letters of congratulation. The Underwriters of Halifax presented him with an Address and a silver plate, value one hundred guineas, and the ladies of the town continued to cosset him unmercifully.

"Sept 29th 1813

"It is high time I should come home, lest I should become too vain. A lady (I don't know who yet) sent me a new velvet cap on Sunday, with some poetical compliments; but I will be modest when I get into Suffolk, and turn farmer, and renounce vanity with my laced coat. I am very well my gentle wife, and shall have a complete head by the time I get home. Adieu! Heaven bless you all in health and joy, soon to meet your affectionate P. B. V. Broke"

The Admiralty, after hearing of his wish to retire to country pursuits for a while, had sent out fresh orders for the *Shannon* to return home, and on 4th October he left his friend Wodehouse for the last time after a poignant scene of farewell and was rowed out to the familiar, weathered old side of his frigate – that magic name on the stern, cut into the very fibres of his being – *Shannon* – he remembered the first time he had been pulled out to his splendid new command in the Thames . . .

The pipes shrilled. The new young officers, his sea children now come of age and hero-worshippers to a man, stood rigid with shiny braid and doffed hats on the quarterdeck as his turban and gay, piratical headscarf in lieu of hair appeared in the gangway entrance. The miracle had happened. Four months ago, almost to the day, he had been lowered from this same gangway, immobile, with his face reflecting the pallor of imminent death; now here he was with the old colour back in his cheeks, and a half-humorous, half-grateful glint briefly in his eyes before he shut it out and became the Captain again – the gold lace of a Captain in the King's Navy – the solitary dignity.

He acknowledged their salutes impassively and walked towards his companionway like an old man; the climb up the side had been more fatiguing than he had expected, and his confounded head was throbbing again. Wallis, searching his face silently, wondered if he would ever be quite the same man he had known – and still loved.

"Lively then —" the bull voice of the new Boatswain shattered the unusual stillness aboard. "Look lively now!"

Many of the hands were new and they were craning their necks, straining and peering from wherever they happened to be in an effort to glimpse this man whose name had already acquired a lustre equal to the Navy's legendary heroes. Everything conspired to make him an object of fascination. He had defeated a Yankee when it had begun to seem impossible, he had achieved it in the shortest time on record for such equal combat and he had led the boarders himself – an unusual circumstance – and then receiving from all accounts a mortal wound at the far end of the enemy's deck, he had fought that too and recovered. Besides all this there were the gunnery innovations in evidence everywhere about the decks, the strange tangent and dispart sights, the unequally cut down carriages, the pendulums, the angles of concentration cut into the deck planking. His methods of daily drill and unremitting attention to the smallest details of aiming and firing had not gone unexaggerated among the old Shannons on board – a proud group who were apt to look down on the newcomers while spinning them wild yarns of prizes left burning in the sea while they hunted in season and out for Commodore Rodgers.

The new hands stared until they were set scurrying about their business again preparing the ship for sea. The pipes began shrilling to weigh anchor – clattering sounds up forward, the cheerful fifer's tune, tramp of feet, crack and stretch of the hawser, the old music again – presently the frigate was leaning and shivering to the press of a north-easterly blow full in her topsails. There was a convoy of dull merchantmen to escort back to England, and she started round them like a seasoned sheep dog, barking with her 12-pounder across their bows and running up signals to encourage them. Broke felt his spirits rising with the activity. The wind was brisk and cold, and carried dark rain clouds low over the mastheads, but the tipping of the deck under his feet again was like the feel of a favourite hunter saddled after long absence – wine after Lent.

"While *Shannon* moves, I am alive!"

When they had the merchantmen safely past the breakwaters and beating as close as their unwieldy lines would permit, he ordered the men to be mustered in the waist and addressed them from the break of the quarterdeck.

"Shannons! Shannons, it is likely that Commodore Rodgers will attempt to waylay us on this voyage – he has notice of our convoy and will know the date we sail." There was complete quiet below him. "If he does so I trust you will deal with him as you did the *Chesapeake*—" There was a rumble of assent. "I look to you to go about your drills and practices with the great guns with the same steady ardour you displayed in action. For it is only with *practical gunnery* that you can keep this ship a most destructive battery, and decide an action even more rapidly than you did before. You know what you must do if you meet the *President* – let us make sure that you can do it *before* we exchange courtesies." And then relaxing his earnest manner, he added, "And if you board again, you must not cut at the Americans but poke them in the guts – for there are some fellows very thick-skulled indeed!" A burst of laughter greeted this sally, and after a few more phrases of encouragement the men were dismissed.

All the old drills and exercises which had made the frigate such a formidable fighting ship were constantly employed as they rode easterly under shortened canvas to keep company with the slow merchantmen; the lookouts scanned the horizon for strange men-of-war.

Broke was annoyed to find that the discharge of the guns still sent pains shooting through his head, and he left more of the supervision to his young officers than had been his wont; there was no doubt he had not the half of his old vigour. He felt strong enough in the quiet of his cabin with his companions the books – but when it came to any exertion the throbbing and dizziness returned. He wondered where Rodgers was.

In the event they saw no hostile ships, and after riding out some autumn gales under bare poles, arrived at Portsmouth on 2nd November to scenes of wild excitement, more salutes from the Naval craft in harbour, more letters of congratulation and the news that he had been raised to the peerage as a Baronet of the United Kingdom. Louisa, however, was not there to share his reception; she was waiting with the children at Plymouth.

"My beloved Loo will be happy to know I am arrived safe here, though the wicked winds would not let us touch at Plymouth. I am perfectly well my love, though must wear my turban yet a little . . . I hope *your Ladyship* will excuse my scrawl. Kiss all the little dears for me. I will have the pleasure of doing so soon myself."

The same day he set off for London; Wallis accompanied him as the gales and responsibilities of the ship and convoy had left him far weaker than he had been latterly at Halifax. They journeyed by easy stages to Limner's Hotel, Conduit Street, and after a warm welcome at the Admiralty from no less a personage than Lord Melville himself returned slowly to Portsmouth, stopping the first night at Guildford and the second at Liphook. Broke was exhausted. And besides his desire to reap the fruits of his long service in peace at Broke Hall it was now very obvious to him and also the Lords of the Admiralty who had received him in London that he was nowhere near fit enough for service afloat – nor would be for some months.

Louisa had meanwhile made the journey from Plymouth and when they arrived Wallis delivered him into her hands. Then he returned a little sadly to the dockyard.

"Having bade each other a fervent farewell, I parted from a man that I loved most sincerely, and from whom I had during nearly two years received I can truly say, affectionate regard. I also believe it to have been owing to his high bearing and sterling worth, added to the kindness of his government (of the men) that our crew were doubly incited to achieve under him a victory he had set his heart upon."

For Broke, the long-awaited reunion with his family was almost too much for him to bear with composure. Louisa was crying with happiness, and the children – *so* much bigger than he remembered them – bounding and bubbling around them. The long years of sea-keeping and endless drill and taut self-discipline seemed to drop away and in his weak state he felt himself being almost visibly transformed into a peaceful land animal again. The years stretched ahead filled with pleasant green prospects of Suffolk and the affection of his family close around him – and his honour with *Shannon* in safe-keeping for all time. His prayers had surely been answered tenfold.

That evening he and Louisa and the older children went to church to give thanks to God, to whom they owed everything. Kneeling beside them, he felt his gratitude and love welling over and filling the lofty silence and peace of His house.

POSTSCRIPT

BROKE stayed a while in Portsmouth and London, showered with honours and invitations to dinners and receptions, at which he was in the habit of answering his eulogisers by saying that his "merit was but of a trifling nature" and "I am convinced there is not an officer in the British Navy who would not have performed the duty with equal zeal." He alternated this frantic society with restful weeks in Suffolk at Shrubland Park, Louisa's family home, or Broke Hall. His head continued to mend, and he was soon able to ride and shoot with all his former enjoyment.

In 1814 he was again offered one of the new class of large frigates built to match the *Constitution* type, and in addition as many of his old Shannons as could be found in the fleet. He resisted this temptation on Louisa's account. His old friend, Sir Henry Hotham, hearing of his decision, wrote, "I rejoice your wife had such fast hold of you and held it so tight, as you must not think of active service again just yet."

In 1815, after peace had been made with the Americans, he settled finally at Broke Hall and took up all the duties of a country gentleman, fond husband and father to which he had been so looking forward. He and Louisa lived simply. He was not a wealthy man. While some of his more fortunate brother officers had made themselves immense riches in prize money, he had served at a time and on stations where British Naval superiority was too firmly established to permit great pickings – and latterly he had been more intent on catching Rodgers than filling his own coffers.

"I shall perhaps, just muster cash enough to make Nacton habitable, and sit down again on the same establishment as before; neither richer nor poorer for all my wanderings."

In one respect, of course, he was immeasurably richer: the capture of the *Chesapeake*, which had netted him £2,449 in prize money – less his agent's commission – had given him both satisfaction and peace of mind. "Though I now retire to a tranquil domestic life, it is with that respectability which my dear father left attached to our family name and which stamps a value even upon my former exertions in my own district (raising and training the corps of volunteers to resist invasion), and proves my constant endeavours in public service to those who would otherwise have looked upon my efforts as merely following the fashion, and my volunteer campaign merely an amusement for idle time."

He continued to keep his pocket diaries regularly as at sea, and also a journal with details of the weather, winds, temperature, his quiet, domestic proceedings and the affairs of his few farms in Suffolk and Essex. These entries tell of riding out with his boys, shooting game, teaching his boys to shoot at a mark, parish meetings, business on behalf of the Tory party at elections, haymaking, buying sheep, attending lamb fairs, speaking at County meetings and shows, house parties, gardening, planting trees – the Naval patriot's pastime – being elected parish overseer and assessor, regular churchgoing.

He delighted in walking with his children, talking to them of his experiences around the world and opening their minds to wider horizons than their schooling and life in Suffolk afforded.

"It was always a treat to be invited to share his walks, for even to us little children he had the happy gift of making his conversation both intimate and interesting." (Loolins.)

He passed on to the children his own love for books and his own faith; on Sundays, instead of reading them a sermon he "would find some portion for us in the Bible to enable us to answer his questions and understand his remarks on the illustrations in the Pictorial Bible, an employment on Sunday evenings we much enjoyed".

On other quiet winter evenings he might amuse himself comparing the butchers' bills of various single-ship actions and even fleet actions with those killed and wounded in his own cataclysmic encounter:

	K & W		
"Indefatigable	0	} $1\frac{3}{4}$ hrs *close*	1796
Virginie	41		
Crescent	0	} 2 hrs close action	1796 . . ."
Reunion	120		

He kept up correspondence with all his friends at sea, helped old Shannons in need of money or patronage and answered frequent applications for certificates of good conduct requested by his former officers and sea children. One of these, who requested a testimonial to the effect that he had been in the *Chesapeake* action, received a stern lecture instead by return. Across his letter Broke scrawled, "Disgraceful! This boy was absent in charge of a prize and not in the *Chesapeake* fight at all . . . !"

He kept up a long correspondence – for his part mainly answering questions about the *Shannon* – with the lawyer turned Naval historian, William James, who subsequently dedicated his *Naval Occurrences of the late War between Great Britain and the United States of America* to him. Broke was also corresponding with various officers at sea who had seen or heard of his gunnery schemes, and who wished to extend them throughout a service which was becoming, in its triumphant state, ever more disinclined to bother about such a tedious, noisy and distinctly offensive affair as gunnery.

Chief among these professional correspondents on a subject that was still very close to his heart were Captain John Pechell, R.N., and Sir Howard Douglas, the latter an army officer in command of the Military College at Farnham, but interested in the sea service through his father, who had been *Rodney*'s flag Captain and a noted innovator in the great gunnery of his day. Both Pechell and Howard Douglas subsequently published works on Naval gunnery, and in both cases Broke's influence shines through between the lines – sometimes his actual words.

Here is a section from Pechell's *Observations upon the Defective Equipment of Ships' Guns*, which contains the essence of Broke's teaching: it is necessary "to have the means of directing a broadside to be fired in a horizontal line when the ship heels under press of sail, the enemy enveloped in smoke, or engaged in a dark night . . ." Pechell went on to refer to the *Chesapeake* fight: "Horizontal fire was, I apprehend, the principal cause of this action being so decisive, and I have no doubt that the same effect would have been produced had the action been fought at night." Broke had no doubts either.

Pechell went on to describe Broke's methods of concentration fire, and the methods of drill which he, Pechell, had introduced in the *San Domingo* after witnessing them aboard the *Shannon*. And he lamented that even now, 1825, few ships had sights fitted to their cannon. "In the Mediterranean squadron destined for the bombardment of Algiers consisting of one ship of the line, five frigates, several sloops and bombs, only two frigates' guns, *Naiad* and *Euryalus*, were disparted, the former only partially."

He ended, "It was the first object of Sir Robert Barlow (H.M.S. *Phoebe*) and Sir Philip Broke to make their guns effective by instructing both officers and men in that part of their duty, which gave them a degree of confidence I defy any man to have who does not follow their example. Having therefore such proof before us, what need we more to excite us to the like . . .?"

Douglas, in his renowned and most influential *Treatise on Naval Gunnery*, adopted many of Broke's observations; Douglas after all was not a sailor and therefore open to the terrible taunt of being a mere 'theorist', and it was natural that he should seek to overcome this with the very practical and proven experience of a man like Broke. Thus many of his remarks on the tactics employed in the frigate actions of the American War, particularly the uselessness of raking fire from a turning ship (*President/Belvidera*, *Constitution/ Guerriere* for instance) are similar to Broke's, as are his stress on the real point-blank range of the pieces, the uselessness of French Naval gunnery in the later years of Napoleon's reign, tending to make British gunnery *appear* superb; his change from advocating theoretical tables of gun ranges to a simple *practical* table making use of the various heights of masts, yards and rigging of the *enemy* ship as points of aim to give the requisite degree of elevation to the guns at different ranges was all from Broke's correspondence.

Howard Douglas' great idea was to form a shore establishment for training a corps of seamen gunners, instead of leaving the sailors to be initiated into the mysteries of the ordnance at the whim of the officers aboard their ships – officers who had themselves received no instruction (unless, like Broke, self-instructed), but had simply 'picked up' their knowledge from observation and service 'lore', handed down from one generation of gunners to the next.

This vision of Douglas', actively supported by Pechell and by Broke, who deplored the lack of interest in practical gunnery shown by many officers, led eventually to the first Naval gunnery school in the world, H.M.S. *Excellent*, whose efforts were to have such a profound influence on the Service. It is interesting that although Broke was enthusiastic about having some such universal system of gunnery training adopted, he put his finger unerringly on the one real disadvantage of a shore establishment that was amply borne out by subsequent history: the creation of a race 'apart from the common run of sailors'.

"Broke Hall, June 7th 1818

"My dear Sir (Howard),

". . . I feel a most sincere regret, I trust you will believe, that I cannot more *fully* and *unquestionably* agree in the *whole* system traced out . . . I must now explain as to my apprehension of the system not being generally applicable *in regard to the men.* There is a pride in our good seaman which would be much broken if the bold and expert young topman raised from the North Sea or foreign trade should find himself precluded from rising to be captain of a gun because he had not been a student on shore. This would destroy his *ambition to command,* which brings so many fine fellows forward and makes them feel a *consequence in themselves* . . . the highest posts would all be filled then by men, who many of them, would be *very inferior characters* in a gale of wind, there would be a danger of them forming an idea that this gunnery knowledge was beneath an old seaman's notice . . ."

Prophetic words indeed. This was exactly what did happen through the century until by the 1890s seamanship and smart drill and paint had become the only criterion of efficiency; gunners were looked down upon as an officious breed, spinners of long words. This happened even more dramatically in the ranks of the commissioned officers, something which Broke did not foresee because he assumed that in the event of Douglas' shore establishment being set up *every* officer would be required to pass an examination in gunnery to obtain his promotion to Lieutenant, and would thereafter pass his knowledge on to the men of his own quarters aboard his ship – *every* officer, not simply one 'long course' man who was the gunnery Lieutenant.

". . . Seamanship and navigation and astronomy and activity and intelligence will constitute a good officer in an East or West Indiaman; they are indispensable in the ship of war, but they will not qualify a man to do his duties as her officer or commander . . . to command ships of *war* he must have the knowledge of warlike science . . . The most assiduous instruction should be given to officers (in gunnery), the elder invited and the younger compelled to make themselves masters of the simple knowledge at least proposed by Sir Howard . . . nothing will be considered as part of a seaman's business which the seaman officer does not teach and practice . . ."

Again sadly prophetic. For reasons outside the scope of this book the seamen officers came to lose all interest in the great guns or teaching their men the theory and practice of gunnery, and concentrated their efforts instead on sail drill and paintwork and boat pulling, cricket, hockey, hunting, polo and many other sporting spurs to competition and physical fitness. The flame of gunnery was only kept alight by the *Excellent* men, a small group specialising in incomprehensible ballistic jargon and weird formal drills, sole repositories of the 'mysteries' of ordnance, which no 'general service' officer could hope to comprehend – a class apart. Thus it came about that when this small group came into its own in the early twentieth century under the dynamic leadership of Percy Scott, who believed, like Broke, that the Navy and the world could only be saved by gunnery, gunnery, gunnery, they bid fair to split the Service down the middle.

"One thing us N.O.s of that period always remember is the autocracy of the gunnery branch. Percy Scott's indoctrination of gunnery specialists at Whale Island (H.M.S. *Excellent*) made them think that ships were just platforms on which guns were mounted for *their* use!"
(Captain G. A. P. Webster, R.N., 1965 of 1905)

Percy Scott and Philip Broke were men from very different moulds, but so far as gunnery went they were carbon copies of one another. Neither was content with the state of the art as generally practised in his day; *Broke:* "Those who are satisfied with the general state of gunnery in British ships of war will never improve others by teaching a system which they deem useless and feel no interest in . . ." *Scott:* "For six years I have urged their Lordships, the Commissioners of the Admiralty, to adopt a system of fighting the guns in parallel; had I not done so and did I not continue to urge it, in the event of war I should feel myself criminally responsible for the defeat we should sustain if our fleet engaged another fleet in which the guns are fitted for firing in parallel."

Broke's first efforts to improve practice were directed to disparting and sighting his pieces in a Service which believed only in getting so close that the guns could not miss whether sighted or not, and he provided the sights out of his own pocket; Scott's first efforts were directed to fitting his cruiser's aiming gun with a telescopic sight when the Service still used a 'V' backsight, later providing telescopes for all his guns out of his own pocket. Broke trained the men in 'hunting the roll' in calm weather by having the barrel of his aiming cannon moved up and down manually while the layer aimed at a fixed target; Scott simply reversed the process and for calm weather practice had the *target* moved manually up and down while the layer aimed at it. Broke had all his guns angled slightly one to another so as to concentrate their fire on one point; Scott calibrated his guns so that each salvo bunched in a small area. Broke had angles for training the guns cut into the deck by each gunport and a master compass on the upper deck by which all guns could be ordered to concentrate on the same spot whether the gun captains could see the target or not; Scott adapted this in his director firing system by fitting all gun turrets with dials showing the training angle ordered from an aloft position – again the gunlayers and trainers did not need to see the target.

So much for the physical similarities. While these expedients may seem obvious now, they were far from obvious when these men initiated them. The similarities of method by which each achieved proficiency with his system is even more striking. First, both men knew that competition was the only way to improve performance, competition between guns' crews, and competition between individual captains of guns in aiming. Broke awarded prizes of tobacco out of his own pocket and gave gun captains the status of Petty Officers and similar shares of prize money; Scott pinned up a list on his notice board showing the gunlayers in order of merit and rewarded his gun captains with positions of honour at ceremonials and parades, and he was instrumental in getting the first cups presented for heavy-gun shooting. Both Broke and Scott used time which in other ships was used for sail drill or painting and polishing to exercise their men at the guns; both men went to infinite pains, *watching* their people at the constant drills and *thinking* about what they saw, making improvements and calling for suggestions from *anyone* who had useful ideas – this was a considerable novelty in the Naval service where Captains asked nothing from subordinates save unquestioning obedience. But neither Broke nor Scott ever went to the length of discouraging their crews by overlong practices; both made it a habit never to interfere with meal breaks whatever the state of the target. Both ran 'taut' ships, but were considerably enlightened commanders by the standards of their day, and carried their officers with them by their own enthusiasm for gunnery, which transformed what otherwise might have been crankiness into leadership of the highest order. Both men had all their officers instructing the men of their own quarters; both stressed the high importance of giving the sailors *confidence* in their pieces when aimed correctly. Both took great pains in the education of their Midshipmen – although Broke was *closer* to his.

Both men were driven by practical enthusiasm and a burning desire for personal distinction.

There the similarity ends. Broke was initiating his improvements at the end of some three hundred years of practically unchanged sea warfare, and, moreover, during a war for the very existence of his country, before gunnery had ceased to be an object with Admirals; Percy Scott made his at a time when new forms of weapons were appearing, after the Service had been lulled by a long peace, and at a time when gunnery was the very least concern of Admirals or, in fact, anyone save the Excellents – whom Broke had helped to bring into being.

Broke was intensely happy in his domestic affairs and had an assured station as an English country gentleman; Scott was latterly not at peace in his home life, and had no station save what he carved himself. Broke made it a point never to disagree with superiors; Scott made an equal point of invariably disagreeing with them unless they shared his views on gunnery. Broke concealed his driving ambition beneath a calm exterior, and went out of his way to be pleasant and easy; Scott was a firebrand with a sharp, cynical brand of humour that made as many enemies as conversions. Broke was strengthened by his absolute faith in God; Scott had nothing to believe in – save perhaps his own genius.

But both these men honoured and loved the Service and held it high above their own interests, recognising the 'proud old union' or the White Ensign as much greater than the sum of its diverse individual parts. And while neither rose to the very top, both made their mark on the incomparable legend of the Royal Navy, and contributions to its real fighting efficiency which are unsurpassed.

·   ·   ·

In 1820 Broke fell from his horse while out riding one day. He landed on the so far uninjured right side of his head, stunning himself for a moment. As he came to he was being dragged along on his back with his foot above him still caught in the stirrup. He remembered freeing it, and then nothing more until he was back in his mother's house about a quarter of a mile away – he was sitting in a chair quietly telling her that he had had a fall, he must have walked from the scene but he couldn't remember. A few minutes afterwards he began to feel dizzy, and when he went upstairs to wash the mud from his hair he discovered that he was scratched and bleeding in several places. As he became fainter afterwards, a surgeon was called and bled him. He vomited and lost consciousness.

By the following day he seemed to have recovered, but in the afternoon began to feel a peculiar coldness in his left leg, foot and hand so that he could not sleep without a worsted glove and stocking over them. And as the weeks passed, this alarming symptom increased to cover the whole of his left side.

> "... the sense of cold appearing to lie internally upon the coating of the bones of the arm, thigh and leg; and that although the flesh was externally warm to the touch and generally in a state of perspiration, and though the skin appeared perfectly fresh and smooth, yet that skin over the whole left side of my person was affected by a singular numbness to the touch."

Ever since the action he had been hampered on his right side by imperfect co-ordination resulting from the sabre blow; he had never quite recovered his old facility with guns or even pen. Now, with the blow on the other side of his head affecting his left side, he became an invalid. An eminent physician, Sir Astley Cooper, examined him.

> "The heart is subject to occasional alteration in its functions from diminished nervous excitability, and hence the pain felt in its region and the sense of strangulation under which Sir Philip occasionally labours.
> "The stomach is also occasionally suffering from its sympathy with the brain, and hence those attacks which drinking warm water alleviates.
> "Congestion in the brain from changes in position and from over exertions of mind, tend to a sudden increase of all the symptons ..."

At about the same time Lady Broke's health, which had never been strong, began to fail completely so that she could only move up and down stairs with help, and spent all her waking hours in a wheelchair. Broke's activities as a country squire, already bounded by his latest incapacities, were further curtailed by his anxious concern for her. He felt that perhaps his own long absences in their early married years may have contributed to this breakdown in her health; he watched over her tenderly, wheeled her out on the lawn on fine days, read her improving books and picked nosegays of flowers to brighten her room.

Then another tragedy overtook them. Soon after the tenth anniversary of the *Chesapeake* affair his second son, William Henry, on holiday from Eton, was drowned while fishing in a small pond not 200 yards from Broke Hall as the rest of the family were eating breakfast. Willy, 'arch little Willy', as he had called him in letters home from the *Shannon*, had been a bright scholar; the rest of the year was clouded with memories of his promise.

His eldest son, Philip, had by this time followed him into the Service via the Naval College, and two years later the third boy, destined to become Admiral Sir George Broke Middleton, and perhaps significantly after the practicality of his father, one of the first Naval officers to volunteer for an engineering training and subsequently for an *engined* ship-of-war, also entered the Service.

His eldest daughter, Louisa, the 'Loolins' of his letters, helped him to look after his crippled wife and the two small boys born after his retirement, and then five orphaned children of a sister of his who came to live at Broke Hall.

Broke still found himself busy with the county business he had taken up on retirement, but the volume he could cope with had lessened, and it all took much longer to get through. Any constant application or writing brought on his old headaches and drained him of energy. He retired more and more into his Horace and his flowers. It was a sad, twilight fulfilment of all his hopes and golden dreams of retirement from the decks of *Shannon*. He built himself a timber-lined study in the shape of his stern cabin in the frigate, and surely looked back nostalgically to those hours in command – in imagination the brave music of water as his ship drove her bows through, the rigging snapping taut to the breeze, never-to-be-forgotten curve and pull of her sails, the trundling cannon, the precision of his arrangements, the good companionship, spice of danger, fine, free times in the intervals ashore with his brother Captains, the poignancy of each mail packet with letters from his delightful Looloo – and all their great hopes before them.

Visits from Wallis, Hyde Parker and his other comrades of those prime years increased in importance as the knowledge that he would never go to sea again fastened upon him. For now both sides of his head were irreparably damaged. Curiously the fall from the horse appeared to have done more mischief than the sabre, for the coldness and numbness it caused had become worse. He was semi-paralysed and could never leave the warmth of his fire without several layers of stockings and outer clothes on his left side.

He was still consulted by serving officers and the Admiralty on gunnery matters, and when the Lord High Admiral, Duke of Clarence, decided to stir up the whole gunnery question in the fleet by sending a form of questions to all ports where H.M. ships were inspected to enquire into the readiness for battle achieved by each vessel during its commission, it was to Broke that his Secretary, Captain the Hon. R. L. Spencer, turned for the specific points to be answered. Broke did not disappoint him. He sent a long reply stressing the necessity of horizontal fire under all conditions of sailing, concentration fire and his 'director' system. Captain Spencer answered:

"Admiralty, Jan 11th 1828

"My dear Sir,

"I must begin by returning my best thanks for your invaluable remarks, especially that part in which you supply me with such cogent and additional reasons for using in my battles, not with an enemy, but with many officers who are nearly as bad, and who will not or cannot be made to understand the use of horizontal and as you properly call it, *blindfold* firing.

"All your questions, and the additions of mine shall be noted in the paper . . . It may at least put men in command of ships a little more in the habit of using their own very extensive and powerful means of helping themselves on board their respective ships to a variety of important things for action. At present it is too much the fashion to trust wholly to what they get from the dockyards, ordnance wharf etc. Whereas in my belief, God help us! If the fighting materials and guns on board any British ships were really made *the best use of*, and an almost exclusive attention paid to them, rather than to whose topgallant yards were across first, there would be nothing more wanted . . ."

Two years later Broke received a letter from Captain Pechell with news of a historic triumph:

"I must however tell you that I have at last the gratification of having accomplished what I have had so long at heart, *viz.* the consent of the Admiralty for the establishment of a depot for instructing seamen and officers in naval gunnery – I was fortunate

213

in finding a foundation laid by the appropriation of the *Excellent* at Portsmouth . . .

"I could not deny myself the pleasure of being the first to apprise you of it, feeling as I do that visiting the *Chesapeake* was the origin of my taking up this subject, believe me dear Sir Philip,

"Very sincerely yours,

"J. S. Pechell."

Broke's two boys rose quickly in the service, lifted by the salt-keenness and gunnery enthusiasm they had learnt from him, and of course by the magic their name still possessed – Broke – of the *Shannon*. They both had the good fortune to see action at the Battle of Navarino, Philip as Lieutenant of the after quarters in a ship of the line, George as a Midshipman. The elderly invalid began to relive all his hopes through them.

". . . Now, my dear George, with a fine frigate, a good Captain and pleasant messmates you are starting all I could wish you; and a pleasant excursion may it be. You have vast variety of station and service before you; so when duty gives you leisure, make yourself happy with all around you. If change of scene or war, or peace send you homewards unexpectedly, you know how happy we shall be in the meeting; but write always as gaily as you can to your tender mama – as I used to do when on very long cruises – telling her all I could to amuse her, and make her think *I was well amused*; but I never said any pretty, sentimental things about 'Home sweet home' till I was pretty sure I should soon be there, and *then* I wrote like a dying lover; but I knew it would not do to awaken all the tenderness before. I am looking now for fine weather to get her amongst the flowers again – the only gay society she is able to enjoy . . . Fair wind and weather and every happiness.

"Your ever affectionate father   P. B. V. Broke."

So the years passed slowly and increasingly painfully; the twentieth anniversary of the *Chesapeake* contest drew near and he noted the uneventful passage of the days just as he had kept his log in better times at sea.

1833, May 28th	64, 56, 61, 69, 62, 61, 64, 63, 53, 50, fine SW. Fuller altered chair. Loo out 2 *hrs* in garden.
29	fine, wind ESE, cold. L not up – resting.
30	Cloudy, NE × N. Got flowers for L, trimmed shrubs, L not up required rest.

June 1   fine SE × S *had bad headache*. I walked at
           8 pm . . .

. . . Thinking. And could he ever forget! "My dearest Looloo, one
happy quarter of an hour has repaid all my ten years' toil . . ."

. . . . . .

"My dear George, . . . Now pray tell us (if a line only from day to
day and not forgetting to *send* it *to the post*) all your prospects as to
sailing etc.; and when you are out you must send all the information you can how *we are to write to you*. I assure you, my dear, that
my utmost hope is to be able to keep on at the *old Hall* so that if I
can afford *nothing else*, there may be always a warm, hospitable
home for all *the old family* when the chances of life bring them
there, that *the old* BADGERS may always have the old earth to bear
up for when they want a home; and this I shall try to do however
humble my establishment – *Broke Hall* – if there is even nothing
there but *brown bread* and *beef*, and *ale* and a blazing log on the
fire, where we may sit when we meet to *talk of old times* and enjoy
whatever we have got left . . .
        "Your ever affectionate father   P. B. V. Broke."
[The old country name for a badger was a broke.]

                                    "Broke Hall, Feb 8th, 1835
". . . Your interesting letter of November 2nd, begun at Trinidad
and finished at Barbadoes, has been lying on my table for months;
but my sad infirmities and the attention requisite to your poor
mother leave me no time for pleasure, or for writing anything but
what imperious necessity forces me to, or I should often . . . have
forgotten my cares and allowed myself, *in imagination*, to have been
wafted over the Atlantic to have a pleasant chat with you, whether
sitting on the carronade, under the awning of your quarterdeck, or
in one of the cool, green verandahs of your tropical casinos; but I
am forever *affairé* with even the little country business devolving
on *even* such an idler as myself. However, great pleasure it *does
give me* to *hear* and to read how happy you are in *your ship*, and
your *comrades* and your station . . . it is a fine thing to be a *happy
fellow*, as you then spread *sunshine* all around you, and harmonise
others into the same, cheerful mood . . ."

                                    "Broke Hall, Aug 31st, 1838
"My dear George, I want you to tell me, when at leisure, what is
the equipment of the French ships with the great howitzers or

                            215

P

Paixhans for the large, hollow shot or shells; and what diameters they are, and if they practise them at all with live shot, or with the fuse only lighted, so as to render the service of them less dangerous, when in actual service and when the shower of sparks (from bursting wads set on fire) come on a ship to leeward from an enemy's fire or come from the same if firing to windward in a fresh breeze? We must use these arms if they do.

"But I do not like the invention, because the most efficient practice of such firing will be in *distant action,* whereas *close quarters* are our shining point. But yet we must have them, as it would be very *disagreeable* to be lying becalmed at half a mile from the enemy whom we could not hurt, and who could very leisurely be making us a *target for practice!*"

"Broke Hall, Feb 27th 1839

". . . Apropos of Ceuta, I never was there, having never been at Gibraltar but during our war with Spain. When you go again and *have time* pray look at the place with your best *warrior's eye,* and tell me if *we held it* with a fair strength as garrison for its size, is it a place secure from any sudden *coup de main* attack by the Moors, supposing their company led by an active Frenchman? . . . consider also whether Ceuta could be held for a month against any regular land attack by a French force of 4,000 or 5,000 men *bien garni*; and also that, if so attacked, the enemy could be prevented occupying *any points* from which they could stop our relief and supplies from Gibraltar by placing batteries . . ."

"Your mother is to write with this to tell you all the *family chat.*
"I am ever, dear George, Your affectionate father,
"P. B. V. Broke."

"You will see by the papers there has been some useful *stir* about *naval equipments,* and that I have another friend at the Admiralty, Sir J. Pechell. He will probably have no power in promotion of commissioned men, but he is a valuable patron *to the noble art of* GUNNERY."

To his own interest in gunnery improvements and inventions he was now adding enthusiasm about steam as the new propelling power for ships. Pechell was stirring this question up too, and wrote to him, "the only check we now experience is from the Navy Board who are so averse to anything like an improvement, but *we* are determined to press on in the introduction of improved machinery and boilers . . ." Broke's other preoccupations were all with Louisa. His brain, although injured in the sensory and motor areas, was as keen as ever, and he brought all the observation and attention to detail which had marked his practical great-gun drills to the simple object of his wife's greater comfort and ease of movement about the house and gardens in her chairs. When he needed to employ a new footman he stipulated that the man must be healthy and strong "and not under 5 feet 7 inches high – that he may be able *well* to draw Lady Broke about the grounds & to help to carry her up or downstairs in her chair . . ."

"Broke Hall, June 12th 1839

"My dear George, . . . Having no one here to assist me in amusing and airing your dear mother, she takes all my time up, and I have none for writing; but she bids me finish this for her. She is as well in health as at her best, and quite cheerful, but no improvement in speech or strength of limbs, spite of all our fresh air and exercise and improved feeding. I fear, at sixty two, we must not expect any further gain, but must thankfully make the best of the increased comforts which we have attained, and by which she is enabled to enjoy so much more of her friends' society within, and of her favourite drives and flowers abroad . . ."

"July 18th, 1839

"I am in all the hurry of packing up for a visit to Shrubland, and what with my own endless wants of strange clothing etc., and your mother's various wheel chairs etc., to send I am as busy as if I, in better times, had suddenly been ordered off, on a day's notice for a station in the East Indies!"

In the autumn of 1840, as the leaves fell from the avenues and bird-chirping copses about Broke Hall, spreading a golden brown carpet over lawn and rosebed, path and parkland, down to the bright Orwell, he prepared for what proved to be his last journey. He had decided, without telling Louisa for fear of alarming her, that he should undergo an operation to relieve the congestion on his brain. After three days of slow packing and setting his affairs in order, and after his daughter had promised that whatever the outcome she would always look after her mother, he started out for the capital on 28th October.

His brother Charles, now Major General Sir Charles Broke Vere, K.C.B., veteran of Albuerra, Badajos, Salamanca, Vittoria, etc., up to Waterloo, accompanied him, and together they stayed at Bayley's Hotel, Berkeley Square, while he was prepared for the surgeons. They were joined later by his eldest son, now Captain Philip Broke, Royal Navy. These two nursed and cheered him through the closing weeks of the year as he lay far from the country sounds he loved.

News came daily from his daughter at Broke Hall, which was a great comfort, and in December there were cheering reports of the British bombardment of St. Jean D'Acre, to which, it was said, the improvements in practice brought about by the new gunnery school, H.M.S. *Excellent*, had contributed greatly.

One of the ships engaged at the bombardment was H.M.S. *Wasp*, First Lieutenant George Broke . . .

"My dear George, I heartily wish you joy of your brilliant victory at Acre . . . I am quietly urging your promotion at the Admiralty, and my friends promise to do their best for you . . .

"Pray inquire and tell me if any of the ships fired *shells* from their large guns. It was a fine opportunity for *practice*! And pray tell me at what elevation the guns were fired in the larger ships as well as little *Wasp*'s carronades, and what your distance was from the nearest battery opposed to you . . .

"Here I am still confined and suffering frequent painful operations, but gain no ground yet; but I have full confidence in my surgeon, and am sure that when *nature* will let him he will effect a permanent cure. My old infirmities were quite sufficient a burden without this distressing torment. My quiet, yet cheerful brother, Charles is the most happy companion for me in my *solitude* and *weariness*, and I have the comfort of hearing daily good reports from home, where your dear sister drives mamma out every day, and keeps up her health and spirits. I shall be very happy to get amongst them again!"

A few days after writing this, he received splendid news.

"My dear George, I was made very happy yesterday by a *private* letter from our kind friend . . . (?), telling me that you were promoted. Hurrah for Commander Broke!

". . . I hear all is well at home today, and they are to send us a little turkey from the old farm for our Christmas dinner, my doctor giving me no hopes of getting home for several weeks yet. God bless you in perfect health, prays,

"Your ever affectionate father,   P. B. V. Broke."

Some ten days after this letter his condition suddenly worsened. The fine constitution which had helped him to fight the dreadful sabre wound aboard the *Shannon* had been worn down from his long infirmities, and the final operation proved too much. He died peacefully in his sleep at 6 in the evening of 2nd January 1841.

"My dearest George," Louisa, his daughter, wrote after hearing the news, "Mamma's submission and resignation are beautiful. Her chief consolation is in knowing that our dear father, when fully aware of his approaching end, expressed his willingness to depart, and his gratitude for all the happiness which he had enjoyed with her and in his family."

Philip wrote to one of the several old Shannons who still made visits to Broke Hall whenever the Service permitted.

"January 8th, 1841

"My dear Wallis, Before this reaches you, the newspapers will have announced that it has pleased Providence to deprive me of the kindest and best of fathers. He was in town previously for two months for the purpose of obtaining surgical advice, and till three days before his death no danger was apprehended. This blow, therefore comes very suddenly on my poor mother and sister and all his relations. It is a consolation to me to have been with him in his last moments, and to know that few men leave this world better prepared than he was to submit with resignation to the Divine will. The funeral will take place here tomorrow, and will be strictly private in order that my poor mother and sister may not be unnecessarily shocked by the sad ceremony being prolonged. *You* will, I know, console with me, and believe me,
"Dear Wallis, Yours ever truly,   P. Broke."

The bells of St. Mary's, Ipswich, beat in muffled waves behind the funeral procession as it wound slowly through the cold, grey streets of the town in the last light of the January afternoon. Behind the hearse and the mutes riding on horses came the family mourning coach and the carriages of friends and the local gentry. Windows along the route and nearby streets were shuttered and the shops closed up as a token of respect.

The coffin and the mourners passed on through the town and into the countryside he had loved, over the old road to Nacton, deep-rutted with winter floods and many wheels, winding in right angles past the lifeless fields without flowers, trees standing gaunt with bare branches shaking against the dusk.

So he made the journey to the old home of the Brokes for the last time in darkness – to the lodge gates, up the long, straight avenue of limes which had offered shelter from the sun to the redhead boy, the Post Captain with his fresh bride, the elderly man with his wounds and his memories and his table linen always packed ready for sea service – under the winter-cold limes to the great oak door of Broke Hall.

The following day his coffin was borne to its last resting place in the little village church close by, and laid in the tomb of his ancestors. Two years later his beloved Louisa followed him there.

.   .   .

And now, if you make the journey to Nacton on the river Orwell just below Ipswich you will still see the church where they lie, and in the Broke Chapel a white marble plaque inscribed:

To the memory of
SIR PHILIP BOWES VERE BROKE
Baronet & K.C.B.,
Rear Admiral of the Red,
who died on the 2d of Jany 1841 in the 65th year of his age
He was an attached husband and an affectionate parent.
In his profession which was his choice from infancy
he was ardent and persevering.
After a long period of service at sea
His professional skill was signally exhibited
on the 1st June, 1813 . . .

"My dearest Looloo, One happy quarter of an hour has repaid all my ten years' toil and enabled me to retire to the enjoyment of that fond society in which only I think life desirable; and that with a reputation which secures me from that restless anxiety which so often disturbs a military man, who, though satisfied he has done his duty, has had no opportunity of proving it to the world. His toils and perseverance, and general services are only known to those of his profession and acquaintance, and people on shore suppose he has done nothing. Indeed, my beloved Loo, our success has been particularly happy; previous misfortune enhanced its value."

". . . My Lords have before had occasion to observe the zeal, judgement and activity which have characterised Captain Broke's proceedings since the commencement of the war, and they now receive with the highest satisfaction a proof of professional skill and gallantry in battle, which has been seldom equalled and certainly never surpassed."

Also of
SARAH LOUISA his wife

CHRONOLOGICAL INDEX AND NOTES

Abbreviations used in Chronological Index:

Brenton. *The Naval History of Great Britain*, Vol. II, by Edward Pelham Brenton, London, 1837.

Brighton. *Admiral Sir P. B. V. Broke, Bart, A Memoir*, by Rev. J. G. Brighton, Sampson, Low, Marston, 1866.

Broke to George. Letters written by Broke to his son, George. The author has been unable to trace these letters in Broke's papers, and they are all quoted from Brighton's Memoir. It is assumed that they are all to George and not to the elder son, Philip, as the latter's time at sea ended in 1835 and the bulk of the letters are dated later.

Broke to Louisa. Letters written by Broke to his wife, now in the Saumarez Papers, Ipswich, prefixed HA 93
1809 877/10; 1810 877/11; 1811 877/12; 1812 877/13; 1813 877/14.

Carden. Memoir of Admiral Carden, written by himself, edited C. T. Atkinson, Clarendon Press, Oxford, 1912.

Chesapeake K. & W. Account of Killed, Wounded & prisoners of officers & crew of the frigate *Chesapeake* in the action with the British frigate *Shannon* – communicated to the United States House of Representatives, 1st March 1826.

Chesapeake Muster Roll. Muster Book of the officers, seamen, O.S. and boys attached to the U.S.S. *Chesapeake*, 1812, Samuel Evans, commander. U.S.N. Archives, Call No. T829 30.

Chesapeake Payroll. Payroll of *Chesapeake* when captured by the *Shannon* 1813 (from 21st May to 1st June 1813 – Jas. Lawrence, commander; J. Chew, purser) U.S.N. Archives as above.

Chesapeake Courts Martial. Courts Martial of various officers and men of the *Chesapeake*. U.S.N. Archives, EXRG 45, Vol. V, 160-99.

Collier. Account of the action by letter from John Collier (Captain Main Top) dated 29th November 1841 (HA 93 877/7).

Collingwood. *Correspondence of Vice-Admiral Lord Collingwood*, ed. G. L. Newnham, James Ridgeway, 1828.

Decatur. *The Romantic Decatur*, by Charles Lee Lewis, University of Pennsylvania Press, Philadelphia, 1937.

Gravière. *Guerres Maritimes*, Vol. II, Capitaine Jurien de la Gravière, Paris, 1847.

Hutchison. *Practical Observations in Surgery*, by Dr. Alex C. Hutchinson, Thomas & George Underwood, London, 1826. (Broke's own copy in the possession of The Hon. Mrs. Llewellen Palmer.)

James. *Naval Occurrences of the late War between Great Britain and the United States of America*, by William James, 1817.

King. *Capt.* (later Admiral) R. H. King's detailed memo of the action, the second half of which is in the Saumarez papers HA 93 877/25, but the missing first half is quoted in part by Brighton in his Memoir of Admiral Broke.

King's Diary. Admiral R. H. King's diary in the possession of New York Historical Society, New York.

Lawrence. *James Lawrence,* by Albert Gleaves, G. P. Putnam's Sons, New York and London, 1904.

Leech. *A Voice from the Main Deck – the Experiences of Samuel Leech,* John Neale, London, 1844.

Marryat. *Captain Marryat and the Old Navy,* by Christopher Lloyd, Longmans Green, 1939.

Nav. Chron. Naval Chronicle.

Pechell. *Observations on the Defective Equipment of Ship's Guns,* by Captain S. J. Pechell, Corfu, 1st December 1825 (included in "Pamphlets on Gunnery" at the Admiralty Library).

Pel Verjuice. *Autobiography of Pel Verjuice,* by Charles Reece Pemberton, The Scholartis Press, London.

Pool Collection. *Don't Give up the Ship,* Catalogue of the Eugene H. Pool Collection of James Lawrence, published Peabody Press, Salem, 1942.

Provo Wallis. *Admiral of the Fleet Sir Provo Wallis – A Memoir,* by Rev. J. G. Brighton, Hutchinson, 1892.

Roosevelt. Roosevelt's Chapter on the Naval War of 1812 in Wm. Laird Clowes' *The Royal Navy – A History* (Sampson Low Marston).

Saumarez Papers. These contain all the Broke papers; they are in the East Suffolk County Archives, Ipswich. Numbers in brackets throughout the chronological index refer to these papers unless otherwise stated, and the prefix HA 93 should be added to each number.

Sermons. *Sermons on the Character and Professional Duties of Seamen,* by James Stanier Clarke, London, 1801. The copy used for this book was Broke's own containing deletions and additions in his own hand (in possession of The Hon. Mrs. Llewellen Palmer).

Shannon's Muster List. List of *Chesapeake* P.O.W.s landed in Halifax to prison or hospital (Public Record Office, ADM 37/4402).

Stack. Account of the action by letter from William Stack (Captain's Cox'n) dated 1841 (HA 93 877/25).

Trade Winds. *Trade Winds,* edited by C. Northcote Parkinson, George Allen & Unwin, 1948.

PROLOGUE

p. 2, line 4, Philip Bowes Vere Broke, born 9th September 1776 at Broke Hall, first son of Philip Bowes Broke and Elizabeth Beaumont, attended Ipswich School, Cheam School and entered Royal Naval Academy, Portsmouth, in 1788.

p. 4, line 7, Joins *Bulldog* sloop, 25th June 1792, Captain G. Hope. Joins

L'Eclair sloop, 6th August 1793, Captain G. Hope, then Captain G. H. Towry from 10th September.

Journal 20th May 1794: "I was discharged into *Romulus* (36-gun frigate) . . ."

"May 25th: joined the *Romulus* with Captain Hope, cruising with the fleet under Admiral Hotham's command . . ."

"June 8th, 1795, I joined the *Britannia* (1st Rate Ship of the line) – Admiral Hotham's flag – Captain Hollowell commander . . ."

p. 4, line 35, Journal, 18th July 1795: "I received a commission for the *Southampton* as third lieutenant."

"July 19th: In the evening joined her under command of Captain Shield . . ."

p. 4, line 40, As an illustration of an "excitement": Broke's Journal 9th June 1796. "Sir J. Jervis discovered a French cruiser working up to Hieres Bay, within the islands, and immediately singling out the *Southampton*, called her commander on board the *Victory*, pointed the ship out, and directed him to make a dash at her through the Grand Pass. The *Southampton* instantly got under weigh and went in, in view of the entire British fleet, which with anxious suspense witnessed the boldness of an attempt that scarcely anything but the completest success could have justified. The Admiral refused even to give a written order for the enterprise . . . the *Southampton* pushed through the Grand Pass, and hauled up under the batteries of the north-east end of Porquerole, under easy sail, in the hope that she might be mistaken for a neutral or a French frigate. The stratagem succeeded, and she arrived within pistol shot of the enemy undiscovered. He (Captain Shield) then cautioned the French Captain through a trumpet, not to make a fruitless resistance. A shot from a pistol at the speaker, and a broadside at the *Southampton* immediately followed. At this instant, being very near the heavy battery of Fort Braganson, the *Southampton* laid the enemy on board; Lieut. Lydiard, at the head of the boarders, entered and carried her in about ten minutes . . . about thirty minutes past one in the morning, the *Southampton* and her prize returned through the Grand Pass and rejoined the fleet . . ."

p. 5, line 15, Fleet Action on 11th October 1798 between Brit. squadron under Sir John Borlase Warren and a French squadron off Irish Coast, seven French ships taken.

p. 5, line 19, Appointed Commander January 1799 to *Falcon* fire brig, unmanned and at moorings at Sheerness. Autumn 1799 appointed Commander *Shark* sloop-of-war, joined North Sea Fleet under Lord Duncan, mostly employed in convoy protection.

p. 5, line 42, Philip Bowes Vere Broke Esq. & Sarah Louisa Middleton married at Crowfield Chapel, 25th November 1802. The marriage settlement from the Middletons £5,000, "the interest of the £5,000 at the rate of £5 per cent per annum . . . by two half yearly payments

... in consideration of the marriage and of the above agreement ..
Captain Broke undertakes & agrees that his solicitor shall deliver
proposals for securing the payment of one annuity clear of all deduc-
tions of £600 to Miss Middleton during her life ... and to be paid by
four equal quarterly payments" (HA 93 877/14).

p. 6, line 4, Nacton, Ipswich, 27th January 1805. To Lord Melville: "My
Lord, Having observed that a great many frigates and smaller ships
have been lately commissioned, I take the liberty of reminding your
Lordship of the promise you favour'd me with in the summer of last
year – that I should be employ'd soon. As your Lordship was pleased
in your letter upon that occasion, to express your approbation of the
manner in which I was exerting myself here, I have continued to support my battalion of peasantry ..." (Brighton, p. 45).

p. 6, line 13, Commission to command *Druid* dated 8th April 1805.

p. 6, line 35, Broke to Louisa from *Shannon* off Boston, 9th May 1813.

CHAPTER ONE

p. 9, line 13, Broke's Journal November to January 1806 (877/51).

p. 11, line 13, Broke to Sir Howard Douglas, 1818 (877/16).

p. 12, line 10, Broke's Journal 1st May 1806 (877/51).

p. 12, line 36, Admiral King's Journal, quoted by Brighton, pp. 55–6.
Author unable to trace Journal. P. 13, 'point of honour ship', King's
Journal ditto. P. 13, gunnery training also King's Journal.

p. 13, line 24, Broke to Sir Howard Douglas 1818 (877/16).

p. 14, line 3, Sights and training of guns. King's Journal above, quoted
Brighton, p. 56: "Captain Broke had placed the dispart sights on the
Druid's guns. The crew were well exercised, and used to handle the
guns with great exactness and celerity ..."

p. 15, line 21, Broke to Sir Howard Douglas 1818 (877/16).
line 38, supposition from the known exercises in *Shannon* and Broke's
Journal in *Druid*.

p. 16, line 14, Broke to George, from Broke Hall, 10th March 1834.
Brighton, p. 387.

p. 16, line 37, Broke to George, 14th February 1838. Brighton, p. 403.
line 40, "Tis DIFFICULTIES that *make* GOOD MEN!" Broke to George,
8th February 1835. Brighton, p. 392.

p. 17, line 5, Broke's Journal (877/51).

p. 17, line 22, Anecdote and quotation feigned illness from Hutchison.

p. 17, line 39, *Providence* anecdote. King's Journal, quoted Brighton,
p. 56–7. Words attributed to Broke here invented by author.

p. 18, lines 7 and 36, Broke's pocket diaries (877/66).

p. 20, line 10, Lord Keith's Standing Orders dated 10th April 1807 (877/53).

p. 20, line 30, Feigned illness from Hutchison, as quotation.

p. 21, line 39, Collingwood, to Vice-Admiral Thornborough 18th October
1807.

p. 22, line 39, Gravière, p. 272.

CHAPTER TWO

p. 23, line 35, List of Occupations, heights, nationalities of *Shannon*'s crew dated March 1809 (877/83).

p. 26, line 2, Pel Verjuice.

p. 27, line 35, Laying the guns horizontal as described by Pechell.

pp. 27–30, Broke's system of gunnery described from three main sources, his own correspondence with Sir Howard Douglas (877/25), Pechell, who copied many of *Shannon*'s systems in *San Domingo*, and King; p. 28, line 9, quotation from Broke to Sir H. Douglas, 1818.

p. 29, line 36, King, p. 31.

p. 31, line 19, Broke to George, 2nd February 1836.

p. 32, line 38, Leech.

p. 33, line 17, Leech.

p. 34, line 1, Remark Book kept on board H.M.S. *Shannon*, quoted Brighton, p. 65, also in Saumarez Papers.

p. 35, line 21, "Beating to Quarters" list (877/83).

p. 37, line 3, Broke to Sir H. Douglas (877/25): "To preserve our firing powder & tubes perfectly was an anxious study always in the *Shannon* & required constant vigilance. We kept our powder in small tin tubes, holding each an ample priming & those prevented the powder ever being damped by the wet fingers of a seaman who, the instant before perhaps, had been handling the tackles or breechings which were wet with spray or water upon the deck."

p. 39, line 2, As above: "In answer to your inquiries concerning our form of exercise for the great guns ... I do not recollect ever hearing of any form being particularly prescribed by authority, the gunner being more generally allowed to exercise the guns in that manner he had been used to ... we had such a variety of modes of exercise to perfect the men in *particular* that it prevents my clear recollection of the *common general* form of working the guns by *word of command*. Few days passed at sea (& *Shannon* was generally there) without some warlike practice of great guns or small arms, frequently *field days*, when in full force we practiced our powers & resources in every position we could suppose the ship placed – engaged with one or more adversaries – either ships or gunboats & in every situation that *la fortune de guerre* could throw us – every man in the ship being used to his small arms & all but the marines (& most of them) & the very dullest of our waisters qualified to serve a great gun – this gave great room for varied practice in the supposition for boarding or repelling boarders & of making the most of our force against an enemy when entangled with us in a position where few guns would bear on him – in our exercises the kind of shot were varied according to the object to which the guns were supposed to be directed & the guns being frequently worked in different divisions for effecting particular sorts of service, as for hulling or dismasting at various distances, the men were prepared for any practice wanted – & also for making the utmost use of their arms in every situation, whether *complete* or more or less disabled by loss of men or by material damage. When the necessity of employing many men upon the other duties of the ship – or when weather prevented us from exercising larger bodies, the captains or 2nd captains were exercised at a gun by themselves each giving the word in turn or were only practiced in continued succession in accurate aiming; in shewing how they *could catch* the *roll* by stopping the gun with the quoin when she bore upon the proper elevation – or in taking aim and elevating by our rough tangent scale – or in *cooly priming their guns*, working their locks, shifting flints etc. – and all the minutiae of exercise, the loaders & other best men at the guns succeeded them in like manner & their partial drill gave excellent opportunities of watching & rectifying errors & teaching these men how to teach others, besides the advantage of frequent *explanations* to them . . . one constant main object was to give a man *confidence* in his gun, & shew him what service he alone might effect against an enemy by cool courage & practical skill – our young officers took their turn in these exercises when the men were all employed so that some *advance* was generally making towards perfect service orders . . . all these studies made a *great round* of practice . . ."

p. 39, line 19, Broke to George, undated, probably 1835, Brighton, p. 395.
p. 39, line 23, Broke's Journal, Brighton, p. 60.
p. 40, line 3, Broke's Remark Book, Brighton, p. 72.
p. 41, line 31, As above, Brighton, p. 78.
p. 43, line 4, Broke's Journal, Brighton, p. 62.
p. 43, line 20, Broke's Remark Book, Brighton, p. 71.
p. 43, line 27, As above, Brighton, p. 84.

CHAPTER THREE

p. 47, line 33, Broke to Sir H. Douglas (877/16).
p. 48, line 7, As above.
p. 48, line 35, Collingwood – to Lady Collingwood, 15th May 1808.
p. 49, line 5, Broke to George, 10th March 1834.
p. 49, line 23, Broke's letter book (877/52).
p. 50, line 38, Broke to George, 29th December 1838: "I have had Captains quarrel with me, but I made it a rule never to quarrel with them, and always to keep in the right . . ."
p. 52, line 17, Broke to George, 4th February 1840.
p. 55, line 33, Broke to Louisa, 25th March 1810.
p. 56, line 4, Collingwood – to Lady Collingwood, 17th June 1809.
p. 57, line 18, Incident invented by author.
p. 58, line 20, From list of small-arms drill (877/83).
p. 60, line 8, Broke to Louisa, 24th June 1810.
p. 63, line 4, Broke to Louisa, 18th September 1810.

CHAPTER FOUR

p. 69, line 42, Broke to Louisa, off Bourdeaux, 19th May 1811.

p. 71, line 20, As above, September 1811.

p. 72, line 15, As above, 22nd September 1811.

p. 74, line 12, Gunnery exercise described by Pechell.

p. 75, line 18, List of fittings (877/83), colour of bulkheads suppositious from other ships of same date.

p. 76, line 15, Sermons.

p. 76, line 31, *Shannon*'s Log. Public Record Office, ADM 51, 2861.

p. 78, line 6, Broke to Louisa, Bermuda, 23rd December 1811.

p. 78, line 16, Brenton, Vol. II, p. 490 footnote.

p. 79, line 4, Broke to Louisa, Bermuda, 1st January 1812.

p. 79, line 29, Provo Wallis.

p. 80, line 5, Brighton, p. 128, who probably had it from King.

p. 82, line 8, Broke to Louisa, 1st August 1813.

p. 83, line 19, Broke to his mother, undated, but marked by a subsequent hand, probably George Middleton Broke, as "written before war was declared with America" (877/6).

p. 85, line 6, Broke to Louisa, 6th May 1812.

p. 88, line 5, Broke to Louisa, 2nd July 1812.

CHAPTER FIVE

p. 89, line 14, *Minerva* anecdote, Brighton, pp. 134–5, who probably had it from King or Wallis.

p. 90, line 37, *Shannon* letter book (877/104). Letters to C-in-C, dated 14th July at sea: "Two fishermen came on board successively as pilots, & were, I believe convinced that they were on board the *Congress* & that our squadron was that of Commodore Rodgers . . . they had heard of *our* taking the *Belvidera* . . ."

p. 92, line 12, Capt., Byron to Broke, letter 20th July 1812 (877/27).

p. 95, line 10, As above.

p. 101, line 39, *The Times*, 24th March 1813.

p. 102, line 4, Broke to Louisa, Sunday, 20th September 1812.

p. 103, line 10, As above, Monday, 28th September 1812.

p. 107, line 5, Leech, p. 31.

p. 107, line 40, Leech: "The First Lieutenant passed through the ship directing the marines & boarders who were furnished with pikes, cutlasses and pistols, how to proceed if it should be necessary to board the enemy . . ."

p. 108, line 40, Anecdote about John Card from Leech, confirmed in *White Jacket*, by Hermann Melville.

p. 110, line 23, Leech.

p. 111, line 26, Carden.

p. 112, line 8, Leech.

p. 112, line 39, Decatur.

p. 113, line 17, Sermons.

p. 115, line 26, *Nav. Chron.*, Vol. XXVIII, 1812, Naval Poetry, p. 422.

CHAPTER SIX

p. 116, line 1, In this connection Captain Lawrence's letter to American Consul dated 22nd December 1812 (877/88) contains a postscript: "The *Constitution* is on the lookout for some vessel we have information of . . ."

p. 117, line 39, Doubt on American wounded figures contained in Lt. Chads' evidence to Ct. Martial aboard H.M.S. *Gladiator*, 23rd April 1813, in which he referred to a statement by his assistant surgeon who assisted American surgeon.

p. 118, line 8, From Chads' and Bainbridge's official letters to respective secretaries, James.

p. 118, line 19, *The Times*, 20th March 1813.

p. 118, line 28, *Nav. Chron.*, Vol. XXIX, 1813, p. 465, Captain W. H. Tremlett, R.N., to Editor, line 33 from same volume, p. 467, "A Naval Patriot" to Editor.

p. 120, line 3, Broke's pocket diaries (877/66).

p. 120, line 11, Brighton, p. 148.

p. 120, line 25, See ref. for p. 39, line 2, Chron. Index above.

p. 123, line 40, Lawrence's Report to Commodore Rodgers from U.S. gunboat *No. 6*, 12th July 1805.

p. 124, line 35, Lawrence. (Note: in Pool Collection this same letter is interpreted as dated 5th May *1813*. The reference to Lawrence's daughter being one year old convinces the author that Gleaves, not Pool, is correct.)

p. 125, line 17, Lawrence.

p. 126, line 12, Lawrence.

p. 126, line 21, Lawrence.

p. 127, line 7, Lawrence to American Consul (877/88).

p. 127, line 31, Admiral Preble quoted in Lawrence.

p. 128, line 1, Marryat (himself serving in *L'Espiegle*).

p. 128, line 30, "Additional Regulations & Instructions relating to H.M. Service at Sea, 1813."

p. 129, line 27, Lawrence.

p. 129, line 33, Bainbridge from U.S. frigate *Constitution*, Boston, 23rd March 1813. Pool Collection.

p. 130, line 28, Broke's Letter Book (877/104).

p. 130, line 39, Broke to George, 27th April 1840. Brighton, p. 417.

p. 131, line 8, King, p. 31.

p. 131, line 34, Broke to Louisa, 27th March 1813.

p. 131, line 31, As above, 27th March 1813.

p. 132, line 6, Hotham to Broke, Bermuda, 7th March 1813 (877/26): ". . . I am so happy at the prospect it (his apptmt. to N. American station) affords me of meeting you sometime, and of serving in the same fleet with you . . ."

p. 132, line 24, Adml. Sir G. Hope to Broke, 13th February 1813 (877/26).

p. 133, line 9, Broke's Letter Book (877/104).

p. 133, line 15, Brighton, pp. 146–7.

p. 133, line 28, Broke's Letter Book (877/104).

p. 133, line 34, Brighton, p. 150.

p. 134, line 33, Supposition from his known extreme frustration as evidenced by all his letters at this time, and his statement in his subsequent letter of challenge to Lawrence: "the pains I took to detach all force but *Shannon* and *Tenedos* . . . and the various verbal messages which had been sent in to Boston to that effect . . ."

Rodgers, when he saw this statement in Broke's challenge, wrote to the Secretary of the Navy that Captain Broke's conduct "was so glaringly opposite (to that claimed in the challenge) as to authorise a very contrary belief."

Broke's Journal has this to say about the escape of Rodgers: "Another week's anxious watch; and then in the evening ran in to reconnoitre. Enemy nearly as before. On the evening of Friday, Apr 30th, the weather being thick & rainy, the American frigates stole out of harbour, evaded the long & diligent watch kept by the *Shannon* & *Tenedos*, & got safely to sea." To his wife, he wrote, "We must have been very close to them; but they did not *seek* us."

Broke's noon positions as recorded in his pocket diaries for the days previous to the escape were:

April 26th "off C. Anne or to 10 leagues E. of it."
　　　27th "Saw C. Anne."
　　　28th "42 13N 69 25W"
　　　29th "42 01N 69 20W"
　　　30th "42 29N 69 31W"
May　1st "42 42N D.R. 70 17W"

That is to say his noon positions for 26th and 27th were in sight of C. Ann and then for the 28th, 29th and 30th, when the wind was recorded as fresh to modte north-easterly, he naturally kept off the lee shore, cruising some 60 miles east of the islands of Boston – a justification for Rodger's comment? Although Rodgers must have known the techniques of blockade. When the wind changed southerly in the evening of 30th, bringing fog, Broke tacked and wafted northerly to make C. Ann once more. It was during this time that Rodgers slipped out past him.

p. 134, line 38, Words of verbal challenge invented by the author.

p. 136, line 15, Broke to Louisa, 9th May, *Shannon* off Boston.

p. 137, line 7, As above.

p. 137, line 34, Lawrence, 26th April 1813.

p. 138, line 14, Lawrence, 6th May, from Navy Department.

p. 138, line 36, Lawrence to Navy Department, New York, 10th May 1813.

p. 139, line 13, As Above, Boston, 20th May.

p. 140, line 10, *Chesapeake* and *Shannon* gunnery details, Broke to Sir H. Douglas (877/16).

p. 141, line 2, *Chesapeake* Court Martial.

p. 141, line 14, Log of *Chesapeake* captured by Broke (877/89) and from *Chesapeake* Court Martial.

p. 142, line 4, Broke's Letter Book (877/104).

p. 142, line 31, Lawrence to Sec. of Navy, 1st June 1813. Lt. Pierce was signed off *Chesapeake*'s payroll on 25th May.

p. 143, line 1, Lawrence to Captain Biddle, 27th May 1813.

p. 143, line 9, Lawrence.

p. 144, line 15, Irishmen and gunnery from *Shannon*'s Log, Broke's pocket diary and Trade Winds.

p. 144, line 36, That Broke drafted his famous letter of challenge on Monday 31st May and not, as generally held, on 1st June is pure supposition. James relates that Broke wrote his letter on *Monday*, but this is probably a slip. However, the style and content appear so nicely calculated as to suggest to the author that Broke had not time to compose the challenge between first sight of the *Chesapeake* a.m. 1st June, and despatching Captain Eben Slocum close to the lighthouse. Of course he was an accomplished writer, and it is quite possible that he did so compose it. But even if he had not actually *written* it out in draft, the author believes he must have been turning the wording over in his mind at least – perhaps from the time when he first learned that Lawrence was the *Chesapeake*'s new Captain.

p. 146, line 38, Eben Slocum anecdote from Stack: "I think we were cruising in the bay 9 or 10 weeks when we captured a sort of cutter which the Captain would have given back again if the Captain in her had not been so saucy to our Captain and told him that if he had a ship of force he would soon drive him off the coast or carry him in to Boston; and as soon as he would go into Boston that thar would be a ship sent to bring us in or drive us off the coast; and he abused our Captain very much so he ordered the captain of the cutter to be gagged and put in irons down below, and in the course of the evening we set the cutter on fire close to the lighthouse, and in a few hours afterwards the captain of the cutter was sent in a fishing boat and our captain gave him a letter . . ."

CHAPTER SEVEN

p. 151, line 12, The number of men aboard the *Chesapeake* when she engaged is still a vexed question. Here are some points:

(*a*) *Chesapeake* K. & W. (see list of abbreviations) lists 48 officers and men killed, 14 wounded, since died, and 320 taken as prisoners of war (total wounded, including 'since dead', 96), or a total of 382 persons aboard the *Chesapeake* for the action. This is the official American figure.

(*b*) *Chesapeake* payroll lists 402 names, 14 of whom were discharged before 1st June; total for action thus 388. The difference between this and official account is thus 6; these six are: John Grant, Joseph Philips, Richard Palfrey, Thomas Ellison, John Smith (2nd) and Charles Bowden.

(*c*) However, all British sources are confident that the number on board the *Chesapeake* was more like 440, which was the figure Broke put in his despatch and which appeared in contemporary Halifax papers. Broke's Journal (877/49) contains the following entry: "June 1st took *Chesapeake*", and on the following page is a pencilled note: "sent to prison & hospital 333, estimated killed 70 – died at sea uncertain number. Men on books were only 389 but complement was 443 some men joined on the day they sailed & were not in the list."

(*d*) Midshipman Smith, one of the Shannons who boarded the *Chesapeake*, wrote afterwards (when a Captain): "Ches crew 391, & volunteered from *Constitution* 50, Total 441." He put the number of Chesapeakes killed and died of wounds 108, and stated that 333 Americans were landed at Halifax, 325 of them as prisoners. (From King's diary and King's detailed memo.) Smith's statement ended: "The *Chesapeake* had most certainly 441 men at the commencement of the action & on the following day were counted 333 or 335."

(*e*) However, Lieutenant Budd, 2nd of the *Chesapeake*, swore in Halifax that the crew had numbered 381 men, 5 boys, total 386.

(*f*) Now here is an extract from Admiral King's diary: "Amongst the *Constitution* volunteers (aboard *Chesapeake*) were three or four Americans who had been in the *Guerriere* and these confessed to 40 men from the *Constitution*! So that upon the whole it is certain that volunteers from the *Constitution* did form a part of the men on board the *Chesapeake*. . . At the time of the capture they were stated generally by all on board the *Shannon* to be 60 . . . There is one strong reason (for this) . . . it was reported & believed by all parties in Boston that the *Shannon* had 60 men lent her from *La Hogue* for the express purpose of making her equal to an American frigate. Of course Captain Lawrence . . . believed this to be a fact and under that belief it was natural & even a duty to admit an equal number of volunteers into the *Chesapeake*." (Note: Broke's letter of challenge, written before the action, contains a statement that reports of 150 men lent to the *Shannon* by *La Hogue* were incorrect.) It must be remembered that Admiral King, although a *Shannon* Midshipman, was absent in charge of a prize on the day of the action.

(*g*) The author has been unable to trace any muster or pay lists from the *Constitution* covering 31st May–1st June.

(*h*) In *Lawrence* it is stated that Lawrence asked Bainbridge for men from the *Constitution* while dining with him on the evening of 31st May, but that Bainbridge refused, saying, however, that he could have men from the dockyard.

(*i*) The author, in an attempt to find the truth from these conflicting statements has checked all the names in the *Shannon*'s muster list of *Chesapeake* prisoners landed in Halifax (to prison or hospital) (P.R.O. Adm. 37/4402) against the names appearing on the *Chesapeake*'s Pay List on June 1st. There are only seven names which do not appear in the *Chesapeake*'s Pay List 1st June. Therefore to believe the British statement that some 60 volunteers came aboard the *Chesapeake* at the last moment and were not included on the Pay List it is necessary to believe that some 53 of these men were killed in action or died before reaching Halifax. In other words that while only 1 in 8 Chesapeakes died in the action 7 in 8 volunteers died. This is plainly unacceptable and it must therefore be assumed that although a few volunteers apparently did come aboard at the last moment they were no more than a dozen at the outside, probably as few as seven or eight.

(*j*) The author's computations are:

Fact: No. of *Chesapeake* officers and men landed from *Shannon* as P.O.W.s at Halifax	332
Fact: Names in U.S. official list of wounded (since died) who do not appear in above (including Lawrence)	13
	345
Add no. killed in action, U.S. official list	48
Therefore no. aboard *Chesapeake* at commencement of action	393

(Plus between say 0 and 3 volunteers who may have been killed in action)

Or another way:

Fact: Officers and men on *Chesapeake* payroll 1st June	388
Fact: Names on *Shannon*'s list of Chesapeakes landed at Halifax who do not appear on above	7
Therefore no. aboard *Chesapeake* at commencement of action	395

Summary: *Chesapeake* engaged with 395 officers, men and marines

Killed in action	50
	345
Died before arrival at Halifax	13
	332 P.O.W.s landed at Halifax

232

6 Chesapeakes including Ludlow died subsequently

Totals: Killed   50
             Wounded, since dead   19
             Wounded and recovered 77

                          146 out of 395 officers and men
                          —— aboard.

This casualty proportion was quite sufficient to ensure the defeat of any man-of-war of the day. No dereliction of duty or cowardice need be attributed to the Chesapeakes.

p. 152, line 4, Stack: "They hove their ship a short . . . ready for tripping the anchor and lowered the two quarter boats down and as their women landed they gave our ship three cheers. They were ordered to remain there – they would take them in again as they brought our ship up harbour. Captain Lawrence gave no more time for the river Chesapeake to overflow the river Shannon than he did to the wasp to sting the peacock to death in fifteen minutes, that is what he said to his men."

p. 154, line 13, The Shannons' state of mind from King: ". . . the men well knew what they could do; they thoroughly appreciated the training they had received under their Captain's own eyes; they *enjoyed* their exercises & prided themselves on their proficiency in the use of all arms. They ardently longed for a meeting with an American frigate quite indifferent as to her size or commander. Without presumption they said, 'if any ship can do it, we are that ship,' and their minds were resolved to endure the severest contest & to conquor."

p. 154, line 27, Author not certain at what time the *Chesapeake* was first seen as under sail from the *Shannon*. According to Smith, (quoted by King) the *Shannon* was six or seven miles from the lighthouse when the *Chesapeake* rounded it. According to the *Shannon's* Log she was farther north, and therefore her sight of the *Chesapeake* as she weighed at noon was probably obscured by islands. The account in the text is a compromise as so many acounts are so contradictory.

p. 155, line 11, Stack: "One of the men by the name of Davis poked his head out of the port and told the Captain it was the *Chesapeake*. The Captain asked him how he knew that; 'sir,' says he, 'I belonged to her for two years . . .' 'Oh, then I know who is Captain of her, 'tis Captain Lawrence,' our Captain said. 'I hope to have the pleasure of shaking hands with him today'."

pp. 160–161, lines 31–22, Broke's speech an amalgam of: Smith to King: "The leading features of Sir Philip's speech to the men before going into action went to remind them that now the time had come to show the superiority in the management of their guns and their long drilling, he glanced at the former unfortunate actions but knew that they were

233

nothing daunted by anything of that sort – he told them of the Glorious First of June and of his sanguine hopes of adding another laurel to that day. He said that the eyes of all Europe were upon them and he had no doubt of the (?) of the coming contest."

Collier: "Previous to the action the Captain stood on the break of the quarterdeck & addressed the ship's company, the men of the upper deck quarters stood all around him by the gangway, the main deck quarters were assembled below. One part of his speech I remember in substance to have been: 'The Americans say and have published it in their papers that the English have forgotten the way to fight but we'll let them know there are Englishmen in the *Shannon* that know how to fight.' A man by the name of Jacob West who had formerly belonged to the *Guerriere* when she was captured by the *Constitution*, but had afterwards been exchanged & joined the *Shannon* at Halifax said to him, 'I hope sir you will give us revenge for the *Guerriere* today.' He replied, 'You shall my man. Go down to your quarters,' which I believe was almost the last words he spoke previous to the action. I had forgotten to say that in one part of his address he had said, 'Don't try to dismast her, fire into her quarters, the main deck quarters into her main deck quarters and the quarterdeck into her quarterdeck. Kill the men and the ship is yours. Don't hit them about the head for they have steel caps on, but give it them about the body,' but we afterwards found it was not as reported as their heads were just as soft as their boddy."

Provo Wallis: "I think Broke's address to the crew shortly before the battle ran in substance somewhat thus: 'Shannons! The Americans have, owing to the disparity in force, captured several of our frigates; but today, I trust, they will find the stuff British sailors are made of when upon an equality. I feel sure you will all do your duty. In a word, remember you have some hundreds of your brother sailors' blood to avenge!'"

p. 161, line 25, Letter, Sir Edward Parry (a recaptured British officer quartered at forward guns on *Shannon*'s quarterdeck for the action) to King (877/27).

p. 163, line 5, Broke to Sir H. Douglas: "I had omitted to remark upon the effect of *raking fire* . . . the failure of it sometimes, even when delivered from the most favourable positions, is so astonishing that it only can be credited from *observed facts*. When indeed a ship is steadily steering down upon another within bearing of her guns she must suffer some damage, unless her enemy's gunners are very bad indeed . . . but it is passing rapidly athwart a ship's bow or stern or in altering the course to rake her that this apparently terrific fire is so frequently impotent, because the object unless very close is much diminished in width & in the ordinary way of training the guns preparatory to such a discharge they will come to bear in rapid succession & as rapidly pass by their object & the smoke of the last gun fired frequently blinds the aim of the others at that anxious moment when they are known to be *nearly at their aim* . . . in a manoeuvring fight the ship crossing the other generally makes a curved line at the very moment she is firing to avoid running too far from her enemy or getting *herself* into a bad position – here the chance of missing is still greater as the helm swings the guns round so instantly in successive bearing that a few seconds of smoke will cloud the whole crisis . . . these circumstances have frequently rendered a raking fire ineffectual & consequently have tended to support the old British system of going right down boldly on the enemy . . ." Broke went on to cite instances of ineffectual fire from a *'whirling plane'*, including Commodore Rodgers' attack on Byron in the *Belvidera*.

p. 167, line 14, Pel Verjuice.

p. 167, line 32, As told to King by *Shannon*'s topman, quoted in text around King's four lithographs of the action (877/26).

p. 168, line 21, Pel Verjuice.

p. 172, line 6, Broke boarding. King: "Captain Broke told the writer that he did not intend to board personally. 'But,' said he, 'the ships touched at so small a point, and seeing that they would very quickly separate it was necessary that every man who could possibly get on board her should go on the instant; therefore I gave the order to board, threw down my trumpet and went on board with the rest as a matter of necessity'."

Stack: "Our starboard most anchor hooked her mizzen rigging. While in the act of heaving some grapeslings aboard to make her fast to our ship, they assembled on the enemy's gangway to board our ship, waiting for the bugle to sound. We fired our 12 pdr carronade along their gangway and fired right among them; the marines fired with a volley. There was a man at that moment from our forecastle jumped on the *Chesapeake*'s taffrail and sung out, 'Captain Broke, now is a fine time to board her, for damn the man that's alive on her quarterdeck.' The Captain that moment called the boarders away; the Captain and me and four others boarded from the work anchor through the mizzen rigging on the quarterdeck." (This account is the only one known to the author which suggests that the Chesapeakes did actually organise themselves for boarding.)

p. 172, line 15, The grenade question is a vexed one. Broke makes no mention of having thrown it, yet some believe he did. Thus, Stack: "After the second or third gun was fired the Captain of our ship threw a hand grenade on board the enemy's ship which fell into a cask of musquet cartridges which lay abaft the mizzen mast on the skylight under the jaws of the main boom, which blew up. They thought the ship was on fire which put them to a stagnation; the blaze running up the luff of the spanker and did no injury."

Chesapeake's pilot, Knox, who left the ship at 5 p.m. was watching the action from a distance; his report places the grenade explosion at the time the ships bumped together: "At that moment an immense explosion took place on board the *Chesapeake*, which spread a fire from the foremast to the mizzenmast apparently as high as the tops on which both vessels were enveloped invisibly in smoke, and on the smoke clearing away the English colours were seen flying on board the *Chesapeake* over the American . . ."

Collier: "Sir Philip ordered me to go below to the gunner's storeroom & bring up a box of hand grenades, which I did, and opened it, placing it by the capstan, they were packets in tow, he ordered me to take them out and put them in a bucket of sand and cover them over for fear of an accident. Just before the *Chesapeake* came alongside I saw him take up one and cut the fuse with his pen knife. I did not see him throw it, but I have every reason to believe that it was the grenade that caused the explosion on her quarterdeck which they say was owing to our shot, and which caused such confusion on board blowing up the arm chest and doing great damage."

p. 173, line 26, *Chesapeake* Courts Martial, evidence by surgeon, Dr. Edgar, and assistant, Dr. John Dix.

p. 176, line 1, Collier: "The first man that attempted to board was killed by a musquet ball. Mr. Holmes, the purser, was killed close to me on our starboard gangway just as we were in the act of boarding & Mr. Stevens the Boatswain was mortally injured at that same moment of time. The number of men who boarded did not exceed 50 in consequence of the two ships clearing each other as soon as they did. There were none on her quarterdeck to oppose us as they had all been driven forward. Just as we came to the gangway a party from the maindeck rushed upon us and drove us back nearly to the binnacle, when we rallied and drove everyone of them off the deck or forward to the forecastle . . . as a few of us were coming along the starboard gangway I happened to be foremost an American sergeant of marines fired at me but struck the next man in the throat. I immediately gave chase to him but he escaped me by running through the bow port into the main deck."

p. 176, line 15, Smith to King: "It was said at the time that several men had jumped overboard and that they were Englishmen, but I'm inclined to think that not more than 2 or 3 perished in this way, the rest who bolted through the head ports got into the bridle ports on the main deck. I have strong reasons however to believe that the most if not the whole of the men who made such a desperate stand upon the forecastle were British subjects and very likely Waters was amongst their numbers."

p. 176, line 36, *Chesapeake* Courts Martial, ev. from Midshipmen Higginbotham & Edmund Russell.

p. 178, line 29, Stack: "So as I came forehead again to the starboard (?)

236

Collier sang out to me, 'One of them fellows has cut the Captain's head,' so in going across the booms I persued him & cut him down as he was going below; the other lost his life by Collier; the forecastle was kept pretty warm for about two or three minutes . . ."

Collier: "Mr. Smith boarded from the *Shannon*'s fore yard arm on to their fore top and drove the Americans down and I have not the least doubt but it was one of them that wounded poor Sir Philip but he met his fate as he deserved for he was immediately killed by one of our marines . . . I did not see Sir Philip wounded but I saw him the instant afterwards with the blood running down his face, but cannot give any particular account of it, only that the man struck him a most cowardly blow without his being able to see him."

p. 181, line 16, Collier: ". . . after the marine, George Hill was killed some of our fellows were firing down her main hatchway he (Falkiner) stepped forward and held up a pistol he said he would blow the first man's brains out that attempted to fire another shot. He then sang out to the Americans that if they did not instantly send up the man that shot our marine he would (as he had 300 men on board) call them up and put them to death one by one which so frightened them that they did not attempt to resist us in any respect for an instant longer."

Stack has: "a man name of Young, a marine, while walking on the grating, he was shot up through the grating."

p. 182, line 17, Provo Wallis to Sir George Broke Middleton, 24th August 1857 (877/77): "When your dear father's wound was being dressed, we found round his neck a little satchel containing hair, and as the doctor gave me his opinion that your dear father could not live, I took charge of the memento intending in due course to deliver it to Lady Broke. But by good decree your dear father lived & when we arrived at Halifax I got my sister to make a new case."

CHAPTER EIGHT

p. 182, line 33, Boston in mourning description from supercargo of an American brig captured by H.M.S. *Sylph*; King's diary.

p. 184, line 22, Wallis memo to Brighton: "The fact being that our lower rigging was all cut through . . ." Brighton, p. 195.

p. 184, line 36, For details of casualties see Chronological Index for p. 151, line 12, concerning numbers of men aboard *Chesapeake*.

p. 185, line 38, Wallis memo to Brighton, quoted in Provo Wallis.

p. 187, line 29, Brighton, p. 228.

p. 188, line 25, Brighton, p. 231.

p. 188, line 37, See Pechell's letter, p. 214, line 4.

p. 189, line 31, Letter written by Dr. Rowlands, 8th December 1841. Brighton, p. 196.

p. 190, line 8, Letter by unnamed writer dated 19th June 1813. Brighton, p. 213.

p. 191, line 6, Wallis memo to Brighton. Brighton, p. 198.

p. 191, line 18, King's diary.

p. 193, line 6, Two of Louisa's letters to Broke (877/14).

p. 194, line 27, *Nav. Chron.*, Vol. xxx, 1813, p. 41.

p. 194, line 31, As above, p. 47.

p. 196, line 18, Brighton, p. 314.

p. 196, line 34, Hotham to Broke (877/26).

p. 197, line 15, Brighton, p. 313.

p. 197, line 23, Brighton, p. 301.

p. 198, line 1, Hotham to Broke (877/26).

p. 198, line 16, Broke to Louisa, 26th June 1813.

p. 201, line 34, Broke's speech to Shannons, part invented by author, knowing that Broke was expecting to meet Rodgers, part quoted Brighton, p. 289.

p. 202, line 25, Broke to Louisa, Portsmouth, 2nd November 1813.

p. 203, line 3, Wallis memo to Brighton. Brighton, p. 199.

POSTSCRIPT

p. 204, line 1, Hotham to Broke, 3rd February 1814 (877/26).

p. 204, line 13, From Broke to Louisa, 6th August 1813.

p. 204, line 19, Broke to Louisa, 5th September 1813.

p. 204, line 39, Miss Broke's recollections. Brighton, p. 458.

p. 205, line 9, Butchers' bills in Broke's hand, in possession of Hon. Mrs. Llewellen Palmer.

p. 207, line 15, Broke to Sir H. Douglas (877/16).

p. 208, line 1, Broke to Pechell, 7th June 1818 (877/16).

p. 211, line 16, Broke to Dr. Lynn. Brighton, p. 344.

p. 211, line 27, Sir Astley Cooper to Dr. Lynn, 2nd November 1822. Brighton, p. 346.

p. 213, line 17, Capt. Hon. R. L. Spencer to Broke, 25th February 18?? (877/26).

p. 213, line 37, Pechell to Broke, 25th February 18?? (877/26).

p. 214, line 15, Broke to George, 23rd March 1834. Brighton, p. 389.

p. 214, line 35, Broke's Journal (877/00).

p. 215, line 5, Broke to George, 10th March 1834. Brighton, p. 389.

p. 215, line 21, Broke to George, 8th February 1835. Brighton, p. 390-1.

p. 215, line 37, Broke to George, 31st August 1838. Brighton, p. 404-5.

p. 216, line 15, Broke to George, 27th February 1839. Brighton, p. 408.

p. 216, line 37, Pechell to Broke, 11th April 18?? (877/26).

p. 217, line 5, Broke to Miss Norfolk, 21st March 1840 (877/26).

p. 217, line 8, Broke to George, Bayley's Hotel, Berkeley Square, 28th November 1840. Brighton, p. 422.

p. 217, line 9, Broke to George, 12th June 1839. Brighton, p. 411.

p. 217, line 20, Broke to George, 18th July 1839. Brighton, p. 412.

p. 219, line 1, Louisa (daughter) to George Broke, 14th January 1841. Brighton, p. 431.

p. 219, line 10, Capt. Philip Broke, R.N., to Provo Wallis, 8th January 1841. Brighton, p. 432.

p. 220, line 9, Inscription on plaque in Broke chapel, Nacton church.

p. 220, line 20, Extract from letter, Broke to Louisa, 5th September 1813.

p. 220, line 31, Final lines on plaque inscription; they are taken from Mr. Croker's letter to Broke, Admiralty Office, 9th July 1813.

ANALYSIS OF THE FIGHT

AMERICANS have always found it hard to stomach the defeat of the *Chesapeake*. The first wild excuses about infernal machines (grenades) being thrown from the *Shannon* (probably true – see Chron. Index, p. 172, line 15) were soon superseded by more pernicious official excuses at the Court of Inquiry into her loss and at subsequent Courts Martial. Tempers run high in war, and all Governments feel compelled to subordinate truth to the spirit of patriotism and the necessity to preserve national morale. And perhaps we should be more amused than sorry at the elasticity of the old gun ratings which allowed both sides in any given contest to claim superior force for the enemy. But perhaps the official and unofficial distortions which follow so many defeats and disasters are more pathetic than the original misfortune.

"No doubt rests with the Court from the comparison of the injury respectively sustained by the frigates that the fire of the *Chesapeake* was much superior to that of the *Shannon* . . . the *Shannon* was reduced almost to a sinking condition . . . while the *Chesapeake* was relatively uninjured, and the Court has no doubt that if the *Chesapeake* had not accidentally fallen on board the *Shannon* . . . the *Shannon* must very soon have surrendered or sunk."

The fact was that the *Shannon*'s fire had been so well directed in a horizontal line that no shot had been wasted below or on the *Chesapeake*'s waterline; all had been aimed to kill and demoralise men, and in this they succeeded admirably. The *Chesapeake* did not fall aboard *accidentally*; the 2 9-pounders for dismantling service had been specifically ordered by Broke to cripple her wheel and then her headsails and they had done their work well.

As for the 'sinking condition' of the *Shannon*, her pumps needed manning in the ordinary course of her cruising, and there is ample evidence of her craziness long before the *Chesapeake* fired at her.

The Court went on to say that the loss of the *Chesapeake* was caused by the almost unexampled early loss of Captain Lawrence and all his principal officers, leaving the deck to one or two inexperienced Midshipmen, and was contributed to by the desertion of the bugler from his quarters. Had the men promptly repaired to the spar deck they would probably have prevented the enemy from boarding, "certainly have repelled them from the cautious manner in which the enemy came aboard"! They went on to attribute superior force to the *Shannon* "of 52 carriage guns and 396 men . . ."

This was all good, clean propaganda. Unfortunately worse was to follow: the Third Lieutenant, Cox, was brought to Court Martial on charges of cowardice, disobedience of orders, desertion from his quarters, neglect of duty and unofficer-like conduct. Although he was acquitted of the first three, he was found guilty of the last two and cashiered with a perpetual incapacity to serve in the Navy of the United States. These findings were not quashed until after his death.

A Midshipman was charged with cowardice and neglect of duty, but acquitted, as was Joseph Russel, captain of the second gun in the first division, who was alleged to have been the first man to pull up the hatchway down to the berth deck, and so lead the panic desertion – but the evidence was inconclusive. The Negro bugler, however, was found guilty of cowardice and desertion and sentenced to 300 lashes (subsequently mitigated by President Madison to 100) and mulcted of all his wages due "and which may accrue to him during the rest of his period of service".

Subsequent American historians and writers have excused the loss of the *Chesapeake* by stating that her crew was newly joined and consequently raw, her officers young and undrilled with them, also that the men were mutinous because they had not been given their prize cheques for the previous cruise (although it is difficult to see how this is compatible with the first statement above!); some writers have even imputed drunk and disorderly conduct to the crew of the *Chesapeake*. In the author's opinion all this is grossly unfair to Captain Lawrence, who would have been almost criminally foolish to go out to do battle with such odds against him. Roosevelt has explained the mass desertion from quarters as the result of a Portuguese Boatswain's Mate pulling up the fore hatch and going below, and other 'foreign mercenaries' and raw natives following him down. However, the man actually accused of lifting the grating was, of course, Joseph Russel, captain of the second gun, and the muster list shows remarkably few non-English names. (See also analysis of numbers on board the *Chesapeake*, Chron. Index, p. 151, line 12.)

Not all the officers fell early; only the Lieutenant of Marines, Sailing Master and Fourth Lieutenant, and subsequently the Captain were mortally wounded, and far from no one realising that 'boarders' had been called because of the desertion from quarters of the bugler, all the three Lieutenants remaining had not only received the order, but had responded to it. The first up on deck with some men of his quarters behind him was Cox, subsequently accused of cowardice, and he naturally, but perhaps unfortunately, helped his mortally wounded Captain below. Lieutenant Ludlow was wounded by a sabre on the head after storming up the main hatchway and driving the boarders as far aft as the binnacle; Lieutenant Budd was wounded in the arm while trying to rally his men on the fo'c'sle.

However, the real evidence of the course of the fight is contained in the list of killed and wounded, and in the wounds suffered by the ships themselves.

The maindeck of the *Chesapeake* had 4 holes from 18-pounder balls by the forward guns and a countless disfiguration of holes which the carpenter estimated as from 30 or 40 balls, both 18- and 32-pounder, in her stern and port quarter; her fo'c'sle and quarterdeck bulwarks showed 9 more clear holes besides beaten-in hammock nettings and severed shrouds, lee and weather at all masts. Beside all this the *Shannon* had only 2 32-pounder and 3 18-pounder holes through the maindeck forward, 2 32-pounders amidships and 1 18-pounder aft; the upper deck had a clear hole from only 1 18-pounder, besides various sections of hammocks beaten in.

The Americans had therefore been exposed to at least 44 round shot in about 6 or at the most 11 minutes (depending whether one takes 5.56 or 6.01 as the time the *Chesapeake* fell aboard), while the British had only suffered from 10 or 11 round shot, most of which had arrived forward in the first 2 or 3 minutes of the action while the ships were still parallel or nearly so. All the rest of the *Chesapeake*'s well-*trained* guns had been pointed too low; thus of 14 bar shot from the American maindeck pieces, nearly all struck the *Shannon* on her coppers just above the waterline and bounced back into the sea. American bar shot expanded into arms as it flew through the air and was designed primarily to dismantle rigging and sweep through men. The fact that nearly all of it, besides a great number of 18-pounder round shot, struck so low is clear evidence that the American guns' crews had little conception of elevating their pieces for horizontal fire. They were firing on the lee side, and under the press of a light breeze on topsails alone they allowed their shot to follow the tilt and camber of the deck down almost to the *Shannon*'s waterline at a separation of only 40 to 50 yards. Altogether they hit the *Shannon* with 39 round and bar shot, but only 11 were effective as killing or demoralising blows – as against the 44 at least from the *Shannon*.

Some of the disparity in the figures is accounted for by the *Shannon*'s superior laying – very few shot went low – but undoubtedly the real excess occurred while the American frigate lay in irons, drifting crabwise, stern-first under half-raking fire. She was punished ruthlessly then without the capability of replying except with those guns right aft which were themselves at the point of the heaviest concentration of shot. The officer of the after quarters fell early. The guns' crews were driven forward; to have remained aft while the metal and splinters flew in clouds diagonally across the deck would have required superhuman or inhuman stoicism.

Thus, when Lawrence's stern windows eventually brought up against the *Shannon*'s anchor and the smoking muzzles of the British cannon, the *Chesapeake* was already virtually a beaten ship. Between 40 and 90 of her company were dead (see analysis of numbers aboard *Chesapeake*, Chron. Index, p. 151, line 12), and 70 or 80 wounded, while a proportion of the rest had all the fighting spirit knocked out of them. Broke and his boarders, to borrow the words of a German military historian, were simply 'presenting the cheque for payment' when they leaped across. (See D. L. Dennis in *Mariners' Mirror*, Vol. XLV.)

The decisive point in the action was not so much the boarding as the *Chesapeake*'s luff into irons, and her disastrous subsequent stern-board. Lawrence has been criticised for allowing this to happen. But did he have any option? Broke had his 9-pounders aimed at the wheel- and the headyards for the purpose of crippling her. Two men were killed at the wheel, which was itself put out of action when the tiller ropes were cut; the jib sheet was cut and the foretopmast tie. And at the end of the action all the lower rigging of the *Chesapeake* was so cut close to the deck that "she could not have made sail or braced her yards about or trimmed her foretopmast staysail for want of the sheets".

Perhaps Lawrence's judgement was impaired by his first wound, but perhaps there was nothing he *could* have done. He came up with rather too much speed and rather overconfident and his guns' crews, although well trained in the handling of their pieces, had not been instructed in laying for horizontal fire, and he found that instead of a weary old cruiser, he was up against a crack gunnery frigate, probably *the* crack gunnery frigate in the British service. When he tried to reduce his speed to that of the *Shannon* with a brief luff, Broke's dismantling guns ensured that the luff continued to the point of no return.

Nevertheless, the *Chesapeake* had put up a good fight. Her crew were far from the raw and undrilled, disaffected, even mutinous and drunken gaggle of spare hands they have so often been painted. They were good *even by American standards* – by French standards superb.

243

They were only allowed about 3 or perhaps 4 minutes of even combat before the guns, starting from forward, were thrown out of bearing by her superior speed and then her luff, and yet in that time they despatched some 15 Shannons (allowing as before for those later killed and wounded in boarding) and wounded nearly 50 others. Even allowing the full 6 minutes before the ships touched, this was a casualty rate of 10 per minute. By contrast, the *Constitution*, a far larger ship with greater guns, had the *Guerriere* helpless for over an hour, raking and sweeping the decks with rifle fire, and only killed 15 and wounded 63 – casualty rate about 1·3 per minute. And when the same ship took on the *Java*, they fought a manoeuvring battle for three-quarters of an hour and a close action for one and a half hours, after which 22 British were killed and 102 wounded. If all these casualties occurred in the last hour and a half the rate was 1·4 per minute. The *United States*, a vessel with even larger carronades than the *Constitution*, took over two hours to kill 36 and wound 68 Macedonians – casualty rate less than 1 per minute. By these standards then – and even allowing for the calmer weather of the *Chesapeake* action – she stands out as a shining example of devastatingly superior gunnery – and a very fit adversary for the *Shannon*.

Indeed, had Lawrence squared his mainyard (according to many historians he did, but it apparently did not have effect early enough) or otherwise reduced his speed without luffing as he came up with the *Shannon*, and so given his gunners a fair chance, the contest would probably have been the bloodiest in the history of frigate warfare, and may very well have ended in a draw and the *Shannon*, so near Boston, subsequently taken by boarding parties from ashore – in which case, would Broke have suffered the verdict of history for fighting so rashly so close to his enemy's port after detaching his companion frigate?

Even as it was, there are few single actions to equal this one for the length of the butcher's bill, and none which come within comparing distance of the casualty rate per minute. In this respect it is quite unique. In those eleven minutes between Cape Ann and Cape Cod more men were killed or wounded per minute than in all of Nelson's and Villeneuve's great battleships combined at the battle of Trafalgar.

SUMMARY OF SHOT AS RECORDED BY MIDSHIPMAN KING

Shannon			*Chesapeake*		
struck by	32-pounders	13	struck by	32-pounders	25
	18-pounders	12		18-pounders	29
	Grape	119		Grape	306
	Bar	14		9-pounder	2
		158			362
			Total *Shannon* struck by		158
			DIFFERENCE		204

King: "Now, looking at the above table the *Chesapeake*'s fire was excellent, for she struck the *Shannon* with 28 shot of all sizes every minute, and this notwithstanding the *Shannon* struck her with 60 shot of all sizes every minute."

SOME USEFUL BOOKS

BESIDES the source material listed in the Chronological Index, and the usual 'background atmosphere' books such as *A Mariner of England*, 1780–1819, by William Richardson, and besides the many books on the American War and the *Shannon/Chesapeake* action itself (ranging from excellent right down to dreadful), I found the following invaluable reference books:

Mahan, A. T.: *Seapower in its Relation to the War of 1812*, Sampson Low Marston

Chapelle, H. I.: *The History of The American Sailing Navy – the Ships and their Development*, Bonanza Books, New York

Falconer, W.: *Marine Dictionary* (modernised by William Burney), Cadell & Davies and John Murray, 1815.

Lever, Darcy: *The Young Sea Officer's Sheet Anchor*, London, 1819 (photolithographed and published by W. Sweetman, New York, 1955)

Gunnery

Douglas, Sir H.: *A Treatise on Naval Gunnery*, John Murray, 1829

Atkinson & Clarke: *The Naval Pocket Gunner*, Robert Scholey, London, 1814

Mountaine, William: *The Seaman's Vade Mecum*, London, 1778
The Practical Sea-Gunner's Companion, London, 1781

Beauchant, T. S.: *The Naval Gunner*, Longman & Co, London, 1828

Admiralty: *Instructions for the Exercise of the great Guns*, 1818 (the first official book of service orders for the great guns)

Chamberlain, Henry: His manuscript book of notes taken while a student in H.M.S. *Excellent*, 1840, delightfully illustrated by himself. A work of art

(All foregoing gunnery books are from the Ward Room Library, H.M.S. *Excellent*, Portsmouth.)

Robertson, F. L.: *The Evolution of Naval Armament*, Constable, 1921

Pope, Dudley: *Guns*, Wiedenfeld & Nicholson, 1965

Of the many articles about the *Shannon/Chesapeake* action, while I am certain I have not seen nearly all of them, that by D. L. Dennis in the *Mariners' Mirror*, Vol. XLV, seems to me the most admirable.